UCD WOMEN'S CENTER

RESHAPING
THE
FEMALE
BODY

RESHAPING THE FEMALE BODY

THE DILEMMA OF COSMETIC SURGERY

KATHY DAVIS

ROUTLEDGE   NEW YORK AND LONDON

Published in 1995 by

Routledge
29 West 35th Street
New York, NY 10001

Published in Great Britain by

Routledge
11 New Fetter Lane
London EC4P 4EE

Library of Congress Cataloging-in-Publication Data

    Reshaping the female body : the dilemma of cosmetic surgery / Kathy Davis.
    p.   cm.
    Includes bibliographical references and index.
    ISBN 0-415-90631-8.—ISBN 0-415-90632-6 (pbk.)
    1. Surgery, Plastic—Psychological aspects. 2. Self-perception in women. 3. Women—Health and hygiene—Sociological aspects. 4. Feminist theory. I. Title.
    RD119.D385 1994   94-19290
    617.9'5'0082—dc20   CIP

British Library Cataloguing-in-Publication Data also available

Material from Chapter 2 has appeared in different forms in Kathy Davis, "Remaking the She-Devil: A Critical Look at Feminist Approaches to Beauty," in *Hypatia* 6, 2 (Summer 1991):21–43; Kathy Davis, "Het recht om mooi te zijn. De vele gezichten van cosmetische chirurgie," in *Lover* 18, 1 (1991): 4–9; Kathy Davis, "Cultural Dopes and She-Devils: Cosmetic Surgery as Ideological Dilemma" in *Negotiating at the Margins: The Gendered Discourses of Power and Resistance,* ed. Sue Fisher and Kathy Davis, (New Brunswick: Rutgers University Press, 1993).

CONTENTS

ACKNOWLEDGEMENTS   vii

INTRODUCTION   COSMETIC SURGERY   1
AS FEMINIST DILEMMA

ONE   THE RISE OF THE SURGICAL FIX   14

TWO   BEAUTY AND THE FEMALE BODY   39

THREE   PUBLIC FACE/PRIVATE SUFFERING   68

FOUR   FROM OBJECTIFIED BODY   93
TO EMBODIED SUBJECT

FIVE   DECISIONS AND DELIBERATIONS   115

SIX   CHOICE AND INFORMED   137
CONSENT REVISITED

SEVEN   FACING THE DILEMMA   159

NOTES   182

BIBLIOGRAPHY   197

INDEX   207

FOR MIEKE

ACKNOWLEDGEMENTS

This book about women's experiences with cosmetic surgery is based on interviews with surgery recipients, physicians, plastic surgeons, and medical inspectors, and on field work in medical settings. To preserve confidentiality, I cannot thank the interview subjects by name. However, the book owes a debt of gratitude to each of them, including the medical practitioners who shared their insights (and, in some cases, doubts) about cosmetic surgery with me and who gave me permission to do field work. I would especially like to thank Iman Baardman, with whom I set up and conducted the clinical study, for a stimulating and enjoyable collaboration. And, finally, my most heart-felt thanks are due to the women who, by generously sharing their experiences with me, helped me understand what cosmetic surgery is about. I hope that they are not disappointed in the outcome of our conversations.

In the course of working on this project, many people kept me supplied with a stream of newspaper clippings, pictures, references, and articles. In particular, I would like to thank Marlou Boots, Sandera Krol, and Juliette Zipper.

Lively and often heated discussions with friends, students, and colleagues have contributed enormously to the development of this book. I would like to thank the participants in the post-graduate course "Interpreting Gender" which was held at Utrecht University in 1993, and the members of the ongoing seminar on text analysis at the Women's Studies Department there for their insights and helpful comments.

I owe warm thanks to the following people for their careful reading and constructive critique of various chapters: Anna Aalten, Jan Davis, Sue Fisher, Lena Inowlocki, Mary Lommerse, Joan Wolffensperger, and Dubravka Zarkov. The copyeditor Neill Bogan was an author's delight who not only polished up the text and kept me on track, but issued the occasional, timely warning against using dubious rhetorical strategies to make my point.

I am indebted to Lorraine Code for encouraging me on several occasions to engage with my critics, and Nina Gregg for reminding me that conflicts—especially among feminists—are worth confronting.

An extra note of thanks goes to Lena Inowlocki for her friendship, her humor, her sensitive commentary, and her numerous impromptu lessons on how to do biographical analysis.

Wieneke Matthijsse spared me the hassle of having to cope with recalcitrant printers and produced a polished manuscript, for which I am grateful.

Most of all, Willem de Haan was the person who read all the drafts, was my toughest but most encouraging critic, and helped me through all the rough patches. He showed me, once again, why I don't ever want to write a book without him.

Amsterdam, May 1994
Kathy Davis

INTRODUCTION

COSMETIC SURGERY AS FEMINIST DILEMMA

This book is about how women account for their decisions to have cosmetic surgery. What kinds of experiences make them want to have their appearances altered surgically? How do they explain the decision and how do they view it in light of the outcome?

Like every book, it is also a personal story. It is the story of how I—a feminist with a long-standing concern about the gendered inequities of medical encounters—became interested in understanding why women want to have their bodies altered by surgical means. What began as my rage at the horrors being perpetrated on women's bodies by the medical system turned to a profound puzzlement after I talked to women who were eager to undergo cosmetic surgery. My inability to put these two emotions together in a meaningful and acceptable way created such a strong sense of unease that I had no other recourse but to tackle my discomfort head on. Being someone who enjoys a challenge, I decided to put my experience to work, using it as a resource rather than an impediment for a feminist analysis of cosmetic surgery.

Several years ago, I attended a conference on body image and identity at the Dutch medical faculty where I had been working for some time in the field of medical sociology. The audience was composed primarily of physicians and medical academics, along with a few social scientists like myself. One of the speakers was a well-known plastic surgeon. This particular surgeon's talk was all about the wonders of cosmetic surgery in helping people overcome a negative body image. He explained that doctors in his specialty had some unique difficulties in diagnosing their patients. In most medical specialties, patients don't know what their problem is, and leave it to the specialist to figure out. Not so with cosmetic surgery. Here, it is the patient who knows what's wrong and the surgeon who often has a hard time seeing it. This leaves him with a dilemma: either he has to send the patient home empty-handed or he has to find some medically acceptable reason for an intervention as drastic as surgery. To illustrate this point, the speaker gave a slide show with—what else?—before and after pictures. To my surprise, the patient was not a middle-aged woman with wrinkles who wanted a face lift, but a fifteen-year old Moroccan girl who wanted her nose done. According to this surgeon, this girl was only one among many similar cases: second-generation immigrant adolescents who were getting harassed at school for having "noses like that." They became miserable, antisocial, and developed feelings of inferiority, he explained. It became difficult for them to become assimilated into Dutch society.

Now, what did this man of science conclude? He decided that he had stumbled upon a new syndrome and, being an enterprising scientist, he immediately gave it a name: inferiority complex due to racial characteristics. Thus, a new diagnostic category was born, many more noses could be "fixed," and, presumably, many unhappy young Moroccan women were enabled to live happily ever after. End of story.

My initial reaction to this incident was outrage. I saw it as a particularly dramatic illustration of the dangers of the medical profession's meddling with women's bodies. This was medicalization and racism in technicolor—under the knife for the sake of white, Anglo-Saxon beauty. A blatant instance of the victimization of women through their

2

bodies and of the racialized aspects of such repression, it confirmed all of my worst feminist suspicions about the dangers of the beauty system. Women are instructed that their bodies are unacceptable: too fat, too thin, too wrinkled, too old and, now, too ethnic.

At the same time, however, I was somewhat taken aback by the fact that a plastic surgeon would reveal such an incident in the first place. As a clinical psychologist with a sociological research interest in decisions concerning women's health, I knew that physicians are notoriously reluctant to admit that their practices are based on anything but objectively derived scientific criteria (Davis 1988). I had never encountered such a public display of medical accountability. The fact that a plastic surgeon would go to such lengths to explain his diagnosis indicated that cosmetic surgery was not an entirely unproblematic endeavor—even for the medical profession.

A second experience occurred several months later and involved a luncheon date with a friend whom I had not seen in awhile. She was an attractive, self-confident, successful professional woman. She was also a feminist. To my surprise, she told me over coffee that she was about to have her breasts enlarged. I must have looked fairly flabbergasted, as she immediately began defending herself. She said that she was tired of putting up with being flat-chested. She had tried everything (psychoanalysis, feminism, talks with friends), but no matter what she did, she simply could not accept it. She saw no other solution but to do something about it. Finally, she said, she was going to "take her life in her own hands."

My friend was well informed about the dangers and side effects of breast implants. She knew, for example, that she had a forty percent chance of some side effects—ranging from lack of sensation in the breasts to scarring to encapsulation of implants (which is very painful and makes the breasts as hard as rocks). She also knew that she had a twenty percent chance that the implants would become infected or rejected by her body and have to be removed and redone. This could leave her in worse shape than she was before the operation. She had even conducted a small study on her own by putting an ad in a local feminist journal and talking to more than twenty women about their experiences, many of which were quite negative.

My friend was a feminist and as a feminist she was very critical of the suffering women have to endure because their bodies do not meet the normative requirements of feminine beauty. She found such norms oppressive and believed that women in general should accept their bodies the way they are. However, she still felt compelled to have cosmetic surgery *for herself.* Despite all the drawbacks of cosmetic surgery, she saw it as her only option under the circumstances. So, here, to my amazement and—I must admit—distress, was a feminist who was actively and knowledgeably opting for the "surgical fix."

As a feminist, I could have rejected my friend's explanation for why she wanted to have cosmetic surgery as the deluded imaginings of another casualty of the beauty craze—an instance of what used to be called "false consciousness." This would have been in line with current feminist thinking about the beauty system as an oppressive way to discipline or normalize women through their bodies. I did not find that approach very satisfactory in the case of my friend, however. After all, she was just as critical as I of the beauty norms and she knew a lot more than I did about the risks and dangers of cosmetic surgery. And, yet she still saw it as the only step she could take under the circumstances. I began to wonder why it was so difficult for me, as a feminist, to hear my friend's account of why she wanted cosmetic surgery as anything other than one more instance of a woman being duped by the beauty system. If she had used the very same rhetoric to justify, say, a divorce ("My marriage is awful. I've had it. I'm going to do something about it. I'm getting a divorce."), I would have heard this as "ideologically correct." In the first case, she is the victim of manipulation and in the second, just another feminist who is taking her life in hand.

Cosmetic surgery was clearly more complicated than I had imagined. I had previously associated it either with well-to-do American housewives who were bored with their suburban lives and wanted to have a face lift or with the celebrity "surgical junkies" who couldn't seem to stop remaking their bodies—Madonna with her collagen-inflated lips ("kiss bumpers") or Cher, who had had so many operations that it was hard to know where the original left off and the artificially constructed began. I hadn't expected to find much cosmetic surgery in The Netherlands and was very surprised to discover that it was not only popular here, but that my own feminist friends were going in for it.

These two experiences formed the backdrop for the present book. The first experience—the surgeon's speech—indicated that cosmetic surgery had become a widespread medical practice with its own discourse of justification—a discourse which seemed to be begging for feminist analysis. It indicated that it was worth looking into how women's bodies became defined as appropriate objects for this particular kind of medical intervention. Understanding such a process, moreover, would require an analysis of the cultural norms of femininity as well as of the specific constraints imposed upon women to "improve" or alter their appearance. The second experience—my talk with my friend—showed that cosmetic surgery is not simply imposed by misogynist, knife-happy surgeons upon women who blindly follow suit. On the contrary, cosmetic surgery is fervently desired by its recipients. Despite myriad dangers and drawbacks, women willingly opt to have their bodies so altered. My puzzlement at my friend's decision convinced me that understanding why women engage in a practice which is painful, dangerous, and demeaning would have to take women's own explanations as a starting point.

In order to make sense of women's involvement in cosmetic surgery, I have attempted a kind of feminist balancing act. My analysis is situated on the razor's edge between a feminist critique of the cosmetic surgery craze (along with the ideologies of feminine inferiority which sustain it) and an equally feminist desire to treat women as agents who negotiate their bodies and their lives within the cultural and structural constraints of a gendered social order. This has meant exploring cosmetic surgery as one of the most pernicious expressions of the Western beauty culture without relegating women who have it to the position of "cultural dope." It has involved understanding how cosmetic surgery might be the best possible course of action for a particular woman, while, at the same time, problematizing the situational constraints which make cosmetic surgery an option.

THE NETHERLANDS: A SPECIAL CASE

It seems almost self-evident that any book about cosmetic surgery should begin in the U.S., where the cosmetic surgery craze emerged (Wolf 1991). Cosmetic surgery tends to be regarded as a typically American phenomenon, conjuring up visions of Beverly Hills surgeons, celebrity "scalpel slaves," and the Oprah Winfrey show. I have situated my inquiry, however, in a country which is rarely mentioned in conjunction with such surgery—The Netherlands. The Netherlands is a special case and it is precisely for this reason that it offers a particularly good place to begin a feminist analysis of the phenomenon.

Like the U.S. and most of Europe, The Netherlands has experienced a general upsurge in cosmetic surgery, both in terms of the number of operations and the number of procedures and technologies available. It is estimated that more than twenty thousand cosmetic operations are performed here every year—more per capita than in the U.S.[1] A multi-million-dollar beauty industry, a history of medicalizing women's bodies, and an Anglo-European cultural norm of feminine beauty ensure that women are the main recipients of cosmetic surgery. In this respect, cosmetic surgery in The Netherlands is not an isolated phenomenon, but is part of the same cultural landscape which makes it endemic to most highly industrialized nations.

The Netherlands is, however, also an exception, having until recently the somewhat dubious distinction of being the only country in the world to have included cosmetic surgery in its basic health care package. For many years it has been available to women who would not have been able to afford it if not for national health insurance. Cosmetic surgery is often expensive. In the U.S., with its fee-for-service medical system, or in European welfare states where cosmetic surgery is not covered by national health insurance, such surgery is limited to people who can afford it. In The Netherlands, however, women from all social backgrounds were potentially able to obtain surgery, provided their appearance was classified as falling "outside the realm of the normal." Despite its availability, cosmetic surgery in The Netherlands was, paradoxically, something of a taboo. In a culture with a Calvinist tradition which cautions against frivolity and excess, cosmetic surgery tends to be problematic, requiring some explanation on the part of the would be recipient. This situation makes it possible to explore women's reasons for having surgery, as well as their difficulties in justifying their decisions, without financial considerations being an issue. While women in the U.S. will presumably have similar experiences and struggles, economic forces and a media-constructed image of cosmetic surgery as acceptable and unproblematic may obscure our view of them.[2] The contrasting Dutch context allows the cultural dimension of women's involvement with the surgery to come to the fore—both in terms of what makes it desirable and of what makes it problematic.

The advantages of the Dutch case for the researcher are not limited to understanding the motives of the recipients, however. In a market system of medicine like that of the U.S., the medical profession is not accountable in the same way that it is in a welfare system. In the U.S., cosmetic surgery is performed at the individual surgeon's discretion. Plastic surgeons seem to have little compunction about plying their trade, providing the technology is available and the patient can pay for it. In a system of socialized medicine, however, health care services have to be justified in terms of medical necessity. As it became increasingly difficult in the context of economic recession for the Dutch welfare system to meet even basic health care needs, cosmetic surgery became the object of heated debate, among the medical profession, the welfare bureaucracy, and the national health insurance system. The need to cut costs made cosmetic surgery increasingly problematic, even for surgeons. An attempt was made to get the problem under control by developing "scientific" criteria to decide which bodies were normal and which were not and a heated public debate ensued, primarily between plastic surgeons and the national health insurance system, concerning the conditions under which cosmetic surgery should or should not be performed.

As any medical sociologist will attest, such public accountability on the part of the medical profession is unusual. It makes The Netherlands an ideal site for exploring how the profession draws upon ideologies of femininity as it defines which bodies are deficient enough to require surgical alteration. Thus, by virtue of its being an exception, The Netherlands provides a good place to explore the cultural and ideological dynamics of decisions concerning cosmetic surgery—dynamics which may be obscured in the U.S., where such decisions are affected both by unrestrained individual choice (possessed by both patients and practitioners), on the one hand, and by the uncontrolled expansion of the beauty industry, on the other.

GETTING STARTED

My inquiry spanned a period of several years and entailed three empirical studies: an exploratory study, a clinical study, and field work. In the first study, I looked for women who had already had or were planning to have some kind of cosmetic surgery. I used what is often called the "snow-ball method" and involves talking to just about anyone who is willing, in order to get acquainted with the phenomenon at hand (Schwartz and Jacobs 1979). This proved surprisingly easy. In fact, every time I went to a party or a social gathering and mentioned my new research project, people would tell me that they knew someone who had had cosmetic surgery and suggest that I talk to them. Some told me that they had had surgery themselves, which was how I discovered that my feminist friend was by no means an exception. After harboring their experience as a slightly shameful secret, many women explained that I was the first person they were really able to talk to about their reasons for having it.

I spoke with women who had undergone everything from a relatively simple ear correction or breast augmentation to—in the most extreme case—having the whole face reconstructed. My only criteria for these conversations was that the surgery be done purely for looks.

I did not talk to women who had had reconstructive surgery as a result of trauma, illness, or a congenital birth defect. The majority were professional women—academics, social workers, teachers—and most lived in Amsterdam. Some were married, some single; some were heterosexual, others lesbian. Many were feminists. In addition to many informal conversations with women (and men), I conducted ten extensive biographical interviews with women who had had cosmetic surgery.[3]

These conversations and interviews enabled me to become familiar with the kinds of accounts women give of their experiences with their bodies and how they explain their decisions to be altered surgically. Since many of my respondents were professional or academic women who had had cosmetic surgery several years prior to the interviews, I became interested in expanding the scope of the inquiry to include a more representative group of recipients. I also wanted to know more about how women actually decide to have cosmetic surgery, and about the process they go through in order to obtain it.

BEFORE AND AFTER

To this end, I embarked upon a second study. This was a clinical study in the plastic surgery department of a small teaching hospital. It was conducted in collaboration with a psychologist who was developing a therapy program for individuals who were dissatisfied with their appearance. This study gave me access to cosmetic surgery recipients from a diversity of socio-economic backgrounds and allowed me to interview them both before and after their operations.

Originally, I had anticipated some resistance from the surgeons there. It is notoriously difficult for social scientists to gain entrance into medical settings, particularly to do research on practices which are as contested as cosmetic surgery. To my amazement, however, we were welcomed with open arms and were immediately given permission to contact patients currently on the waiting list for surgery, as well as to conduct research in the clinic.

After talking to the surgeons, I realized that they were faced with some difficulty in legitimating operations performed for strictly aesthetic reasons on otherwise healthy bodies. They explained how difficult it was to develop scientific criteria for determining which patients were candidates for cosmetic surgery. They seemed skeptical, in particular, about their female patients' motives, citing the misguided middle-aged woman who hopes to hold on to her errant husband by having her breasts augmented as a case in point. The twin spectre of the surgical junkie and the dissatisfied patient loomed large. Symptom displacement was the underlying fear, implying as it did that the surgeon had not tackled the problem at its root. Thus, whereas other medical specialists might be reticent about allowing critics a peek into their kitchen, we were treated by the surgeons as potential helpmeets who might be able to provide them with some additional psychological criteria for the vague and subjective process of determining which patients were suitable for cosmetic surgery.

The clinical study focussed on breast augmentation as a paradigm case for investigating women's decisions to have cosmetic surgery. Breasts are irrevocably linked with cultural notions about femininity. Particularly in Western culture, femininity and voluptuous breasts go together, making breast augmentation a way to enhance femininity (Ayalah & Weinstock 1979; Young 1990b). This is a form of cosmetic surgery which is only performed on women—or transsexual men who want to become women—and, unlike breast reduction, it is done strictly for looks. Moreover, breast augmentations are the single most frequently performed cosmetic surgery in The Netherlands (and in the U.S., second only to liposuction).

In addition to contacting thirty women who had had breast augmentations in the hospital within the previous five years, twelve women who were currently waiting for operations were interviewed prior to the surgery, immediately after it, and one year later. The respondents came from a variety of backgrounds, ranging from a seventeen-year-old woman living with her parents to a forty-three-year-old woman, married, with teenage children. All were white and most came from working-class or lower-middle-class backgrounds. Some had outside employment as, for example, cashiers, saleswomen, or home helps; others were full-time housewives. With one exception, their operations were covered by national health insurance.

This clinical study allowed me to expand my initial explorative study in several important ways. It enabled me to explore the motives of women from working-class as well as professional or middle-class backgrounds. Moreover, because I could talk to these women prior to the surgery, I could compare their reasons for wanting surgery with how they felt about it after the fact. I was able to follow them through the ordeal of the surgery itself, which provided me with considerable insight into what women have to go through in order to have their bodies altered. Although I conducted several informal interviews with plastic surgeons in the course of the project, I was not permitted to sit in on their consultations. As they explained—quite truthfully, as was later confirmed by the patients—the time spent in consultation was "too short to make it worth my while." In order to understand the actual process of determining which bodies are suitable for cosmetic surgery, I had to turn to another medical setting—the national health insurance system.

"NORMAL" BODIES

During a period of a year and a half, I did a third study which involved participant observations in consultations where the decision was made whether cosmetic surgery would be covered by national health insurance. These consultations took place between a medical inspector and various applicants for cosmetic surgery. The requests might involve anything from the removal of unwanted body hair or tattoos to nose or ear corrections, face lifts, tummy tucks, breast surgery (augmentations, reductions, or lifts), or corrective surgery to repair the results of previous cosmetic operations which had not been successful. The applicants were primarily women and they came from a wide range of socio-economic, educational, and ethnic backgrounds.

This field work allowed me to observe firsthand how patients present their cases as well as how representatives of the medical profession determine which bodies are "abnormal" enough to warrant surgical intervention. It also enabled me to gain insight into how such decisions are later justified. The medical inspector was under some constraint to cut back expenditure for cosmetic surgery. He had, together with plastic surgeons, developed criteria for sorting out the illegitimate from the legitimate candidates—criteria which he would explain to me as he went along. I was able to observe some of the difficulties he had in making the actual decision. His criteria proved notoriously vague. Even when the patient's appearance did not meet the criteria required for coverage, her account of her suffering often made it difficult for the inspector to refuse. This often resulted in a kind of tug of war between the patient and the inspector. In the course of my field work, he often asked me what I thought about an assessment or whether I would have made it differently, indicating that the guidelines did not automatically enable him to make decisions. It also showed that he was compelled to explain and, in some cases, defend his actions against potential criticism. The consultations, along with informal conversations with the medical inspector, enabled me to observe how decisions concerning which bodies require surgical alteration are negotiated, as well as how practitioners defend and, in some cases, struggle with these decisions.

ABOUT THE BOOK

The book has been organized around three themes which are the threads running through each of the chapters, serving to tie them together and helping to make sense of women's involvement in cosmetic surgery. The first theme is *identity*. It concerns the problem of ordinariness and of how a person's subjective sense of self is negotiated in the face of what is perceived as a bodily deficiency. The second theme is *agency*. It concerns both the problem of giving shape to one's life under circumstances of social constraint and the degree to which cosmetic surgery may be a resource for empowerment for an individual woman. The third theme is *morality*. It concerns the problem of suffering and of whether there are circumstances under which cosmetic surgery might be regarded as a legitimate solution for emotional pain which has gone beyond an acceptable limit.

Chapter One sets the stage with a brief historical sketch of the recent expansion of the surgical fix. Cosmetic surgery has not only become the fastest growing medical specialty, it is one of the most risky. This has necessitated its increasing legitimation on the part of the medical profession and the welfare state. The forms this legitimation takes depend on the way the health care system is organized. The Dutch case will be drawn upon here as the exception which proves the rule; namely, that even socialized medicine with its discourse of need cannot solve the problem of whether and under what circumstances the surgical alteration of the body for aesthetic reasons can be justified.

Chapter Two deals with explanations for women's involvement in beauty and their practices of body improvement. Social psychology, psychoanalysis, and sociology have looked to women's propensity toward conformity, low self-esteem, and narcissism, or to their position as brainwashed consumers in late capitalist society for such explanations. What is missing from these accounts is an analysis of gender and the cultural constraints of the feminine beauty system. I locate this analysis in several traditions of contemporary feminist theory on femininity and the body, which treat women's preoccupation with beauty as a cultural phenomenon, linking the constraints of beauty practices to the reproduction of femininity and to power asymmetries between the sexes and among women. I draw upon this work to develop a theoretical perspective for explaining women's involvement in cosmetic surgery without relegating them to the position of cultural dope—a perspective which highlights women's agency and their active and knowledgeable struggles within the cultural and structural constraints of femininity and the beauty system.

The next four chapters form the heart of the book. Starting from the three empirical studies described above, the trajectory which a woman follows in order to have her body altered by surgical means is explored. The three themes—identity, agency, and morality—will serve as heuristic devices for understanding women's biographical reconstructions of their suffering over appearance, of their decision to undergo cosmetic surgery, of the surgery, and of its aftermath.

In Chapter Three, the problem of "normal" appearance is explored. Medical attempts to develop scientific criteria are contrasted with women's accounts of why they decided to have their bodies altered surgically. Prerequisite to these women's decisions is a long history of suffering with bodies which are experienced as unacceptable, different, or abnormal. Their accounts dispel the notion that those who have such surgery are simply the duped victims of the beauty system. Cosmetic surgery is, first and foremost, about identity; about wanting to be ordinary rather than beautiful.

In Chapter Four, cosmetic surgery is explored as a strategy for interrupting the downward spiral of suffering which can accompany a woman's problematic relationship to her body. Based on the narrative analysis of one woman's experiences with surgery, I show how the intervention enables her to renegotiate her relationship to her body and through her body to herself, becoming, paradoxically, an embodied subject rather than "just a body."

In Chapter Five, women's decision-making processes are explored in more detail. While suffering precipitates the decision to undergo cosmetic surgery, it is by no means seen as a sufficient reason for it. I show how women struggle with their own anxieties and persuade often reluctant family members and medical professionals that their problems are serious enough to merit surgical intervention. The decision process is central and I explore it in terms of agency; that is, of how cosmetic surgery can be a way, if a problematic one, for women to take their lives in hand.

Chapter Six describes surgery and its aftermath. Drawing upon interviews with women a year after their operations, I continue to examine how such operations change (or do not change) their relationship to their bodies, themselves, and the world around them. In some cases, this change entails coming to terms with results which are bitterly disappointing. In a discussion based on women's attempts to make sense of both decisions and outcomes, the issues of choice and informed consent are considered.

I argue that while decisions to have cosmetic surgery are rarely taken with complete knowledge or absolute freedom, they are, nevertheless, choices. Cosmetic surgery can be an informed choice, but it is always made in a context of limited options and circumstances which are not of the individual's own making.

Chapter Seven returns to the question raised at the outset of the book, namely, how can women's involvement with cosmetic surgery be critically situated in the cultural context of femininity and the beauty system, without attacking women for having it? While the present inquiry shows how this might be done, I conclude with a discussion of some of the methodological, theoretical, and ethical dimensions of the undertaking. A case is made for resisting a politically correct feminist response to cosmetic surgery in favor of an approach which takes ambivalence, empathy, and unease as its starting point.

ONE

THE RISE OF THE SURGICAL FIX

PLASTIC SURGERY IN RETROSPECT

Plastic surgery has a long history. As early as 1000 B.C., the first plastic surgery was reported in India, where a person's nose might be cut off as a form of punishment or, in the case of an adulterous Hindu wife, bitten off by the wronged husband. Procedures which displayed remarkable similarity to present rhinoplasties were developed to reconstruct the noses of such errant individuals (Gabke and Vaubel 1983: 29). Plastic surgery appeared on the European continent considerably later. In the early fifteenth century, the Sicilian physician Branca began doing nose surgery, using a flap of skin from the patient's arm which was immobilized by binding it to the nose until the graft could take. Other forms of plastic surgery began to appear around the early sixteenth century and were sporadically performed up until the late nineteenth century on individuals with congenital abnormalities or with deformities due to diseases like leprosy or syphilis. Harelips and cleft palates could be repaired, ears corrected, and breasts amputated in the case of tumors.

Although techniques for surgically altering the appearance of the human body have been available for centuries, the development of the field has, nevertheless, been slow. This is hardly surprising. The emergence of plastic surgery is linked to the development of medicine as well as to changing cultural notions about the alteration of the body. Prior to 1846 when ether and chloroform were discovered, surgery had to be done without anesthesia. Surgeries done under these conditions would have inevitably been traumatic for the patient and probably for the physician as well. If patients did not die from shock or loss of blood, the chance that they would perish from infection was imminent. Before the discovery of antisepsis in 1867, it is a wonder that patients managed to survive surgery at all.[1]

In addition, the body was thought to be the corporeal manifestation of the relationship between God and man, with disease and deformity being due to the consequences of immorality (Turner 1984; Finkelstein 1991). Leprosy or small pox were divine punishment for sins committed, a monstrous infant the result of the mother's promiscuous behavior. In this context, surgical intervention took on a slightly blasphemous character as it disturbed the natural order of things and eliminated the marks of punishment. Early facial surgery, a case in point, was frequently employed to repair the ravages of syphilis. The lowly status of the surgeon, who was up until the seventeenth century little more than a local barber, further accounts for plastic surgery being regarded as a slightly disreputable practice.

With the development of medicine as a science, surgery underwent a general rehabilitation. Surgeons were required to have a university education, setting them apart from other lay practitioners. Medical science replaced traditional beliefs linking the physical body to the person's moral character and propagated the merits of observation and classification. Under the all-encompassing medical gaze, every aspect of the body became a welcome object for scrutiny, including abnormalities in bodily appearance. While the status of surgery improved, it took the phenomenon of mass warfare to eliminate the moral onus attached to plastic surgery and to enable it to emerge as a full-fledged medical specialty.

The Crimean war and both world wars produced a large number of casualties. Thousands of young men were severely burned or disfigured during battle. Surgeons were sent to the front en masse to fix mutilated faces, reconstruct severed body parts, and repair burns, thereby gaining invaluable practice in their craft. Enormous strides were made in developing techniques for reconstructing limbs and hands and for repairing badly scarred or burned skin. In the process, plastic surgery underwent something of a moral face lift as well. It became associated with deserving heroes, injured in the course of doing their patriotic duty, rather than with the mere victims of an unkind fate who were expected to bear their suffering with fortitude (Minker and Scholtz 1988). In short, plastic surgery became a respectable field of medicine.

In the years that followed, surgery continued to be performed for reconstructive purposes—that is, for restoring physical dysfunction or for minimizing disfigurement due to disease, congenital deformity, or accident. The emergence of cosmetic procedures in the mid-twentieth century dramatically altered the field of plastic surgery, marking a new phase in its history. Whereas nearly all plastic surgery in the first part of the century was done to alleviate deformities due to disease, birth, or mishap, in the second half of the century this was no longer the case. Plastic surgery began to be performed for the aesthetic improvement of otherwise healthy bodies and the number of operations increased dramatically.

The rise in cosmetic surgery was spurred on by improvements in surgical procedures and technologies. Air drills for cutting bone and planing skin, binocular magnifying lenses, precision instruments, and refined suturing materials all enabled surgical interventions to be performed with better results and less trauma for the patient (Meredith 1988). Improved technology is only part of the explanation, however. With the advent of cosmetic surgery, the rationale for surgical intervention in bodily appearance changed and, along with it, the kinds of technologies being developed. It was not only done for different reasons, but the scale on which it was performed shifted. The extension of plastic surgery into the realm of body improvement has led to a veritable boom in cosmetic surgery—a kind of "Surgical Age" (Wolf 1991). Cosmetic surgery became, for the first time, a mass phenomenon. Today cosmetic operations make up well over forty percent of all plastic surgery, and where previously patients were men disabled by war or industrial accidents, now the recipients are overwhelmingly women who are dissatisfied with the way their bodies look.[2]

In this chapter, I explore the rise of this surgical age. I consider how cosmetic surgery could become such a popular phenomenon as well as the risks and dangers associated with it. Finally, I examine how the tensions between the enormous expansion of cosmetic surgery and its shadow side are dealt with in public discourse, contrasting how the surgical fix is dealt with in the U.S. and abroad.

PLASTIC BODIES

The development of cosmetic surgery technology is inextricably connected to a market model of medicine, on the one hand, and to a consumer culture, on the other. With the rise of medicine as a profession, medical cures and services become something which could be obtained for a fee. In an open market system, the patient is a consumer and, like consumers of other products, free to choose any treatment, provided it can be paid for. The body is no longer simply a dysfunctional object requiring medical intervention, but a commodity—not unlike "a car, a refrigerator, a house—which can be continuously upgraded and modified in accordance with new interests and greater resources" (Finkelstein 1991: 87). It can be endlessly manipulated—reshaped, restyled, and reconstructed to meet prevailing fashions and cultural values.

Modern cosmetic surgery technology sustains and is a product of the notion of the body as "cultural plastic"—"a construction of life as plastic possibility and weightless choice, undetermined by history, social location, or even individual biography" (Bordo 1990: 657). The technologies of cosmetic surgery assume the makeability of the human body, expanding the limits of how the body may be restyled, reshaped and rebuilt. A twin "disdain for material limits" and an "intoxication with change" (ibid., p. 654) make the possibilities for surgical intervention seem both desirable and endless. Nowhere is this more tellingly manifested than in the use of computer technology whereby potential recipients are given a preview of how they might look after a face lift, nose job, or breast augmentation. The patient is photographed and the image is duplicated on the screen. The surgeon (God and artist, all in one) uses an electronic pencil on a special board to make the desired changes while the patient watches. Flesh is added or taken away, wrinkles disappear, breasts are inflated, or body shape is transformed. The makeability of the body and the power of medical technology are visually sustained in each demonstration (Balsamo 1993).

Cosmetic surgery is the cultural product of modernity and of a consumer culture which treats the body as a vehicle for self-expression (Featherstone 1983; 1990; Turner 1984; Finkelstein 1991; Bordo 1990; Giddens 1991). By engaging in a wide array of available body

17

maintenance routines, individuals are encouraged to seek their salvation through altering their appearance. ("You are the way you look.") Along with the beauty, fitness, and diet industries, medical technologies can be drawn upon to help turn back the biological clock—to combat the natural deterioration of the body which accompanies age and the rigors of everyday life. The notion of Nature-as-the-ultimate-constraint is replaced by Nature-as-something-to-be-improved-upon. Whereas plastic surgery was formerly aimed at repairing bodily deficiencies which made a person noticeably different from the rest of the world, it increasingly came to be seen as a normal intervention for essentially normal bodies. Bodies no longer have to be damaged or impaired to merit surgical alteration. Growing older, gaining or losing weight, or simply failing to meet the transitory cultural norms of beauty are now sufficient cause for surgical improvement. Cosmetic surgery allows us to transcend age, ethnicity, and even sex itself.[3]

FROM CELEBRITY JUNKIE TO THE GIRL NEXT DOOR

Cosmetic surgery has increasingly become a mass phenomenon, with the media playing an essential role in making it acceptable for an ever growing population. Initially, it was associated with the rich and famous (the jet set, celebrities, pop singers). Tales of the surgical exploits of Farah Dibah, Raquel Welch, Sophia Loren, Jane Fonda, Michael Jackson, Joan Collins, and others abounded as the media regaled us with descriptions of lavish clinics where they enjoyed gourmet meals and private suites, along with their face lifts and body sculpting.[4] Models, news commentators, or actresses whose work puts them in the public eye have come to consider cosmetic surgery part of the job. In Beverly Hills, plastic surgeons have their own publicity firms and even accept Visa and MasterCard.[5] The undisputed queen of cosmetic surgery is the pop singer and actress Cher, who has reputedly undergone dozens of operations. She has spent over seventy-five thousand dollars on altering her body ("My body is my capital."), having her stomach corrected to give her navel a "girlish look," her dimples enhanced with silicone, and, most dramatically, two ribs removed to emphasize her waist. By chronicling the operative histories of individuals who are already considered by the public to be beautiful, the media makes its message clear: no one is so beautiful that she cannot become even more so with the help of surgery.

The first articles on cosmetic surgery began to appear between 1965 and 1975, and the end of 1975 marked the beginning of a new era with an increase of nearly two hundred percent in the number published (Dull and West 1987: 3). Upscale glossies like *Vogue, Cosmopolitan*, or *Self* as well as most daily newspapers today regularly feature advertisements for clinics specializing in such surgery. Women's magazines frequently provide personal testimonies of the "before and after" variety, which depict women's experiences with various kinds of operations. A typical article describes an ordinary, young, professional woman who "just wants to feel a little better" by having her breasts augmented.[6] She is not portrayed as a celebrity ("My breasts never dominated my life, not like other women.") and her motives seem imminently reasonable—after all, who wouldn't want to feel better? The reader is subsequently taken behind the scenes as she goes through the procedure. Potential unpleasantness and difficulties are downplayed in pictures which show the patient lying bare-breasted and smiling on the operating table with circles drawn where the surgeon will cut. ("Here is C., right before the operation. . . . [I]n just over an hour, the silicone implants will be sitting pretty.") Having a breast augmentation becomes a kind of adventure, something to look forward to in pleasant anticipation. The story has a happy ending, the patient emerging with a new body and a boost to her self-confidence as well.

Although magazines occasionally feature a personal testimony about a failed operation ("My life was ruined after having a nose job."), the mishap tends to be attributed to medical malpractice rather than to problems inherent in the operation itself. The patient is simply unfortunate in having run into the one bad apple in the otherwise exemplary bunch of plastic surgeons. In general, surgery is presented as a relatively harmless way to improve appearance—an acceptable path toward happiness and well-being.

There is, of course, the problem of the "plastic surgery junkie"—the individual who indulges in "plastic surgery the way some of us eat chocolate—compulsively."[7] Undeterred by the cost, pain, or terrible bruising, those who are pathologically addicted to having their bodies remade or beautified through surgery cannot be stopped. Although cases of repeated cosmetic surgery receive considerable media attention, the addiction of the recipients tends to be normalized in such public discourse. In her discussion of television's treatment of the cosmetic surgery boom, Dull (1989) shows how "scalpel slaves" may be used to promote the advantages of cosmetic surgery to the general public. For example, in 1986 Oprah Winfrey invited people who had had as many as nine cosmetic operations to share their surgical resumes on her show. As the program progressed, the audience's horror and skepticism were gradually transformed. They no longer viewed this involvement as a sign of addiction, but began to see it as simply a matter of being "prosurgery"—an imminently reasonable choice among all the other choices available to the modern individual.[8]

In short, the media constructs cosmetic surgery as an option which is not only available to everyone, but which bears the promise of an exalted life—one can partake in what was formerly available to the chosen few. Or, as Featherstone (1983) puts it:

> [T]he imagery of consumer culture presents a world of ease and comfort, once the privilege of an elite, now apparently within the reach of all. An ideology of personal consumption presents individuals as free to do their own thing, to construct their own little world in the private sphere (p. 21).

In such a climate, it is not surprising that cosmetic surgery would seem to be more and more of an option for everyone. Despite its costs, it is available for even those who would normally doubt that they could afford it.

THE COSMETIC SURGERY BOOM

Cosmetic surgery is big business. In the U.S., it takes its place alongside the twenty billion dollar cosmetics industry and the thirty-three billion dollar diet industry as one of the most rapidly expanding fields in the beauty system today (Wolf 1991). Three hundred million dollars are spent every year on cosmetic surgery and the amount is increasing annually by ten percent. Operations are expensive, ranging from two hundred fifty dollars for a chemical face peel to over five thousand dollars for an abdominoplasty or tummy tuck.[9] The average plastic surgeon makes a profit of $180,000 a year, earning nearly double the income of a family practitioner, pediatrician, or internist and considerably more than what the average obstetrician or gynecologist would earn.[10]

In 1988, more than two million Americans underwent some form of cosmetic surgery. This figure was up from 590,550 in 1986 and it continues to skyrocket.[11] In the U.S., the number of operations doubled every five years, until it tripled between 1984 and 1986 (Wolf 1991: 251). The situation is no different in many European countries. Within the last decade, cosmetic surgery has doubled in Great Britain. As Wolf graphically describes it: "a city the size of San Francisco gets cut open every year in the United States; in Britain, a village the size of Bath" (p. 251). In Germany one hundred eighty million marks are spent annually on cosmetic surgery. More than one hundred thousand Germans have such surgery each year, including ten percent from former East Germany (a "new face for a new boss from the West").[12] In The Netherlands, it is estimated that between ten and twenty thousand cosmetic surgery operations are performed every year. Since 1982, all operations have doubled in frequency and eyelid corrections and tummy tucks are up five hundred and three hundred percent respectively, since 1975 (Starmans 1988).

Nearly ninety percent of the operations are performed on women: all breast corrections, ninety-one percent of face lifts, eighty-six percent of eyelid reconstructions, and sixty-one percent of all nose surgery. In 1987, American women had 94,000 breast reconstructions, 85,000 eyelid corrections, 82,000 nose jobs, 73,230 liposuctions, and 67,000 face lifts—nine times more operations than men had (American Society for Plastic and Reconstructive Surgeons 1987). The only procedures which are performed primarily on men are hair transplants (ninety-five percent) and ear surgery (forty-four percent). (National Center for Health Statistics 1987). Despite reports that men are having faces and necks lifted and sagging eyelids corrected to give them a "competitive advantage" in the business world, women continue to be the primary objects of surgical intervention.[13] Whereas the majority of cosmetic surgery operations have been performed on white women, in 1990 it was estimated that twenty percent of the cosmetic surgery patients in the U.S. were Latinos, African Americans, and Asian Americans. Of these, over sixty percent were women (Kaw 1993).[14]

Cosmetic surgery is the fastest growing specialty in American medicine (Faludi 1991: 217). Whereas the total number of physicians has little more than doubled in the last quarter of a century, the number of plastic surgeons has increased fourfold. At the end of World War II, there were only about one hundred plastic surgeons in the U.S. In 1965, there were 1,133 plastic surgeons and in 1990, the number of certified plastic surgeons had reached 3,850.[15] In Southern California alone, there are 289 practitioners. By 1988, the caseload of registered plastic surgeons had more than doubled, to 750,000 operations annually. Since at least ninety percent of cosmetic surgery is performed in a physician's office or a private clinic,[16] it is not necessary to be a licensed plastic surgeon to be able to perform cosmetic surgery. Face lifts, eyelid corrections, or chemical peeling may be performed by a dermatologist, while otorhinolaryngologists (ENT-specialists) are engaging in nose and ear corrections. There are no standard procedures for preoperative screening and less concern for quality control than would be the case in a hospital setting.[17]

NEW TECHNOLOGIES

Cosmetic surgery began with the application of reconstructive procedures to recipients who were not disfigured through birth, disease, or accident, but were concerned with improving their appearance. Although this distinction is not always easy to make, plastic surgeons now emphasize the difference between surgery for reconstructive purposes and surgery for aesthetic or cosmetic reasons. In fact, plastic surgeons in the U.S. belong to separate professional organizations from cosmetic surgeons and have different access to medical insurance. Consequently, they have different kinds of patients as well as different status. Although reconstructive surgeons earn less money, their work does not carry the commercial taint attached to surgery for aesthetic purposes. Nor do they face the difficulties of having to justify doing surgery without a clear-cut medical indication.[18]

While much of the growth in plastic surgery has been in cosmetic surgery, it often seems to be a matter of taking earlier reconstructive technologies and putting them to new uses. For example, rhinoplasties, the oldest form of plastic surgery, are now performed in response to the patient's desire to meet a cultural ideal (Millard 1974)—creating the "the nose best suited for the individual face."[19] Nose contouring is currently regarded as a solution for "teen angst," and is an increasingly popular graduation gift for adolescents concerned that their noses are too large/too flat/too ethnic to meet the current standards of facial appearance.[20] Ear surgery (otoplasty) has also expanded its horizons (Huffstadt 1981). A relatively simple operation which was frequently performed on the "jug ears" of school-age children is now being perfected to ever more refined interventions. Earlobe reductions have become the "latest nip-and-tuck": overly-long earlobes ("a much overlooked sign of aging") are trimmed down to twenty-five percent of the total ear (a more "ideal" format).[21] Once done to alleviate vision impairment due to sagging eyelids, double eyelid surgery is increasingly employed to westernize the eyes of Asian businessmen, consumer-conscious Korean housewives (Finkelstein 1991) and, more recently, Asian American women (Kaw 1993). Braces and the capping of teeth, which used to be the province of orthodontists, has now been transformed into cosmetic dentistry—a rising specialty which can involve a radical reconstruction of the entire face and jaw for aesthetic purposes. In each case, old techniques are refined or applied to different kinds of patients.

In addition, new medical technologies and procedures have been developed since the early sixties which belong exclusively to the domain of cosmetic surgery. For example, face lifts, breast augmentations, and fat removal or body contouring are the most frequently performed procedures. They are done almost exclusively on women for aesthetic or cosmetic reasons.[22] Because these newer procedures mark a shift in both the practice of surgically altering bodily appearance as well as in cultural discourses about the human body, I will discuss them in more detail.

FACE LIFTS

Although face lifting was first developed in France in 1919, it took another fifty years before it was done to any great extent (Huffstadt 1981). In the U.S., rhytodectomies (the word comes from the Greek word for wrinkle) are now the third most common form of cosmetic surgery. They are performed to smooth out wrinkles or eliminate the sags and puffiness associated with age or the ravages of sunbathing, poor nutrition, smoking, or excessive drinking. The operation involves making an incision from the temples to the front of the ear and then behind the ear to the back of the head. The facial and neck skin are then lifted from the underlying skin and pulled toward the incision. The overlapping skin is cut off and the new edge is sewed to the scalp. It has been compared to "lifting off a wrinkled piece of plastic wrap, smoothing it out and putting it back again."[23]

Face lifts are not the solution for everyone and, as Finkelstein (1991) notes, the ideal candidate often seems to be the one who least needs it. To be ensured of success, the patient should be "of slender build, with soft, smooth skin and minimal sub-cutaneous fat, with a family history of youthful aging, without serious illness, emotional trauma, or weight fluctuation after operation, and with the desire and skill to augment the surgical improvement by makeup, hairstyling, and enhancing clothes" (Goldwyn 1980: 693). Surgeons, in fact, recommend that face lifts should only be performed on patients who already have demonstrated a concern for their appearance. For those who do not display the "appropriate concern for their appearance," a trip to the local beauty farm is recommended instead (Huffstadt 1981).

Despite these restrictions, more than sixty-seven thousand American women had their faces lifted in 1987—nearly ten times more than the seven thousand male recipients in the same year (American Society of

Plastic and Reconstructive Surgeons 1987). The typical face-lift candidate is described as a well-to-do, fashionably-dressed, middle-aged woman between the ages of forty-five and sixty who anticipates having to attract a new mate after a divorce or simply wants to hold her own on the job in the face of younger competition.[24] However, face lifts are increasingly being done on younger women as well. Ever on the lookout for new recipients, one enterprising surgeon found prisons provided a new market for his services. Some female prisoners suffered from "premature aging of the skin due to extensive use of drugs and poor nutrition;" others wanted to have needle marks removed.[25]

Face lifts often go hand in hand with additional surgical procedures. Eyelid corrections take care of telltale sagging or eliminate puffiness associated with fatigue, heavy drinking, or depression. Silicone may be implanted into chin or cheeks to fatten up faces shrunken by age or simply not lush enough to meet current standards of beauty. Dimples can be created surgically in cheeks or a chin enhanced with a ruggedly handsome cleft (Rees and Wood-Smith 1973: 510–511). Collagen treatments which involve pumping a protein directly into the skin to plump out the fine lines or enlarge lips are becoming increasingly popular.

Face lifts and associated procedures do take off years, but they are not permanent. They have to be redone. For example, surgeons recommend that the patient should have her or his first face lift in the early to mid-forties, the second in the fifties, and the third in the sixties and so on (Rees and Wood-Smith 1973). Moreover, since collagen is quickly absorbed by the body, this kind of treatment is only of temporary benefit and has to be repeated, sometimes more than once a year. It becomes, literally, a form of body maintenance—not unlike getting a permanent or having a facial.[26]

For individuals who cannot afford this kind of maintenance—maintenance which can run up to a total of eight thousand dollars—less drastic procedures for rejuvenating the face are available. Chemical peeling (dissolving the top layers of the skin with acid) or dermabrasion (sanding down the skin with a machine-powered wire brush) can delay face lifts or be used to eliminate fine facial wrinkles caused by exposure to the sun or smoking, acne scars, and other blemishes (Meredith 1988).

BREAST AUGMENTATIONS

Breast corrections (mastopexy, reduction, argumentation) also have a long history. In medieval times, breasts were amputated for tumors and the first case of a breast reduction for aesthetic reasons was reported in

1560.[27] It wasn't until the late nineteenth century, however, that breast reductions were performed to any significant degree. The practice of enlarging breasts did not appear until mid-twentieth century.

Augmentations were first performed in the early 1950s in Japan, but it was not until the early sixties that they became a commercial success. A topless cocktail waitress working in San Francisco became an instant media star in the late fifties when she allowed twenty shots of silicone to be injected directly into her breasts. The press had a field day exploiting Carol Doda's—now forty-four double D—chest. Enthusiasm for this method waned when it was discovered that paraffin or silicone injected directly tended to migrate to other parts of the body, causing cysts and necrosis of the skin. Sponges made of terylene wool, polyvinyl or polyethylene were then introduced to replace the injections. These new materials were an improvement, but they often hardened, protruded or caused fluid to accumulate in the breasts, which then had to be drained.

By 1963, inflatable silicone implants were becoming increasingly popular as a way to enlarge small breasts or correct asymmetrical breast development. The implants consisted of bags containing silicone gel or, less commonly, saline solution. Some were coated with a polyurethane foam, although these were later taken off the market by the manufacturers themselves because of their possible carcinogenicity (*FDA Medical Bulletin* July 1991). Silicone implants could be inserted by means of a small incision in the armpit, nipple, or underneath the breast. These implants had the advantage of feeling like real breasts and were less likely to be rejected by the body's immune system, particularly if used in conjunction with steroids. A pocket was created below or behind the chest muscle so that the implant could be inserted.

Although silicone implants also had drawbacks, breast augmentations became one of the most popular forms of cosmetic surgery (Meredith 1988). It is estimated that over one million women in the United States have had their breasts "enhanced," usually by means of silicone implants. Each year one hundred thirty thousand women embark on this operation in the U.S.—the single most commonly performed operation next to liposuctions. The situation is similar in other countries. In Britain, six thousand silicone implant operations are carried out every year. In The Netherlands, there has been a fifty percent increase in the number of augmentations performed since 1982 (van Ham 1990: 99)—more breast augmentations per one hundred thousand inhabitants than in any other country in the world.

Most breast augmentations are performed on women between the ages of twenty and thirty. However, increasingly younger women are having them (two percent of the breast augmentations in the U.S. are performed on women under the age of eighteen) as well as women well into middle age whose breasts have begun to sag after pregnancies and breast feeding. Breast augmentations are increasingly a prerequisite for any job which places a woman in front of the camera.[28]

FAT REMOVAL AND BODY CONTOURING

In a culture which suffers under a "tyranny of slenderness" (Chernin 1981) and where the diet industry has reached epidemic proportions, an increasing number of people consider themselves overweight. In the U.S., for example, more than seventy-nine million Americans claim that they weigh too much (Spitzak 1990: 9). In this context, it is not surprising that various techniques in cosmetic surgery have been developed for eliminating fat and trimming overweight bodies. Procedures range from tightening abdominal skin that has lost its elasticity due to weight loss, pregnancy, or the normal aging process, to abdominoplasties that involve cutting off an apron of excess skin which has caused discomfort and irritation.

Originally, cosmetic surgery was not considered a substitute for dieting. In recent years, however, a technique has been developed which makes dieting a thing of the past. The liposuction or suction lipectomy has been developed to remove fatty tissue. Imported from France in 1982, this procedure involves injecting a saline solution, which liquefies the fat, into the area in question. A small incision is then made and fatty deposits are sucked out with a kind of vacuum cleaner. The procedure may be performed in conjunction with abdominoplasties or locally to eliminate saddlebag thighs, trim hips and buttocks, and even get rid of "pudding knees."[29] The most extreme form of body contouring or sculpting involves trimming, tucking and remodeling the entire body in a series of nearly simultaneous operations. The advantage to the patient is that she only has to be put under anesthesia once (Pitanguy 1967). For example, fat can be removed from hips and ankles, sagging skin in upper arms and tummy tucked, and a neck lift performed—all in one sitting.

Liposuctions are the fastest growing form of cosmetic surgery in the U.S. In 1986 alone one hundred thousand operations were performed— a number which rose by seventy-eight percent between 1984 and 1986.[30] By 1989 one hundred thirty thousand women alone underwent liposuctions and more than two hundred thousand pounds of body tissue was suctioned out of them (Wolf 1991: 261).[31] Although liposuctions are far from safe and have even been know to cause death when too much body tissue is removed, they continue to enjoy an unprecedented popularity.[32]

PROBLEMS AND PITFALLS

Without doubt, cosmetic surgery is popular. It is, however, also painful and risky. The most minor intervention causes discomfort, ranging from the dead crust of skin left by a chemical peel to the swelling and inflammation of a face lift. Other operations like abdominoplasties, breast corrections, and liposuctions fall under the category of major surgery, requiring hospitalization and sometimes even intensive care. Recovery periods can be long and arduous—painful drains and a slow healing process for breast corrections, wearing a tight girdle after a liposuction to keep the skin from sagging, or having the jaws wired together for two months following cosmetic dentistry are all routine postsurgical experiences. While these discomforts may force the recipient into hiding until her bruised and swollen body returns to some semblance of normalcy and she can show herself to the outside world, there is more involved in most cosmetic surgery than just discomfort.

Most operations have side effects, many of which are serious and even permanent. Although statistics are not kept, the list of complications accompanying cosmetic operations is long (Goldwyn 1980). For starters, infections, wound disruption, and erosion of overlying skin are a routine byproduct of any operation. Scar tissue can harden or darken. There is no way to prevent this kind of disfigurement and it is estimated that over twenty percent of all cosmetic surgery involves repairing scar tissue left over from previous operations.[33] Negative reactions to anesthesia are so common that they are called routine complications, although in some cases they can be fatal.[34]

Each operation has its own specific dangers. Pain, numbness, bruising, discoloration, and depigmentation frequently follow a liposuction, often lingering up to six months after the operation. Face lifts can damage nerves, leaving the person's face permanently numb. More serious disabilities include fat embolisms, blood clots, hypovolemia (fluid depletion), and, in some cases, death. While a breast augmentation is relatively minor surgery and can even be performed on an outpatient basis, it is, nevertheless, a risky undertaking. Health experts estimate that the chance of side effects is between thirty and fifty percent, some of which are very serious. The least dramatic and most common side effects include decreased sensitivity of the nipples, painful swelling or congestion of the breasts, hardening of the breasts which makes it difficult to lie down comfortably or to raise the arms without the implants shifting position, or asymmetrical breasts (Gurdin 1972). While such side effects are common, they are usually temporary and not health threatening. More serious is the problem of encapsulation, whereby the body reacts to the presence of foreign matter by developing an enclosing capsule of fibrous tissue around the implant. This happens in nearly thirty-five percent of the cases. The implant becomes doorknob-shaped, rock hard, and painful. In some cases, a firm massage on the part of the surgeon (euphemistically called "fluffing them up") will break up the tissue—at great pain to the patient. If this does not work, however, the implants have to be removed—a formidable procedure sometimes requiring that the hardened implants be literally chiselled from the patient's chest wall. More rarely, the implant's outer envelope ruptures or there is gradual leakage of silicone into the body ("gel bleed")—a process which can impair the woman's immune system permanently, leading to arthritis, lupus, connective tissue disease, respiratory problems, or brain damage (Walsh et al., 1989; Weiss 1991; Goldblum et al., 1992). There is still debate about whether the detection of cancerous abnormalities in mammograms is impaired by the presence of an implant or that the implants themselves can cause cancer.

Cosmetic operations often have to be redone. While face lifts fall and have to be repeated every five years, silicone breast implants need to be replaced after fifteen years. Fat which has been removed from thighs or buttocks may return, requiring another liposuction, or the skin may bag and have to be cut and redraped.

Finally, the recipient of cosmetic surgery faces the very real possibility that she may emerge from the operation in worse shape than she was before. Unsuccessful breast augmentations are disfiguring. They leave the recipient with unsightly scars instead of a bigger chest size. An overly tight face lift produces the zombie look—a countenance utterly devoid of expression.[35] Following a liposuction, the skin can develop a corrugated, uneven texture or dents so that the recipient looks worse than she did before the surgery.

SITUATED CRITIQUE

Making sense of both the popularity and the problems of the surgical fix requires situating cosmetic surgery in the cultural and social context from which it emerged. Cosmetic surgery belongs to the cultural landscape of late modernity: consumer capitalism, technological development, liberal individualism, and the belief in the makeability of the human body. It is in this context that cosmetic surgery could emerge as an acceptable means for altering or improving the appearance of the body.

In recent years, however, cosmetic surgery has become increasingly controversial as well. Cosmetic surgery involves a surgical intervention in otherwise healthy bodies. It is a painful and dangerous solution for problems which are rarely life threatening and seldom evoke physical discomfort. And, last but not least, cosmetic surgery is expensive. In an age when cutbacks in health-care expenditure are the order of the day, it is a problematic medical practice.

While cosmetic surgery has become a source of contention in both the U.S. and Europe, these controversies take a different form, depending upon the organization of health care and the political commitment to welfare in each country in question. The organization of health care delivery not only sets limits on who may or may not indulge in the surgical fix, but it shapes the cultural discourses through which the controversial dimensions of cosmetic surgery can be expressed. Like other controversial medical procedures and technologies (in vitro fertilization, fetal monitoring, organ transplants or even female genital excision), cosmetic surgery is justified and criticized for different reasons.[36]

In order to deepen our understanding of how cosmetic surgery is problematized (as well as of what is left out of the critique), I shall now take a look at two different models of medicine—a market model and a welfare model—and the discourses through which cosmetic surgery in each case tends to be criticized.

A MARKET MODEL: THE DISCOURSE OF RISK

In a market model of medicine, health care is provided on the basis of fee-for-service (Cockerham 1992).[37] Government regulation of services and technologies is limited. Specialists are free to provide services, just as patients are free to choose the health care they desire, provided they can pay for it. Public access is not guaranteed. By encouraging competition among providers, a market model is supposed to enhance the quality of health care. The issue of equality in the distribution of health care is largely unaddressed.[38] Patients see themselves as consumers, regarding health care as a privilege rather than an entitlement. However, as consumers, they expect value for their money. The medical profession is responsible for providing quality health care while keeping risks at a minimum.

In a market model of medicine, controversies about care tend to center around the problems of risk, informed consent, and malpractice. Patients are free to embark upon dangerous or even experimental medical practices, provided they know what they are getting into and can knowledgeably calculate the risks.[39] The medical profession, and more indirectly, the regulatory bureaucracy, are expected to keep patients posted concerning the advantages and disadvantages of medical services so that they can make informed decisions. Patients are not supposed to be exposed to medical experimentation unless they have had access to this information and their consent has been obtained in advance. The malpractice suit insists that the medical profession toe the line, giving patients the possibility of compensation in cases of medical failure.[40]

In the U.S., the drawbacks of cosmetic surgery have been discussed in terms of risk and informed consent. Nowhere is this more tellingly illustrated than the recent controversy concerning silicone implants for breast augmentation surgery. The development of breast implants has always been an enterprise fraught with difficulties (Pickering et al., 1980). In the 1960s, the Food and Drug Administration (the FDA) banned the direct injection of silicone into the breasts. By the early seventies, the rubbery implants of the sixties were succeeded by implants filled with silicone gels which were less likely to be rejected by the body. Silicone implants were on the market even before they were officially approved in 1976. Like many other medical devices—for example, the infamous Dalkon shield— silicone implants were grandfathered by the FDA, meaning that manufacturers could continue to sell the implants while scientific data were being collected (*FDA Medical Bulletin*, July 1991). It was known as early as 1965 that silicone might be carcinogenic. By 1972, information was available that silicone migration could cause serious damage to the immune system. However, this information was not made public and manufacturers—most notably, Dow Corning—continued to distribute silicone implants for breast augmentations to women on a large scale. The FDA ignored the matter for another twelve years, relying on drug companies to keep the public informed and on physicians, in turn, to advise women about the risks and benefits of implants before scheduling surgery.

In 1984, the silence surrounding the dangers of silicone implants was broken when a federal court awarded a Nevada woman one and a half million dollars in punitive damages after her implants had leaked silicone into her body. The manufacturer was held responsible for withholding information about the dangers of the implants. In the decade that followed, more successful law suits against implant manufacturers followed. Atrocity stories about silicone began to accumulate.

Consumer-advocate groups filed complaints with the FDA regarding misleading information in the literature published by the makers of breast implants. Pressure ensued from congressional critics as well as the media. Allegations were made that Dow Corning—the primary manufacturer of silicone implants—had violated federal laws regarding the labeling of medical devices and had failed to warn consumers about risks which they had known of since 1968. In the decade which followed, negative test results continued to trickle in. Congressional committee hearings were held and, finally, in 1991, the FDA, by now a little hot under the collar about implants, demanded that they be taken off the market until the contradictory data could be more thoroughly evaluated. Since 1992, use of silicone implants has been limited to cases of "urgent need"—usually meaning reconstruction following mastectomies—and to candidates enrolled in clinical studies. It is unclear how many women will be able to get implants through these trials, and, indeed, how many will want to have them since the negative findings on silicone have been made available to the general public.

The crux of the silicone controversy was not that the implants were risky per se. Data about side effects has been contradictory and inconclusive.[41] Moreover, despite the drawbacks of the implants, studies abound which show a high level of patient satisfaction.[42] The controversy concerned how the implants had been made available. By withholding information, the manufacturers and, later, the FDA by association, made themselves guilty of fraud. Patients had not been able to weigh the risks against the benefits of the implants. It was argued that women as consumers had a right to be informed that the implants were risky and to decide whether or not they wanted to be guinea pigs for a procedure which was still being tested.

The case of the implant illustrates both the strengths and the weaknesses of a discourse of risk, and, by implication a market model of medicine, for coming to terms with the problems associated with cosmetic surgery. On the one hand, it sustains—at least, in theory—the notion that the individual patient, including the woman who wants cosmetic surgery, has the right to expect quality service (as long as she can pay for it), is entitled to complete information about the service, and is capable of making her own decisions (Parker 1993). This right could be mobilized by consumers as a resource in their struggles for satisfactory health care, both individually through malpractice suites or collectively through pressure from consumer organizations.

On the other hand, the issue of why silicone implants should have been available in the first place is more difficult to raise in a market model of medicine. Determining the safety or efficacy of a device after it has already been developed is not the same as deciding whether it is desirable or necessary, or why certain individuals feel that it is necessary for their well-being. When cosmetic surgery is treated as a private matter, the issue of why individuals might regard the surgical alteration of their appearance as a precondition for their happiness and well-being is left unexplored. And, of course, the issue of why most cosmetic surgery recipients are women is not addressed.

In most European countries where a welfare model of medicine prevails, medical technology and procedures are evaluated within a discourse of need and scarcity of resources for public health services. Since cosmetic surgery tends to be limited to the private sector (just as it is in the U.S.), it is not discussed within this discourse. The exception is The Netherlands where cosmetic surgery was, until recently, covered by national health insurance and included in the basic health care plan. I shall now turn to the welfare model of medicine with its discourse of need in order to explore another problematic dimension of cosmetic surgery—a dimension which tends to be ignored in a market model of medicine with its discourse of risk.

A WELFARE MODEL: THE DISCOURSE OF NEED

Most industrialized European countries have a welfare model of medicine, ranging from socialized medicine to decentralized health care (Cockerham 1992). Despite differences—notably in how directly the government regulates services and payments to providers—welfare models of medicine offer comprehensive health care for all citizens. In theory, a patient has a right to any form of health care he or she needs. Health care is not simply a privilege to be enjoyed by those who can afford it, but an entitlement for every citizen, regardless of his or her social position.

In practice, however, many health care services are too expensive for the state to fund. The most common dilemma in the European welfare model of medicine is the increasingly articulated need for particular services and technologies and the equally pressing necessity to limit government expenditure on health care (Ginsburg 1992). A discourse of need shifts attention from risk to whether a particular medical service or procedure is really necessary in a context of scarcity. There is generally an implicit or explicit consensus that unnecessary services cannot be included in the basic health-care package and must, therefore, be abandoned or made available through other means.

Controversies about medical procedures and technologies center around the problem of equal distribution rather than the quality of the service itself. If quality is an issue, it tends to be raised in the context of attempts on the part of the welfare bureaucracy to cut costs. Patient organizations are less concerned with information about the risks of procedures and more concerned with filling up the holes in a crumbling welfare system by setting up support groups, hot lines, or alternative health care centers.

In most European welfare systems, cosmetic surgery is considered a luxury. It is performed in private clinics and is not covered by national health insurance unless there is a clear-cut medical indication. Despite the increase in the number of cosmetic surgery operations performed in Europe, the expansion is often referred to as a "typically American" phenomenon. Wolf (1991), the leading American critic of the cosmetic surgery craze, echoes this sentiment:

> Procedures . . . we have come to tolerate in America still sound nauseating in Great Britain and revolting in The Netherlands, but next year British women will be able to keep their gorge from rising and Dutch women will feel merely queasy (p. 251).

European reactions to the implant controversy are a case in point. In Britain, for example, the FDA decision to ban silicone implants was denounced in the media as a "typical instance of Americans being frightened of malpractice suits."[43] In The Netherlands, plastic surgeons and policy makers reassured the public that there was no real evidence that silicone implants were dangerous. The Secretary of the Health, Education and Welfare Department was quoted as saying he saw no reason to conduct a large-scale follow-up on women with silicone implants as he had "full confidence that the plastic surgeons who use implants have fully informed the recipients of the risks involved."[44] Instead of generating a full-scale controversy, the problems associated with the silicone breast implant were minimized ("We don't have that problem here") or left to the medical profession and welfare bureaucracy, who predictably kept the problem under wraps. Thus, silicone implants continue to be distributed in Europe.

This example suggests that the European response (or lack of response) to the drawbacks of cosmetic surgery may be more than a matter of time lag, as Wolf has suggested. Problematizing cosmetic surgery requires a discourse from which arguments can be drawn. Whereas a welfare model provides the discursive means for evaluating the drawbacks of medical technology in terms of necessity, this discourse did not apply in the case of breast implants since cosmetic surgery as a privatized form of health care did not fall under the auspices of socialized medicine. While the risks of silicone implants could be and, to some extent were, acknowledged, there was no cultural discourse of risk which could be drawn upon by a concerned public to debate them at length. Thus, in most European welfare states, the risks of cosmetic surgery tended to fall between the cracks of public discourse.

The Netherlands was the exception. Unlike the U.S. and most European countries, cosmetic surgery was not available only on a private basis. It became controversial precisely because it could be considered in terms of welfare as a medical service which was—at least in some cases—necessary for patients' health and well-being and, therefore, should be covered by national insurance.

THE DISCOURSE OF NEED REVISITED: THE DUTCH CASE

In The Netherlands, cosmetic surgery began as a small, but acceptable branch of plastic surgery. Like any other medical practice, it was included in the basic health care package, providing the surgeon thought it was necessary. Initially, plastic surgeons did not justify performing cosmetic surgery in terms of the patient's physical characteristics. Instead, they reiterated that appearance is a source of psycho-social problems and can cause an unacceptable degree of damage to the person's happiness and well-being.[45] They defended cosmetic surgery patients against charges of vanity or hypochondria. On the contrary, there may be deep psychological reasons for wanting surgery. "Loss, feelings of inferiority, sexual frigidity, and other expressions of despair" were cited (Van de Lande and Lichtveld 1972: 428). Modern society imposes norms of appearance, so that children with "jug ears" run the risk of being teased by their classmates. Women with sagging breasts may be afraid to go swimming with their children. Problems with appearance can lead to antisocial or even suicidal behavior (Huffstadt et al., 1981). Thus, cosmetic surgery is not a luxury, according to this argument, but a necessity for alleviating a specific kind of problem. The term "welfare surgery" was born.

Cosmetic surgery became problematic, however, when, in the early eighties, the demand for operations began to double. For a welfare state already in crisis, this expansion was bad news. In an attempt to stem the flow of applicants for cosmetic surgery, the national health insurance system, together with plastic surgeons, decided that guidelines were necessary for deciding when and under what circumstances cosmetic surgery was necessary (Starmans 1988).

They began by establishing three categories of problems which merited cosmetic surgery and should be eligible for coverage by national health insurance: [46]

- A functional disturbance or affliction (for example, eyelids which droop to such an extent that vision is impaired).
- Serious psychological suffering (the patient is receiving psychiatric treatment specifically for problems with appearance).
- A physical imperfection which falls "outside a normal degree of variation in appearance" (the patient's appearance does not meet certain aesthetic standards as determined by the medical inspector).

The first two categories were straightforward. Functional or physical disturbances could be unproblematically delineated within medical discourse. Recipients rarely applied for cosmetic surgery due to "severe psychological suffering" because it meant bringing a report from a psychiatrist. In practice, the majority of the cosmetic surgery recipients fell under the third category: "outside a normal degree of variation in appearance."[47] It was also this category which proved something of a headache for the national health insurance system and, indirectly, for the medical profession.

Initially, medical experts, together with the national health insurance system, attempted to develop guidelines for abnormal appearance. They looked for criteria which could be objectively observed, classified, and applied to all candidates for cosmetic surgery. Undeterred by the adage that beauty is in the eye of the beholder, these men of science seemed convinced that appearance—as any other feature of the body—could be assessed scientifically.

Some problems did, indeed, seem to be amenable to classification. For example, ears could be measured in centimeters; i.e. how far they protruded from the side of the head. Other problems received more praxeological (rule of thumb) criteria. For example, a breast lift was indicated if the "nipples were level with the recipient's elbows." A "difference of four clothing sizes between top and bottom" was sufficient indication that a breast augmentation or liposuction was in order. A sagging abdomen which "makes her look pregnant" was enough reason to perform a tummy tuck. For a face lift, the patient had "to look ten years older than his or her chronological age."

To be sure, these criteria seem to be based more on common sense than science. This was, however, only part of the problem. More seriously, the guidelines were inadequate in the practical context of deciding which kinds of cosmetic surgery should be covered by national health insurance, as the following example dramatically illustrates.

It concerns a relatively minor form of cosmetic surgery: the removal of tattoos. Initially, it was agreed that tattoo removal should not be covered by national health insurance. The argument was that tattoos were a clear example of elective cosmetic surgery. Since the patient had presumably had the tattoo put on voluntarily, it was only reasonable that he or she should have it taken off in the same way. This seemed very straightforward until a large number of Moroccan immigrant women began coming in to have their tattoos removed. The medical experts began to falter, wondering—as they put it—just how voluntary tattoos had been in this particular case. Whereas tattooing in The Netherlands was viewed as an expression of an individual's right to experiment with his or her body, experts viewed the same practice as a symbol of cultural constraint when performed in Morocco. They reasoned that since tattoos were not done voluntarily and were, furthermore, detrimental to immigrant women's integration into Dutch society and, by implication, their well-being, an exception had to be made. The criterion for tattoo removal was changed. It was covered by national health insurance, provided the recipient was not Dutch-born.

No sooner had this new guideline been established, however, when the next problem arose in the form of a highly publicized rape case where the victim had been drugged, and awoke to find her assailant's name tattooed on her stomach. When she attempted to have the tattoo removed surgically, she was denied coverage on the grounds that she was Dutch. The press got hold of the incident, much to the embarrassment of the medical inspectors. After several behind-closed-door meetings, they decided that, once again, an exception should be made and agreed to grant this particular recipient coverage.

The tattoo episode is but one example of the difficulties surrounding cosmetic surgery. However, it highlights the difficulties the medical profession faced in deciding when such surgery was necessary and when it was not. Attempts to develop general rules for applying guidelines to particular cases failed in the face of the myriad exceptions. Confronted with the exceptions, the medical profession was forced to go beyond its own discourse and draw upon subjective or commonsensical arguments. Or, more problematically, it made use of the ideological discourses available to them which meant, at least in The Netherlands, liberal individualism and ethnocentrism.

Plastic surgeons began admitting publically that cosmetic surgery was a subjective enterprise and that they often could not see what the problem was. Medical inspectors for the national health insurance system complained about having to make practical decisions on coverage without having adequate guidelines. And, more seriously, after nearly a decade of trying to get cosmetic surgery under control, the rise in the number of operations showed no signs of abating.

The medical experts and welfare bureaucrats were forced to admit defeat. After a short, heated, but somewhat belated public debate, primarily among plastic surgeons, the proponents of welfare surgery were overruled. Since the medical profession was unable to back up the welfare argument with a plan for stemming the flow of operations, there was no other recourse but to hand the issue over to the government and let it decide. Unsurprisingly, the government allowed financial considerations to prevail and decided to limit the state's responsibility to those few cases which could be justified unproblematically within medical discourse—cases of functional or psychiatric disturbance. The solution to the problem of cosmetic surgery was, therefore, to drop it from the national health insurance system and limit cosmetic surgery for strictly aesthetic reasons to the private sector.[48]

In conclusion, the Dutch case, like the U.S. case, has left some pieces missing when it comes to understanding the rise in cosmetic surgery despite its drawbacks. In the U.S., the problem of risk became a matter of public concern and the importance of the individual being able to make an informed choice was acknowledged. The problem of why individuals would want to embark on such a risky undertaking to begin with, however, was not addressed.

In The Netherlands, individual welfare and the necessity of making choices in the collective provision of health care were central concerns. Although no workable solution was found for making such decisions, the discussion itself raised the issue of need. Problems with appearance were acknowledged as a source of such suffering that cosmetic surgery could, in some cases, become necessary for the welfare of some individuals. Cosmetic surgery remained a problematic solution, however—something which should not be left to individual whim or the market economy, but should rather be treated as a matter of collective concern. Ironically, the Dutch discussion faltered because cosmetic surgery was treated as a strictly medical matter. It was left to medical practitioners to justify cosmetic surgery and, as we have seen, they were unable to come up with a convincing defense within their own discourse.

What is missing from debates about cosmetic surgery in both the U.S. and The Netherlands is the recipient. Little attention is paid to why patients are willing to take the risk of having cosmetic surgery. Nor have they been consulted in discussions about cosmetic surgery as a matter of welfare. Social policy tends to be made without enlisting the aid of those who are most effected by the outcome. Moreover, the debates have been noticeably silent about the fact that the recipients of cosmetic surgery are primarily women. Why are women so dissatisfied with their appearance that they are prepared to undergo a dangerous operation to have it altered? Why is it taken for granted by the medical profession, the welfare bureaucracy and, for that matter, the general public, that it is the female body which needs surgical alteration?

A discussion of gender and the relationship between beauty and the female body is clearly in order. This will be the subject of the next chapter. In the chapters which follow, I will explore what the recipients themselves have to say about the advantages and the disadvantages of the surgical fix.

T W O

BEAUTY AND THE FEMALE BODY

Beauty and the female body go hand in hand. In Western culture, beauty was treated as a virtue which was associated with the female sex (Lakoff and Scherr 1984; Suleiman 1985). Since Plato, feminine beauty has been idealized as representing moral or spiritual qualities. The medieval cult of chivalry extolled the fair damsel as a symbol worth fighting and even dying for. During the Renaissance, the female sex was linked to the divine. The female nude represented beauty in its purest form. Throughout the nineteenth century, Romantic poets, novelists and philosophers sought their inspiration in beauty, adopting a beautiful woman as their muse.

The alteration of the physical body in the name of beauty also has a long tradition—a tradition which has fluctuated in accordance with changing configurations of power. Although beauty practices are at present primarily the domain of women, this has not always been the case. Historically, both sexes went to great lengths to beautify and decorate their bodies. The French historian Perrot (1984) provides an arresting account of shifting practices in the alteration of the body in Western Europe. For example, in the eighteenth century the cultivation of appearance was limited to the aristocracy. There was little difference between the wealthy Parisian lady and her male counterpart. Both sported heavily powdered faces, brightly painted lips, false hair and enormous whigs, and high heels. The French revolution abolished this accentuation of class difference through appearance. In the late eighteenth century, sexual difference became the central organizer of social asymmetries of power (Laqueur 1990). This was reflected in changes in appearance. Men began to dress soberly, paying little attention to their physical appearance, while women were increasingly concerned with altering and beautifying their bodies. The corset became the symbol of the nineteenth century—literally imprisoning women in their bodies (Kunzle 1982). Assembly line production of clothing and the department store made fashion available to the masses, the beauty salon was born, and the invention of the camera made it possible for images of beauty to proliferate on a mass scale—from women's magazines to the movie industry (Lakoff and Schorr 1984; Wilson 1985; Bowlby 1987).

By the twentieth century, the cultivation of appearance had become a central concern for women of different classes, regions, and ethnic groups, simultaneously uniting them in the desire for beautification, and setting up standards to differentiate them according to class and race (Banner 1983). For example, Peiss (1990) shows how the burgeoning cosmetic industry used a combination of a universal standard of feminine beauty ("beauty through the ages") and cultural constructions of gender, class, and race to sell beauty products. The exotic vamp with the Cleopatra look became a cult figure emulated by thousands of American women, while the association of light skin and straight hair to social success, refinement, and superiority held women of color in its sway. By exploiting the tension between the appearance of Anglo-Saxon gentility and foreign exoticism, advertisers could appeal to women of different class and ethnic backgrounds, while, at the same time, creating a conception of beauty which drove a wedge between them.

As the twentieth century progressed, the standards for feminine beauty shifted in rapid succession. In the U.S., for example, the stately Gibson girl with her hourglass shape made way for the perky, flat-chested flapper of the twenties. The businesslike, assertive beauties of the forties as represented by Hollywood stars such as Joan Crawford, Katherine Hepburn, and Bette Davis were replaced by the sex symbols and Playboy bunnies of the fifties. Thin was in with Twiggy in the sixties and muscles and the healthy look were added in the late seventies as the fitness craze emerged and Jane Fonda became the symbol of feminine beauty (Banner 1983; Lakoff and Scherr 1984; Marwick 1988).

Despite the changes in cultural beauty ideals, one feature remained constant; namely, that beauty was worth spending time, money, pain, and perhaps life itself. Beauty hurts, and it appeared that modern women were willing to go to extreme lengths to improve and transform their bodies to meet the cultural requirements of femininity. Comparing contemporary Western beauty practices to the ostensibly more painful practices of other cultures (like binding feet, stretching lips, elongating necks, or filing the teeth to sharp points), Lakoff and Scherr (1984) note that:

> the pain tends to be of a long, even lifelong duration: rather than the quick prick of the needle, we have the squeezing of the tight-laced corset, the stab of the pointy toe, the asphyxiation of the collar and tie, or the scrape of the razor blade, day in and day out. The pain is perhaps less agonizing at any one moment in our beauty rituals than in theirs, but over time it evens out (p. 60).

Whether a practice is labeled mutilation or decoration, bizarre or normal depends more upon the discourses of beauty in a particular culture than any innate quality of the practice itself. Moreover, the amount of damage inflicted in the course of beautifying the body tends to be directly related to the development of technology. As Perrot (1984) has noted, the nineteenth century corset may have been unhealthy, causing breathlessness, fainting spells, and shifting organs, but the twentieth century has produced an even more constraining corset—the woman's own skin. Cosmetic surgery has become, if not routine, at least acceptable as a method of body improvement for contemporary Western women.

This chapter deals with women's willingness to suffer for the sake of beauty. First, I take a brief look at explanations put forth in the social sciences for this phenomenon, showing how these accounts are inadequate primarily due to their neglect of issues concerning gender and power. I then turn to several feminist theories which place the relationship between beauty and the female body in the context of the social reproduction of femininity and power relations. Drawing upon a critical appraisal of these theories—as well as a dash of feminist fiction—I assemble a theoretical perspective which can help me tackle women's involvement in the most drastic beauty practice of all—cosmetic surgery.

SOCIAL PSYCHOLOGY AND BEAUTY

In social psychology, appearance has been a standard topic. Empirical studies abound which show that beauty is linked to a host of positive social and cognitive characteristics (Berscheid et al., 1971; Berscheid and Walster 1974; Hatfield and Sprecher 1986). The attractive person is happier, more successful, more well-adjusted, and generally better liked. In a society where first impressions are increasingly important, attractive people get preferential treatment in everything from getting jobs to finding a residence. Good looks are important throughout the lifespan for shaping self-esteem, ensuring happiness, and determining how a person will be treated by others.

Although social psychologists portray attractiveness as advantageous for everyone, they are quick to note that there are sex differences. Studies show that men seem to profit more from being attractive and care less, while women, regardless of how they look, have difficulties reaping the benefits of physical attractiveness (Hatfield and Sprecher 1986). Men have consistently better body images than women. Even at an early age, girls admit to feeling less attractive than their sex peers and this sense of physical inferiority increases with every passing year (Freedman 1986). Women consistently perceive their bodies inaccurately or experience them as having an abnormal shape, size, or appearance (Miller et al., 1980). This faulty body image is related to a host of typical female body disorders like anorexia nervosa, obesity, agoraphobia, frigidity, and depression. It contributes to psychosomatic symptoms, stress, and feelings of shame and guilt (Freedman 1986).

Many researchers cite women's lack of self-esteem as the reason they do not profit from the advantages of physical attractiveness. Social norms of female inferiority have been internalized to the extent that even physical beauty does not bolster a woman's pride (Sanford and Donovan 1984). The beautiful woman is never really free of the fear that she will loose her looks or that she is only valued for her body. Marilyn Monroe is the paradigm example of the difficulties which can befall the beautiful woman (Lakoff and Scherr 1984). The general female propensity toward feelings of self-worthlessness make the plight of both beautiful and plain women remarkably similar. Whereas attractive men can enjoy their appearance, attractiveness is not a source of well-being for the female sex.

This is particularly disturbing in the light of findings that both sexes value physical attractiveness more highly in women than in men (Freedman 1986). Women believe that beauty is important in their everyday social interaction as well as their relationships, while men are more likely to find their attractiveness of importance in intimate relationships alone. Men especially value beauty in their partners, while women put qualities like kindness, empathy, or having the same interests on the top of their lists (Lakoff and Scherr 1984). It is assumed that women are aware of this discrepancy and in the interest of finding a male partner will be prepared to invest time and energy in maintaining their appearance.

Social psychology tends to explain such sex differences in terms of role socialization. If society—for whatever reason—requires physical attractiveness in women, girls will be socialized to comply with the norms of beauty. Sex-specific expectations concerning appropriate behavior or feelings will be internalized by the individual woman who will find beauty essential for her well-being. In a context where female inferiority is the norm, women will suffer from a low self-esteem, making them vulnerable to what others think about them.

Social psychological explanations treat women's preoccupation with their appearance as an individual, psychological problem. They do not explore the social pressures on women to be beautiful; nor are they concerned with why the social sanctions on women to comply with the norms of beauty have emerged at this particular moment in time. It therefore remains unclear why women are willing to go to such lengths to improve their appearance. By the same token, it is difficult to explain why women who have managed to defy social conventions in other areas of their lives are unable to resist the norms of beauty. In short, social psychology tends to minimize the problematic dimensions of beauty for women, while blaming the individuals who become overly concerned with their appearance.

PSYCHOANALYSIS AND BEAUTY

In psychoanalytic thought, the cultivation of appearance is associated with narcissism. Freud (1957) referred to narcissism as the "original disposition of the libido" (ibid., 81) whereby the individual achieves gratification through looking at or touching her or his own body—literally, treating it as though it were a sexual object. Children of both sexes start out with a capacity to take pleasure in their own bodies and a certain degree of narcissism is considered necessary for both sexes as a defense against feelings of worthlessness or shame. Narcissism, however, can take on a pathological hue when the individual has to shore up his or her psychic boundaries through an omnipotent sense of self-worth or an insatiable need for admiration from others (Kohut 1977). Grandiosity becomes a neurotic cover-up for a fragile identity which is too easily overwhelmed by feelings of shame or despair.

Although narcissism has its origins in the Greek myth about a young man who fell madly in love with his own reflection while bending down to drink from a pond, the narcissistic cultivation of appearance is most often associated with women, conjuring up the image of "a woman primping in front of a mirror imagining her sexual desirability to real or fantasized men" (Garry 1982: 148). Indeed, psychoanalytic thought regards narcissism as essential to women's sense of self—along with masochism and passivity, the sine qua non of femininity (Freud 1933; Deutsch 1930). Narcissism begins with the girl's fatal discovery that she lacks a penis. She is castrated; her body is deficient. This crushing blow to her pride in her body and, more generally, her self-esteem initiates a lifelong cycle of excessive vanity, alternating with bouts of shame and self-hate.

As one psychoanalyst succinctly puts it:

> I assume that the little girl who compares her genitals to those of the little boy finds her own ugly. Not only the greater modesty of women but their never ceasing striving toward beautifying and adorning their bodies is to be understood as displacement and extension of their effort to overcompensate for the original impression that their genitals are ugly (Reik, quoted in Firestone 1970: 66).

In psychoanalysis, feminine narcissism is treated as a necessary defense and even a partial corrective to the problems of femininity. By taking an excessive pride in her appearance and enjoying her own image as seen through the eyes of another, a woman can defend against the feelings of shame and inferiority which are her anatomical lot in life. Female beauty becomes a consolation prize for phallic loss.

The line between narcissism as a normal feature of femininity and narcissism as a character disorder is a thin one, however. The pride a woman takes in how she looks is, after all, little more than a thin veneer, covering a deep-seated sense of unworthiness. The cultivation of bodily appearance is a form of adaptation to the difficulties central to woman-hood—a way to keep depression at bay, at least for the moment. It does nothing, of course, to eliminate the wound which women receive to their core feeling about their bodies and sexual identities. Femininity, by definition, creates a precarious balance between narcissistic gratification and an ever-present dissatisfaction, fuelled by a deep-seated self-hate.

Unlike social psychological explanations for women's concern with their appearance, psychoanalysis asserts that women have little choice but to pursue beauty. Their very identity, not to mention their happiness and well-being, depend upon how they look. However, by treating narcis-sism as an essential feature of femininity, it gives it an ahistorical, univer-sal quality, independent of specific constellations of power or cultural contexts.[1] And, finally, psychoanalytic approaches to feminine narcissism construct and reproduce a double standard of mental health: to be nor-mal, a woman must be feminine. However, being feminine, she auto-matically becomes maladjusted and disturbed (Broverman et al., 1970; Smith and David 1975). A woman who cultivates her appearance is damned-if-she-does and damned-if-she-doesn't.

SOCIOLOGY AND BEAUTY

Although women's relationship to their bodies and their problems with beauty were on the agenda of feminist sociologists for nearly two decades (Henley 1977; Millman 1980; Chernin 1981; Brownmiller 1985; Collins 1990; Smith 1990b), the body seems only very recently to have become a topic for the sociological mainstream (Turner 1984; O'Neill 1985; Featherstone 1991; 1992; Finkelstein 1991; Giddens 1991; 1992; Scott and Morgan 1993; Shilling 1993). Sociology is pri-marily concerned with institutions, social structure, the constitution of society, and social change—subjects which were apparently far removed from the individual's relations to his or her body. As Turner (1984) explains:

> The human body as a limiting point of human experience and consciousness seemed less important than the collective reality of the social world within which the self was located. The legitimate rejection of biological determinism in favor of sociological deter-minism entailed, however, the exclusion of the body from the sociological imagination (p. 31).

Bodies, however, are back. Frank (1991) traces this sudden return of the body as a respectable topic for sociological inquiry to the contradictory impulses of modernity as carried forward in postmodern theory. This is the backdrop for considerable research on the importance of beauty in consumer society as well as on women's particular involvement with the cultivation of appearance.[2]

Interest in the body is the product of a typically modernist conflict. On the one hand, modernity spawned positivism which treats the empirical world as an objective mirror of reality. On the other hand, it launched the Enlightenment quest for a transcendental reason which would provide the stable foundations for knowledge and politics. At the same time, however, the actual (post) modern world is characterized by impermanence, fragmentation, and constant flux.[3] There are many versions of reality in it and the tendency toward political relativism and even nihilism lurks just around the corner. The contradiction between modernist certainty and (post)modernist uncertainty is played out in sociological perspectives on the body. On the one hand, the body is treated as the biological bedrock of theories on self and society. It is the "only constant in a rapidly changing world, the source of fundamental truths about who we are and how society is organized, the final arbiter of what is just and unjust, human and inhumane, progressive and retrogressive" (Frank 1990: 133). On the other hand, the body itself seems to provide the most convincing proof for radical constructionism. It has become increasingly untenable to speak of a natural body. The work of social scientists like Douglas (1966; 1973) and Goffman (1959; 1963; 1967; 1976) demonstrate that the body's surface and comportment as well as the cultural beliefs and technologies concerning its maintenance, alteration, or improvement vary radically, both within and between cultures. The body as social construct appears to be suited for use as a ground for launching criticisms against claims of universality, objectivity, or political correctness.

The contradiction between the body as bedrock and the body as construct can also be found in postmodern theory. For example, in the "high theory" of Barthes (1985), Lacan (1977; 1982), Deleuze and Guattari (1983), and Baudrillard (1988), the material body makes room for the body as metaphor, but the tension remains.[4] The body is treated as the ideal location from which to criticize Enlightenment philosophy and its tendency to privilege the experience of a Western masculine elite which had devalued the body. By "embody-ing" knowledge, these critics deconstruct the faulty universalist pretensions of such narratives as merely one version among many.

In the work of Foucault (1978; 1979; 1980; 1985; 1986; 1988), which has made an even greater impact on recent sociological theory, the body is treated as a primary site for investigating how power works. Modern power is no longer deployed from above, but works at the micro-level of the body, through discipline rather than oppression. The body is a good place to explore how different subjectivities are constructed and authorized as the truth through the disciplinary discourses of power. Thus, the body in postmodern theory is both reference point in a world of flux and the epitome of that flux (Frank 1991:40).

The revival of interest in the body has formed the backdrop for recent studies on the importance of appearance in Western consumer culture (Turner 1984; Featherstone 1983; 1991). Postwar improvements in organization of production, a general increase in wages, the improved distribution of commodities through department stores and buying on credit, and the rise of advertising all contribute to the creation of a mass consumer market for personal goods and services. The Protestant ethic of the nineteenth century, with its emphasis on hard work, thrift, and sobriety, makes way for an ethic of leisure, consumption, and "calculating hedonism" (Jacoby 1980).

> The imagery of consumer culture presents a world of ease and comfort, once the privilege of an elite, now apparently within the reach of all. An ideology of personal consumption presents individuals as free to do their own thing, to construct their own little world in the private sphere (Featherstone 1983: 21).

The locus of control has shifted from society to the individual (Crawford 1984). An emphasis on life style change holds individuals responsible for their own fate. They expect to be happy, to achieve a glamorous life style, and to cultivate an attractive body through discipline and denial. Controlling appearance through the daily regime of body maintenance (jogging, diets, keeping fit) is a primary means for the individual to eke out his or her identity under the conditions of modernity (Giddens 1991). Through the cultivation of the body, individuals enact and display their desire for control.

> We cut out the fat, tighten our belts, build resistance, and extend our endurance. Subject to forces that lie beyond individual control, we attempt to control what is within our grasp (Crawford 1984: 80).

47

Although these social scientists frame their analysis of body maintenance and improvement as a general phenomenon in Western consumer
culture, something affecting the modern self, they willingly concede that
women are the primary targets and "most clearly trapped in the narcissistic, self-surveillance world of images" (Featherstone 1991: 179).

The explanation for the feminine susceptibility to the promises of
happiness through body improvement is sought in the sexualization of
the female body by the media in order to sell products. Bombarded
with images of themselves on billboards, in magazines, and on the
screen, women are easy prey for the lures and false promises of consumer culture. However, lest we become too alarmed, we are assured
that cosmetic and fashion industries are currently directing their efforts
at a male market. It is presumably only a matter of time before men
and women enjoy "dubious equality" in the area of body cultivation
(Featherstone 1991: 179).

Taking this argument a step further, some have suggested that
women are not merely the primary objects of consumer culture but
that culture itself is in the throes of "feminization" (Huyssen 1986;
Featherstone 1992). The masculine or "heroic" values of action have
been replaced by the "idols of consumption." The world of Hollywood
celebrities, soap opera stars, and royalty—the cultural favorites of the
female consumer—are the new cultural symbols—admirable for who
they are rather than what they can do. They are ideally suited to pro-
moting the glamorous life, replete with fancy hair styles and makeup,
electrolysis, teeth capping and cosmetic surgery. In the feminization of
culture, women are the victims and the perpetrators, all in one.

Other sociologists place women's concern with appearance in the
context of their emancipation (Turner 1984; Giddens 1991; 1992). Having broken free of the constraints of domesticity and entered the public
sphere of waged labor, women have for the first time the material means
to enjoy themselves. The sexual revolution and feminism provide the
finishing touches, encouraging them to make the most of themselves
and take their own needs seriously. Women continue to be excluded
from full participation in the public realm, however, and the cultivation
of the body becomes one of the only ways they can achieve the exciting
life which they had come to expect was within their reach. As the contemporary epidemic of anorexia nervosa attests, controlling the body can
become a dangerous and destructive way to master an insecure environment. In a world of many promises and few real options, freedom under
conditions of modernity is, at best, a "risky business" (Giddens 1991:
107–108)[5] and, at worse, only a "pseudoliberation," with the old chains

of patriarchal authority replaced by the new ones of consumer culture and neuroticism (Turner 1984: 203).

Unlike social psychological or psychoanalytic approaches, sociological perspectives on beauty do not individualize women's concern with appearance as a personal lack of self-esteem or as a woman's psychosexual predisposition toward narcissism. The cultivation of appearance is treated as an artefact of consumer capitalism which, in principle, affects us all. The specific relationship of women to their bodies, however, tends to be ignored or overemphasized as the feminization of culture in general. Women are treated as the brain-washed victims of media hype or of their own deluded search for emancipation. Sociologists, like psychologists, tend to blame the victim rather than explore how women actually experience and negotiate their bodies in a context of many promises and few options. Beauty is linked to women's illusory quest for happiness rather than the more mundane reality of discomfort and suffering which most actual beauty practices entail. Power relations between the sexes tend to be glossed over or dispatched conveniently to some shadowy and distant patriarchal past. Although some concession may be given to the "greater premium" placed on physical attractiveness for women as opposed to men (Giddens 1991: 106), the significance of gender for these different beauty norms (or the norms for sexual difference) is left unexplored. Thus, while sociological approaches provide insights into the social and cultural context in which body improvement is situated, its explanations fail to account for women's specific relationship to their bodies and for their involvement with the practices of body improvement. To do so would require a perspective which links a sociological analysis of the contradictions of modernity and consumerism to an analysis of the social construction of femininity, the control of women through their bodies, and the politics of beauty.

FEMININITY AND THE POLITICS OF BEAUTY

Within feminist scholarship, women's preoccupation with their appearance is invariably explained as an artefact of femininity in a context of power hierarchies between the sexes and among women of different social and cultural backgrounds. Feminists have tended to cast a critical eye on women's quest for beauty, which is described in terms of suffering and oppression. Women are presented as the victims both of beauty and of the ideologies of feminine inferiority which produce and maintain practices of body maintenance and improvement. Originally, the culprit was sought in what was described as a system of cultural beauty norms. These norms demanded eternal youth and impossible beauty from women: slender but voluptuous shapes, faces unmarked by the passage of time, and, most of all, an appearance in keeping with the conventions of upper-class, Western femininity (Perutz 1970; Henley 1977; Millman 1980; Baker 1984; Brownmiller 1985; Chapkis 1986; Wolf 1991).[6] By linking the beauty practices of individual women to the structural constraints of the beauty system, a convincing case was made for treating beauty as an essential ingredient of the social subordination of women. Beauty was seen as an ideal way to keep women in line by lulling them into believing that they could gain control over their lives through continued vigilance over their bodies.

In recent years, feminist scholarship on beauty as oppression has begun to make way for a more postmodern approach which deals with beauty in terms of cultural discourses (Suleiman 1985; Probyn 1987; Haug et al., 1987; Diamond and Quinby 1988; Jaggar and Bordo 1989; Jacobus et al., 1990; Spitzak 1991; Bordo 1993). In this framework, routine beauty practices belong to the disciplinary and normalizing regime of body improvement and transformation, part and parcel of the production of "docile bodies" (Foucault 1980). The focus is on the multiplicity of meanings attributed to the female body as well as the insidious workings of power in and through cultural discourses on beauty and femininity. The body remains a central concern, this time, however, as a text upon which culture writes its meanings. Following Foucault, the female body is portrayed as an imaginary site, always available to be inscribed. It is here that femininity in all her diversity can be constructed—through scientific discourses, medical technologies, the popular media, and everyday common sense.

Although the theoretical perspectives for understanding women's beauty practices differ in their emphasis on beauty as oppression or as cultural discourse, the focus remains on how these practices work to control or discipline women.[7] In the first perspective, femininity is defined in terms of women's shared experiences of which the most central is oppression. Power is primarily a matter of male domination and female subordination. In the second perspective, the unified category "woman" is abandoned in favor of a diversity of femininities. Femininity is regarded as a (discursive) construction with power implicated in its construction. Power is no longer a matter of top-down repression or coercion, but the vehicle through which femininity is constituted at all levels of social life. In both perspectives, women's preoccupation with their appearance is viewed as part of a complex system of structured social practices, variously referred to as the politics of appearance (Chapkis 1986), the technologies of body management (Bordo 1989), the beauty system (MacCannell and MacCannell 1987), the aesthetic scaling of bodies (Young 1990a), the fashion-beauty complex (Bartky 1990), or the beauty backlash (Wolf 1991). This system includes the myriad procedures, technologies, and rituals drawn upon by individual women in their everyday lives, the cosmetic industry, the advertising business, and the cultural discourses on femininity and beauty. Beauty is central to femininity, whereby Woman as sex is idealized as the incarnation of physical beauty, while most ordinary women are rendered "drab, ugly, loathsome or fearful bodies" (Young 1990a: 123). This ambivalence concerning the female body is implicated in the reproduction of unequal power relations between the sexes. It aids the channeling of women's energies in the hopeless race for a perfect body. As Bartky has noted, the "fashion-beauty complex," like the military-industrial complex, is a "major articulation of capitalist patriarchy" (Bartky 1990: 39–40).

The beauty system also articulates social hierarchies based on class, race, and ethnicity (Lakoff & Scherr 1984; Chapkis 1986; Collins 1990; Peiss 1990; Young 1990a; Bordo 1993). In Western culture, dominant discourses of the body enable privileged groups—notably, white, bourgeois, professional men—to transcend their own material bodies and take on a god's eye view as disembodied subjects. They become the ones who set the standards and judge, rather than the ones who are judged against standards they can never hope to meet. Subordinate groups are defined by their bodies and are defined according to norms which diminish or degrade them. Those designated by the dominant culture as Other (old, homosexual, disabled, fat, and/or female) become imprisoned in their bodies.

Beauty standards set up dichotomies of Otherness and power hierarchies between women.

> Blue-eyed, blonde, thin white women could not be considered beautiful without the Other—Black women with classical African features of dark skin, broad noses, full lips, and kinky hair (Collins 1990: 79).

White, Western women are trapped by the promise that they are special, which gives them a vested interest in maintaining the beauty system. The norms which equate the light-skinned, Western look with beauty permeate relations between white women and women of color, as well as between women and men of color. Women of color are bombarded with cultural messages which not only link whiteness to feminine beauty, but, more importantly, to "gentility, female domesticity, protection from labor, the exacting standards of the elite, and Anglo-Saxon superiority" (Peiss 1990: 164)—in short, to power.

In conclusion, feminist approaches place the social production of femininity and power processes of domination and subordination at the heart of their analysis of beauty. I shall now take a closer look at how women's involvement in the norms and practices of the beauty system has been analyzed in the two main perspectives within feminist scholarship on beauty: beauty-as-oppression and beauty-as-cultural-discourse. Feminist scholarship from these two perspectives is predictably diverse and rarely fits neatly into one perspective. I have chosen to focus on two specific examples which are particularly good representatives of each perspective. In addition to showing how beauty can be analyzed in terms of gender and power, they enable me to explore the strengths of each framework for understanding women's specific participation in the beauty system.

BEAUTY AS OPPRESSION

In *Beauty Secrets* (1986), Wendy Chapkis tackles beauty as a central feature of women's oppression. Her primary aim is to analyze beauty as a political phenomenon—a "politics of appearance"—and to this end, she employs two strategies. First, she takes women's concern with appearance out of the realm of individual psychology. She shows how advertising, the communications media, and the cosmetic industry have joined forces to become a "global culture machine," which makes a Western model of beauty and the Good Life mandatory for women all over the world (Chapkis 1986: 37).

Second, she explores the beauty secrets of women of various ages, ethnic backgrounds, and social classes. Adopting a "personal is political" stance, she uses their everyday battles with hated bodily features (facial hair, blemishes, bulges) as a starting point for a powerful commentary on the suffering which women experience when their bodies do not meet the standards of conventional femininity. She uncovers the diversity of expensive and painful rituals which women routinely undertake in the name of beauty.

According to Chapkis, the cultivation of appearance is one of the primary ways that gender difference is created and maintained. Beauty belongs to the sex/gender system (Rubin 1975), whereby both sexes negotiate conflicts between gender identity and anatomical reality through the alteration of appearance.[8] For example, the mustached woman contemplates depilatories or electrolysis to avoid being addressed as "sir." The small-chested woman receives a breast augmentation in the hopes that she will feel more "womanly." The professional woman dresses for power, while looking for ways to maintain a "feminine look." Men, too, must toe the line, however. The short man wears elevator shoes or takes up body building; the balding man buys a toupee or has a hair transplant. In short, gender and appearance are mutually sustaining.

Like other proponents of the oppression model, Chapkis employs a top-down model of power. She treats the beauty system as a repressive collection of structures and practices which work through the mechanism of internalized oppression. Women are lulled into believing that by controlling their bodies they can control their lives. They are compelled to conform with standards of feminine beauty which are not only impossible to meet, but have to be met, paradoxically, "naturally"—that is, without effort or artifice. Herein lies the most pernicious feature of most beauty rituals: they are performed in secrecy. For the feminist, of course, such rituals are especially shameful. Knowing that the beauty norms are oppressive and yet hopelessly caught up in them herself, she is in for double trouble. As Chapkis notes, describing her own experiences with electrolysis:

> I am a feminist. How humiliated I then feel. I am a woman. How ugly I have been made to feel. I have failed on both counts (Chapkis 1986: 2).

Despite women's entrapment in the beauty system, Chapkis is convinced that there are possibilities for change. She illustrates this optimism with instances of women who manage to find ways to beat the system—for example, by dressing to please themselves or celebrating their wrinkles, flat chests, or stretch marks. The key to liberation lies in women casting aside the oppressive yoke of femininity—and along with it their own self-defeating obsession with beauty—and accepting themselves and their bodies as they really are. This means breaking the silence and subjecting our beauty secrets to a clear-headed feminist analysis.

The major strength of Chapkis's analysis and, more generally, the oppression model from which she draws, resides in placing a hitherto privatized phenomenon like beauty on the political agenda. She shows why beauty is relevant for all women—including feminists. Appearance is one of the central ways that gender difference is constituted in a sexually, racially, and economically divided society. By drawing upon women's personal experiences, Chapkis makes a convincing case for the importance of linking the structural and cultural constraints of the beauty system to women's lived experiences with their bodies. She situates resistance to the beauty system in refusal and provides examples of individual women who, indeed, manage to free themselves from the dominant norms of feminine beauty. Although her solution to women's beauty problems is utopian—a feminist aesthetic of appearance—her portrayal of their everyday struggles indicates that even in a context of oppression there are always some possibilities for action.

BEAUTY AS CULTURAL DISCOURSE

Like Chapkis, Susan Bordo assumes that beauty cannot be understood without taking gender and power into account. She does not immediately link the feminine quest for beauty to oppression, however. Instead she focusses on images of the female body as a site for exploring how gender/power relations are constituted in Western culture (Bordo 1993). Drawing upon Foucauldian notions on power, Bordo treats the female body as a kind of text which can be "read as a cultural statement, a statement about gender" (Bordo 1989: 16). In order to understand why women are preoccupied with their appearance, she describes several intersecting cultural discourses, showing how they converge in contemporary bodily phenomena associated with femininity—hysteria, eating disorders, agoraphobia, and the more routine beauty practices like dieting and body building (Bordo 1988; 1989; 1990b; 1990c).[9]

The first discourse centers around the mind-body dualism which permeates Western thought, dividing human experience into a bodily and a spiritual realm. The female body becomes a metaphor for the corporeal pole of this dualism. Images of the dangerous, appetitive female body, ruled precariously by its emotions, stands in contrast to the masterful, masculine will, the locus of social power, rationality, and self-control. The female body is always the "other": mysterious, inferior, threatening to erupt at any moment and challenge the patriarchal order (Bordo 1990a: 103).

The second discourse focusses on the preoccupation with control and mastery in highly industrialized Western societies. Like the sociologists mentioned earlier, Bordo situates the explosion of techniques for body maintenance or improvement in the "collective cultural fantasy" that death and decay can be defeated and an increasingly unmanageable culture brought under control (Bordo 1988: 100). The notion that the body can be controlled through a little will power ("mind over matter") sustains power relations between the sexes. Women believe that by controlling or containing their bodies and their appetites, they can escape the pernicious cycle of insufficiency, of never being good enough. Moreover, by controlling their bodies they can take on "male" power— power-as-self-mastery (Bordo 1990a). Thus, women paradoxically feel empowered or liberated by the very beauty norms and practices which constrain and enslave them.

The third discourse focusses on femininity. The female body is a medium through which different cultural discourses of femininity are expressed. Whereas the norms for femininity, and by implication, beauty and how women should adorn or alter their bodies, have varied immensely, the discourse of feminine beauty works to erase differences between women under the homogenizing banner that any body will do (as long as it is different than the one you have.) For example, corn-rows on the unimpeachably white Bo Derek lend an "exotic touch of Otherness" while a black woman is magnanimously offered the "choice" of having her hair straightened. This ostensible sameness in opportunity ignores a history of racist body discriminations and acerbates inequalities based on ethnicity, class, or sexuality (Bordo 1990b: 659). The erasure of specific cultural meanings robs beauty practices of their political significance and makes them ideally suited to the normalization of femininity in all its forms.

Bordo is more pessimistic than Chapkis about women being able to beat the system. Their preoccupation with beauty is not something to be shed with a little feminist rhetoric along the lines of accepting the "real me," that autonomous feminist subject lurking underneath or outside the constraints of culture. Women are embedded in and, indeed, cannot help but collude in the beauty system which oppresses them. Gender power is oblivious to the goals and motivations of individual women. As feminist strategy, Bordo advocates analyzing the "collusions, subversions, and enticements through which culture enjoins the aid of our bodies in the reproduction of gender" and recovering the body as a "political battleground for feminist practice" (Bordo 1989: 28). It is not at all clear, however, how any practices, feminist or otherwise, might escape the hegemony of cultural discourses in which the female body is enmeshed. While Bordo distances herself from an exclusive focus on cultural representations of the body to the detriment of women's practical relationship to their bodies, she remains oriented to how women collude or comply with the norms and practices of feminine beauty.[10] It is easy to lose sight of how women manage, individually or collectively, to resist or even subvert the beauty system.

The major strength of Bordo's analysis resides in her sophisticated framework for linking individual beauty practices to a broader context of power and gender hierarchies. By analyzing the complex and contradictory workings of cultural discourses around the body, control, and femininity, Bordo shows why women are especially susceptible to the lures of the beauty system. Since women do not stand outside culture, Bordo makes a convincing case for why feminists have to be suspicious of the possibility of discovering an authentic feminine self who is able to free herself from the constraints of the beauty system. She alerts us to how women's attempts to liberate themselves are continually in danger of being reabsorbed into repressive discourses of femininity.

In conclusion, feminist perspectives take social scientific explanations for women's concern with their appearance a step further. The feminine predilection for body improvement is not reduced to undesirable role behavior, to be shed with a little more willpower. Nor is women's concern with their appearance relegated to an immutable and pathological feature of femininity itself. The feminine beauty system is not simply a gender-neutral artefact of consumer capitalism, the feminization of culture, or of the contradictions of modernity; it is central to the production of relations of domination and subordination as well. By adding gender and power to their theoretical frameworks, feminist approaches can uncover why women engage in the beauty system and how their participation perpetuates the constraints and disciplinary effects of femininity without blaming them for their collusion. Both the oppression and the cultural discourse perspectives on beauty provide valuable insights into why women persist in improving or altering their bodies despite the dangers and drawbacks of most beauty practices. For this reason, they are foundational for analyzing women's involvement in cosmetic surgery. At the same time, however, they leave several questions unanswered. It is to these questions that I now turn.

THE PROBLEM OF THE CULTURAL DOPE

I began this book with a story about my own discomfort and puzzlement when a feminist friend informed me that she wanted to have cosmetic surgery. Confronted with the contradiction between my critical stance toward cosmetic surgery as dangerous and demeaning for women and my desire to take my friend at her word that it was, nevertheless, the best course of action for her under the circumstances, I looked to feminist theory for help. I wanted to take my friend's reasons for having cosmetic surgery seriously without condoning cosmetic surgery as a practice. While contemporary feminist scholarship on beauty enables me to be critical of cosmetic surgery and the beauty system it sustains, it falls short when it comes to making sense of my friend's experience. For example, how can I reconcile her determination and even exhilaration at having decided to have cosmetic surgery with her knowledge of its risks and dangers? How can I explain that she avidly subscribes to the feminist case against the beauty system and yet defends cosmetic surgery as the only solution to her own problems with her appearance? How can I take her suffering seriously, without undermining as mistaken or misguided her decision to alleviate this suffering?

The feminist approaches described above do not do justice to these kinds of questions—questions which concern women's active and knowledgeable involvement in practices which are also detrimental and/or degrading to them. Despite their differences, both oppression and cultural discourse models of beauty account for such ambivalencies by assuming that women who choose to have cosmetic surgery do so because they have had the ideological wool pulled over their eyes. They are cultural dopes.[11]

It is my contention that there are (at least) three reasons why a cultural-dope approach to beauty obstructs an understanding of women's involvement with cosmetic surgery.

First, it reinforces dualistic conceptions of feminine embodiment. Contemporary feminist theory has paid considerable critical attention to the masculinist underpinnings of epistemologies which split mind from body (Jaggar and Bordo 1989). Ironically, however, women's active and lived relationship to their bodies seems to disappear in feminist accounts. Cosmetic surgery becomes a strangely disembodied phenomenon, devoid of women's experiences, feelings, and practical activities with regard to their bodies. Without embodied subjects, there is no space for experiences of excitement or triumph which might be part of the act of altering one's body surgically. Cosmetic surgery can only be a transformation of the body as object, never as self.

Second, it rests on a faulty conception of agency. Whether women are viewed as oppressed victims of patriarchal capitalism or as embedded in the cultural discourses of feminine inferiority, cosmetic surgery cannot be explored as something which can, at least in part, be actively and knowledgeably chosen. Women's actions can only be construed as compliance, serving to reproduce the conditions of their subservience. It is impossible to even entertain the possibility that cosmetic surgery might be a solution for a particular woman under the circumstances.

Third, it ignores the moral contradictions in women's justificatory practices. Given the totalizing and pernicious character of the feminine beauty system, women's reasons tend to be heard as ideologically contaminated, having nothing of relevance to offer for a feminist response to cosmetic surgery. By ignoring how women defend, legitimate, but also criticize their decision to have cosmetic surgery, those feminist approaches make it difficult to imagine not only what tips the scales in favor of cosmetic surgery, but also what makes the surgery problematic for the recipients themselves. Feminist intervention in cosmetic surgery becomes restricted, on the one hand, to the moralistic strategy of propagating self-acceptance in the hope that women will see the error of their ways or, on the other, to waiting until some miraculous shifting in the discursive constellations enables this particularly nasty cultural phenomenon to make way for other—less oppressive, it is hoped—cultural practices.

In conclusion, while contemporary feminist scholarship has made a strong case for linking beauty to an analysis of femininity and power, it has been less successful in finding ways to understand women's lived experience with their bodies, how they actually decide to have cosmetic surgery, and how they access their actions after the fact. Thus, my brief foray into feminist scholarship on beauty leaves me with a problem. While I am now armed with a critical perspective on cosmetic surgery, I am left empty-handed in terms of how to take women who have cosmetic surgery seriously. In order to avoid relegating women who have cosmetic surgery to the position of cultural dopes, I would need to be able to explore their lived relationship to their bodies, to recast them as agents, and to analyze the contradictions in how they justify their decision to have cosmetic surgery.

I found the theoretical antidote I was looking for in the work of Iris Young, Dorothy Smith, and Sandra Bartky. Each has dealt with the practices and discourses of the feminine beauty system. Although they also draw—albeit somewhat eclectically—from the oppression and cultural discourse perspectives described above, they avoid the pitfalls of a cultural-dope approach to beauty. Although they do not explicitly deal with cosmetic surgery—and, indeed, stop short in applying their theoretical insights to that particular phenomenon—they provide the theoretical building blocks for a critical analysis of women's involvement with cosmetic surgery without undermining the women who decide to have it.

EMBODIED SUBJECTS

The political theorist Iris Marion Young (1990a; 1990b) provides a theoretical framework for understanding how women negotiate a sense of self in relation to their bodies. Drawing upon phenomenological theories of embodiment (Merleau-Ponty, Sartre, de Beauvoir), she explores the typical tensions of feminine embodiment as women attempt to become embodied subjects rather than "mere bodies."[12] On the one hand, women participate in a gendered social order where they are continually defined through their bodies. The female body is the perennial object of the intentions and manipulations of others. Women often adopt this attitude themselves, viewing their own bodies at a distance through the critical eyes of others.[13] It is easy for women to feel "mired in materiality," to experience their own body as a thing or as an encumbrance to their projects (Young 1990b: 155). On the other hand, women, like men, experience their bodies as vehicles for enacting their desires or reaching out in the world. Whereas they do not transcend their bodies as men presumably can, as subjects women can never be entirely satisfied with a rendition of themselves as nothing but a body.[14] This tension accounts for the unease many women experience with their bodies and, through their bodies, with themselves.

> [B]ecause she is a human existence, the female person necessarily is a subjectivity and transcendence, and she knows herself to be. The female person who enacts the existence of women in patriarchal society must therefore live a contradiction: as human she is a free subject who participates in transcendence, but her situation as a woman denies her that subjectivity and transcendence (Young 1990b: 144).

Young takes the tension between the female body as object and the embodied feminine subject as a theoretical starting point for understanding women's everyday struggles with their bodies and imagining how this tension might provide possibilities for subverting or disrupting the objectification of women's bodies. Her analysis of the feminine

59

experience of "being breasted" is a case in point, particularly in view of the rising incidence of cosmetic breast surgery (Young 1990b: 189–209). In Western culture, breasts are probably the most visible symbol of femininity and, therefore, central to women's identity and bodily self. More than any other body part, breasts are "up for judgement," problematic, and subject to various forms of correction, ranging from the padded bra to the surgical lift or augmentation (Young 1990b: 190). Breasts are also a source of pleasure for women, a part of their body which distances them—at least in part—from the cultural norms of beauty. "However much the patriarchy may wish us to, we do not live our breasts only as the objects of male desire, but as our own, the sproutings of a specifically female desire" (Young 1990b: 192). Women's breasted experience can disrupt the patriocentric dichotomization of mothering and female sexuality, for example, in the experience of nursing where the image of the nurturant, giving mother is united with the image of the sexual, desirous woman who takes her pleasures without a man. Thus, Young's analysis shows that breasts do not have to be viewed as symbols of women's objectification, but can be seen as a source of empowerment and subversion as well.

Young's notion of feminine embodiment enables me to situate women's experience of their bodies as potential objects for surgical manipulation in a broader context of the tensions of feminine embodiment in Western culture. I can explore cosmetic surgery as symptomatic of a culture where it is possible to view one's body as separate from who one is or would like to become and as site, particularly for women, to negotiate their identities in a context of structured hierarchies of power. Cosmetic surgery becomes both an expression of the objectification of the female body and of women's struggles to become embodied subjects rather than mere bodies.

SECRET AGENTS

The sociologist Dorothy Smith (1990b) is concerned with femininity as an active and knowledgeable accomplishment of the female agent. Like Chapkis, Smith situates women's dissatisfaction with their appearance as well as their involvement in the beauty system in the context of patriarchal and capitalist relations of ruling. Women's energies and activities are channeled into the all-consuming business of creating an acceptable feminine appearance, while, at the same time, waiting passively and with apprehension for the male stamp of approval. Smith rejects the notion, however, that women blindly internalize the dictates of femininity. On the contrary, women are always agents—agents who, as she puts it, "give power to the relations that 'over-power' them" (Smith 1990b: 161). Like Bordo, Smith treats femininity as a discourse. However, she is not primarily concerned with cultural discourses per se, but rather with the ways that femininity is discursively mediated through women's practical activities.[15] While femininity is textually mediated, women are not simply entangled in its discourses; they have to actively "do femininity."

Smith shows how even the most mundane texts—for example, an advertisement, a fashion photo, or instructions for cosmetics—require complex and skilled interpretative activities on the part of the female agent. For example, in order to create an acceptable appearance according to the current norms of femininity, a woman must possess specialized knowledge about makeup and fashion. She must be able to indexically imagine how her present body looks as well as how it would look following the application of a particular product or procedure. She has to plan a course of action, making a series of on-the-spot calculations about whether the rigorous discipline required by the techniques of body improvement will actually improve her appearance given the specifics of her particular body. In short, she has to know what she is doing for the text to have any impact at all (Smith 1990b: 201).

Smith does not limit agency to women's ability to process texts on feminine beauty, however. She shows how the texts themselves are organized around the notion of a female agent. By projecting an ideal image of the female body (perfect skin, slender figure, expensive clothing), a woman is confronted with the imperfections of her own body. Dissatisfaction breeds the desire for transformation, for a different body than the one she has. At the same time, the text instructs her in how her body can be improved upon. The body is remediable, once the female agent has discovered how to go about it.

> Discontent with the body is not just a happening of culture, it arises in the relation between text and she who finds in texts images reflecting upon the imperfections of her body. The interpenetration of text as discourse and the organization of desire is reflexive. The text instructs her that her breasts are too small/too big; she reads of a remedy; her too small breasts become remediable. She enters the discursive organization of desire; now she has an objective where before she had only a defect (Smith 1990b: 185–186).

61

The female agent is the sine qua non of the feminine beauty system. Without agency, texts would fail to motivate women to participate in activities of body improvement. By creating a gap between a woman's perceived bodily deficiency and an objective which promises to overcome it, her dissatisfaction becomes an active process. Rather than immobilizing women, bodily imperfections provide the opportunity for action. Women relate to their bodies as objects—not as sex objects for others—but rather as objects of work, as something to be improved, fixed, or transformed. While women cultivate the appearance of beauty without effort and adopt a passive attitude of waiting until the masculine subject finds them attractive, such appearances are deceiving. In reality, women are agents, albeit secret ones.

> There is a secret agent behind the subject in the gendered discourse of femininity; she has been at work to produce the feminine subject-in-discourse whose appearance when read by the doctrines of femininity transfers agency to the man (Smith 1990b: 202).

Smith's notion of agency allows me to tackle several issues concerning women's involvement in cosmetic surgery which are obscured by a cultural-dope approach to beauty. I can explore women's decisions to alter their bodies surgically in the context of their having to "do femininity." I can begin to look at how they actively and knowledgeably transform the texts of femininity into a desire for cosmetic surgery. Cosmetic surgery becomes viewable as a possible remedy—a way for women to do something about their dissatisfaction. And, finally, I can explore the decision to have cosmetic surgery as a way for women to take action—paradoxically, perhaps, to become female agents.

ONTOLOGICAL SHOCKS

The feminist philosopher Sandra Bartky (1990) has offered a penetrating analysis of how women actually grapple with femininity as moral actors rather than the victims of false consciousness. Like Smith, she regards agency and the sense of mastery which accompany women's involvement in the beauty system as essential to femininity. And, like Young, she draws upon phenomenological frameworks to explore how women's struggles with femininity might actually feel. Unlike Smith and Young, however, Bartky is particularly concerned with how women become embroiled in the moral contradictions posed by practices which are both desirable and denigrating, seductive and dis-empowering (Bartky 1990: 2). Taking the prototypical experiences of masochism, narcissism, and shame as objects for her analysis, she shows how women's everyday struggles to make sense of needs which are in conflict with their (feminist) principles can be a resource for a critical intervention in the oppressive practices of femininity.

Her analysis of shame is a case in point. Shame is one of the most profoundly disempowering features of feminine experience. It is the gut-level sense of being flawed or at fault which structures a woman's image of her body, her perception of who she is, her interactions with others, and her capacity to move about freely in the world. It can be read in women's bodily demeanor: their hunched shoulders, bowed heads, hollowed chests, or flushed faces. Without being linked to a specific act or a negative reaction, it evokes silence, hiding, evasion, and the "confused and divided consciousness" which sabotages wom-en's intentions and politics (Bartky 1990: 93–94). In short, shame is the feminine emotion par excellence.

In view of this pervasive sense of bodily deficiency, it is not surpris-ing that women become committed to the rituals and practices of body improvement: the "sacraments" which provide "the closest thing to a state of grace" (Bartky 1990: 41). Femininity is a need which is no less real for being repressive. Despite the "repressive satisfactions" of femininity and the "fashion-beauty complex," women would feel lost and abandoned without them.

The experience of having to make sense of needs which are both heartfelt and harmful is morally unsettling, however. The contradictory lures and oppressions of femininity can be experienced as "ontological shocks"—that is, disjunctures between a woman's values and beliefs and her practical or lived consciousness of being-in-the-world, between how she thinks she *should* feel and how she, in fact, *does* feel.[16]

Bartky is critical of attempts to resolve these troublesome ontologi-cal contradictions discursively—for example, by propagating the freedom of the individual to "do her own thing" without concern for the structural constraints of femininity or by providing a radical code of ethics for feminist behavior "which divides women within the movement and alienates those outside of it" (Bartky 1990: 61). Both solutions are inadequate for coming to terms with women's struggles as moral actors to make sense of the troubling or painful dimensions of their experiences. She proposes instead an approach which takes wom-en's "ambiguous ethical situation" (Bartky 1990: 20) as an opportunity for reflection and, ultimately, for "exorcising one's own demons."[17]

Although Bartky's approach might be seen as pessimistic and non-utopian, it offers a program for feminist analysis which is grounded in women's everyday moral experience in a gendered social order.[18]

In conclusion, Bartky's work is useful for uncovering women's ambivalence concerning cosmetic surgery. It can help me pinpoint the ways that a woman's gut-level sense of bodily deficiency might sabotage her reservations about cosmetic surgery as well as her critical stance toward the feminine beauty system in general, enabling me to understand what makes cosmetic surgery both desirable and morally problematic for the recipients themselves. I can treat women's ongoing struggles to justify a contradictory practice like cosmetic surgery as a resource for developing a feminist response which speaks to women's experiences rather than simply reiterating the correct line on women's involvement in the beauty system.

Taken together, the work of Young, Smith, and Bartky provide the theoretical tools necessary for a feminist analysis of cosmetic surgery which avoids viewing recipients as the duped and passive victims of the feminine beauty system. They show that embodiment, agency, and moral contradictions are central to understanding women's problems with their appearance as well as their decisions to have their bodies altered surgically. Interestingly, none of these authors extend their theoretical insights to women's involvement in cosmetic surgery. While their reluctance to explore this particular phenomenon is somewhat puzzling—and I will be returning to possible causes for this hesitation later (Chapter Seven)—I see no reason why their theoretical insights concerning embodiment, agency, and women's struggles with morally problematic practices might not be applied to understanding cosmetic surgery. Drawing upon feminist perspectives on femininity, power, and the cultural norms and practices of the beauty system, I attempt an analysis of cosmetic surgery which is critical without undermining the women who have it. Before getting started on this endeavor, however, let me leave feminist theory for the moment and take a brief look at some feminist fiction as—paradoxically—a way to get closer to the facts of women's involvement in cosmetic surgery.

THE DEMISE OF THE CULTURAL DOPE

Fay Weldon's *The Life & Loves of a She-Devil* is a feminist satire about cosmetic surgery. The heroine of the story, Ruth, is a fat, ugly, middle-aged housewife, mother, and drudge, whose husband Bobo leaves her for Mary Fisher—rich, beautiful, successful, and, of course, thin. Initially devastated, Ruth gathers together her courage and decides to get even. Her revenge involves, among other things, a series of cosmetic surgery operations. Over a period of several years, she has her entire body remade surgically, transforming her into a beautiful woman and enabling her to vanquish her rival. She exacts her revenge, winning her husband back. This time, however, he is a broken man who is firmly and irrevocably under her thumb.

Weldon's novel leaves the reader with several puzzles. It is a feminist novel about sexual politics, replete with shocking examples of female oppression and male treachery. However, it a tale with a surprising twist—a female protagonist who wins; that is, who comes out on top in the battle of the sexes. It is the story of a woman who suffers to such an extent under cultural norms of feminine beauty that she is willing to undergo the pain and expense of cosmetic surgery to alter every part of her body. However, the heroine also uses cosmetic surgery as a source of empowerment, a way to regain control over her life. Ruth is both a victim of the feminine beauty system and one of its most devastating critics. Her decision to undergo cosmetic surgery supports the status quo of feminine inferiority, while, at the same time, it shifts the power balance—temporarily, at least—in her own relationships.

Ruth could, of course, be discarded as merely a fictional character, hardly representative of women who really undergo cosmetic surgery. Her quest for power and beauty then would become just another instance of feminist (science) fiction, to be enjoyed but otherwise ignored. However, before relegating Weldon's heroine to the world of make-believe, I propose taking the imaginary more seriously. It is my contention that her book contains some important lessons about why women might insist upon altering their bodies surgically, even at great cost to themselves—lessons that could profitably be incorporated in feminist accounts of femininity and beauty.

To begin with, Weldon's tale is a bitter commentary on the constraints of normal femininity as well as the institution of heterosexual love. Discussing her plans to have cosmetic surgery, Ruth compares herself to Hans Christian Andersen's little mermaid:

> I am paying with physical pain. Hans Andersen's little mermaid wanted legs instead of a tail, so that she could be properly loved by her Prince. She was given legs, and by inference the gap where they join at the top, and after that, every step she took was like stepping on knives (Weldon 1983: 148).

This is a fairy tale which links, as no other, women's subordination in heterosexual relationships with beauty. It is about women's compliance with the beauty system and their willingness to undergo terrible suffering for the love of a man. The tale has a subtext, however. It is also a story about feminine wiles and subterfuge—the woman who applies deceit knowledgeably and with forethought in order to get her way. The little mermaid knows the rules of the game and plays by them. So, too, does Ruth.

> "Of course it hurts," she said. "It's meant to hurt. Anything that's worth achieving has its price. And, by corollary, if you are prepared to pay that price you can achieve almost anything" (Weldon 1983: 148).

This is no cultural dope, blinded by social forces beyond her control or comprehension. She does not see cosmetic surgery as the perfect solution and she is well aware of the enormous price for women who undertake it. Under the circumstances, however, it is the best she can do. For she knows only too well that the context of structured gender inequality makes this solution—as perhaps any solution—at best, a temporary one. In other words, she plays the game, assessing the situation with its structural constraints and making her choices, knowledgeably, within the context in which she lives. She knows what she wants, but, at the same time, she knows how limited her choices are. Within the context in which she lives, Ruth makes her choices—perhaps not freely, but at least knowledgeably.

Cosmetic surgery thus becomes a resource of sorts in the power struggle between the sexes. Whereas no one (including Ruth herself) particularly likes the means to the end, it cannot be denied that, by the time the book comes to a close, Ruth has a better bargaining position than she had earlier. She not only has more control over her immediate circumstances, but she has gained a different perspective on her future. As she notes at the end of the book, it was, after all, just a matter of power: "I have all, and he has none. As I was, so he is now." (Weldon 1983: 240). In this way, Weldon's novel offers a scathing portrayal of the feminine beauty norms without reducing women to the position of deluded victim. Her protagonist is a "she-devil" and, if we might wish her a better life, the matter of her agency cannot be ignored.

Weldon's portrayal of cosmetic surgery provides a view of the subject which does not fit into feminist perspectives on beauty. Ruth is

neither as embedded as Bordo would have us believe, nor has she liberated herself along the lines that Chapkis would suggest. Caught off
guard by a literary ploy—"a comic turn, turned serious" (Weldon
1983: 240)—the reader must begin, perhaps in spite of herself, to
entertain issues that tend to be skipped over in the more straightforward rhetoric of academic feminism. Previously held notions of the
docile female, trapped by the constraints of beauty, are forgotten—at
least for the moment—in favor of a vision where women as knowledgeable agents and cosmetic surgery can go together. By combining
the contradictory and disturbing dimensions of cosmetic surgery with
a feminist critique of the power relations between the sexes, Weldon
shows how ambivalencies can be embraced rather than dismissed or
avoided. It is precisely at this point of discomfort—our own and other
women's—that a feminist analysis of cosmetic surgery needs to begin.
We need to find ways to explore cosmetic surgery as a complex and
dilemmatic situation for women: problem and solution, oppression and
liberation, all in one.

THREE

PUBLIC FACE/PRIVATE SUFFERING

The scene is the examining room cum office of a medical inspector for the national health insurance system. It is the morning for applicants seeking coverage for cosmetic surgery. This can be anything from epilation or removal of tattoos to major surgery like tummy tucks, breast corrections, or corrective surgery for previous operations. The Inspector, Dr. Berg, sees up to fifteen applicants in a morning during which he must determine whether their problems meet the criteria for full coverage (see Chapter One).[1] In practice, most of the requests for cosmetic surgery for medical reasons have already been weeded out in advance. ("We hardly call in the ears any more.") Applicants who seek cosmetic surgery for strictly psychological reasons rarely appear. Most of the cases are candidates for "normal variation in appearance." I am intrigued by the opportunity to observe firsthand how the medical profession actually determines which (female) bodies are abnormal enough to merit surgery. In other words, I expect to discover just how beautiful a woman has to be in order to be regarded as "normal." As we drink coffee before the consultations begin, the Inspector explains with some pride that he has developed some "pretty sound criteria" for sorting out the cases where there "really is an abnormality" from those which are only "psychosocial." For example, women who want to have their breasts enlarged in order to "keep their husbands interested" or to be able to wear a bikini at the beach belong to the latter category. Coverage is in order for cases like: abdominal folds which "look like the early stages of pregnancy," sagging eyelids "which make the person look like he's been hanging around in bars," or a nose which "is *too* Negroid." As he puts it, "I start with what I *see*."

Preparing myself for a look at these criteria in action, I seat myself next to the door with notebook in hand. Dr. Berg calls in the first patient. I glance at the pile of cards on his desk, wondering what is in store for me. I have no idea what to expect as the patient enters the room. She is a slender, pretty woman in her early twenties who looks a bit like a blonde Nastassia Kinski. I am taken aback—what could possibly be wrong with this vision of loveliness? I scan her closely as she walks across the room and takes a seat opposite the Inspector. I am still unable to discover the problem. I notice that she is wearing a heavy leather jacket although it is a warm spring day. She takes off the jacket to reveal a bulky black sweater. The Inspector glances at his card and says, "Well, Ms. P., you've been referred to us by Dr. J. (a plastic surgeon) for a breast augmentation. Perhaps you can begin with your reasons for wanting a breast augmentation?" Hunched forward and with eyes cast downward, she begins in a halting and barely audible monotone to explain that she is "unhappy with what she has." She explains that her breasts are so small that she is ashamed. She can't seem to stop comparing herself to other women; everywhere she goes, she is confronted with women who have "more" than she does. She is always noticing other women's breasts—every time a woman raises her arm to fix her hair, for example, she is reminded of her own problem. It is this "daily confrontation," she explains, which wears her down. She has developed an "inferiority complex." "I know I shouldn't keep comparing myself to other women," she whispers, "but I just can't help it." The Inspector asks her whether she has considered getting psychotherapeutic help at which point she looks up briefly and snorts. She does not reply.

The Inspector, apparently somewhat at a loss, shuffles his cards together and tells her to step behind the partition next to his desk so that he can examine her. I can see her head and shoulders just above the partition as she pulls off her sweater, followed by three more t-shirts. The Inspector walks over and begins to examine her, walking around her and scrutinizing her breasts. "What exactly is so bad about your breasts?" he asks. I see her blush; she avoids his eyes. "Oh, they're awful, can't you *see*?" The Inspector takes another look and then tells her to get dressed. He returns to his desk and, a minute later, she takes her seat. He explains that this is clearly surgery for "aesthetic reasons" and in such a case, national health insurance only covers half of the costs. She breathes a sigh of relief and says that it doesn't matter; she'd "pay anything to have it done." Trying to be helpful, Dr. Berg suggests that she might want to have the surgery done on an outpatient basis as that would be cheaper. She smiles happily and thanks him profusely.

After she is gone, the Inspector shakes his head, saying: "Those were *fantastic* breasts, real *beauties*." "It's a shame to tamper with them," he explains, "but what can you do? It was on the tip of my tongue to advise her against it, but that's not my job, so . . ." Still shaking his head, he stands up and calls in the next applicant.

This episode was not an exception. In the course of my field work, I watched fifty-five people, fifty women and five men, enter the room for various kinds of cosmetic surgery.[2] With one exception, a man with a cauliflower nose, I was never able to guess what the person had come in for. In some cases, I had a suspicion, as, for example, when a woman with a rather prominent nose appeared, only to have them dashed when she explained that she wanted an eyelid correction because her five-year-old son was always asking her "why she had been crying." My first impression confirmed that applicants for cosmetic surgery looked no different than the run-of-the-mill woman (or man) on the street and some were even decidedly attractive. Their appearance did not seem to warrant corrective measures as drastic as cosmetic surgery.

Nevertheless, all of the applicants were highly convincing in their accounts of the suffering they endured due to some part of their appearance. With the occasional exception—for example, the applicant who came in because she "had heard about it from her neighbor and wondered whether she could have the same thing done, too"—most applicants explained that they had spent years trying to accept bodies which they hated. They wanted to have a liposuction because they "loathed" their stomach/hips/thighs ("I look like someone who is always pigging out on cake, but I'm not . . ."), or they wanted to have their eyelids corrected because they looked tired or because people were always joking about them drinking until all hours of the morning. One man explained that he had to have a face lift because the lines around his mouth made him look "hard"—"like one of those criminal types." Many explained that they had already tried everything—diets, lotions, exercising, or just plain stoicism, but nothing had helped. They had reached the end of the line, an impasse. Over and over again, I heard different variations of what seemed to be the same plea for help: "I just can't go on like this."

I also watched them go through the humiliation of having to share their suffering with a stranger. They had to negotiate the seriousness of their problems and, in many cases, convince the Inspector that their bodies were deficient enough to merit cosmetic surgery. This required being able to discern which reasons the Inspector would find satisfactory. Not everyone was equally skilled in this and, in some cases, an applicant would inadvertently spoil her case. For example, a middle-aged Surinamese woman justified wanting a tummy tuck because she suffered from stomach pains. When the Inspector did not respond, she went on to explain that her "mother and sisters back home are all fat and I can see which way *I'm* heading." She attempted to enlist Dr. Berg's sympathy by referring to cultural stereotypes which he, as a member of the white Dutch majority, might be expected to entertain. ("You know how much *we* like rice.") Ultimately, coverage was denied—not because the applicant did not meet the physical criteria for abdominoplasty, but because her strategies for convincing the Inspector disqualified her.[3]

In addition to the precarious business of convincing the Inspector that they needed surgery, applicants often had to undergo the embarrassing ritual of a physical examination. This not only entailed having to disrobe and allow the Inspector to scrutinize the offending body part, but it meant being poked, prodded, and, in some cases, weighed. Applicants for abdominoplasties or liposuctions were invariably asked to climb onto the scales. After asking the applicant how much she thought she weighed, the Inspector would make a point of any discrepancies—"Oh dear. How can that be? The scale says seventy-five kilos. That's four kilos more . . . ." Flustered at being caught in the act of self-deception, many applicants would begin making excuses. ("It's because I went out to eat last night" or "some scales just make you heavier.") After listening politely, the Inspector would explain that whereas "there definitely was a problem," the applicant would have to diet before being eligible for a tummy tuck or liposuction. If she managed to lose some weight, she could come back and "we'll see what we can do about it." As he explained to me later, "*First* some effort, *then* the reward."[4]

The willingness of applicants to put themselves through such ordeals is an indication of how great their desire for cosmetic surgery was. Interestingly, many were not deterred, even if they did not obtain coverage, and insisted that they would find a way to have the operation. "I don't care about the money," they explained. "I just want to have this operation. If I have to go without a vacation this year, well, that's just the price I'll have to pay."

My field work left me with several puzzles. To begin with, it removed any illusions I might have entertained that women who have cosmetic surgery do so because of some observable defect in their physical appearance. I discovered that perfectly ordinary looking and even attractive women wanted to have cosmetic surgery. Not only did I rarely notice what the applicants were coming in to have done, but once I knew what the problem was, I found myself feeling astounded that anyone could be willing to undergo such drastic measures for what seemed to me such a minor imperfection. At the same time, however, I was confronted with the applicant's suffering and her insistence that an imperfection which I found minor, nevertheless, cast a shadow over her entire life, influencing how she felt about herself, her relationships, her sexuality, her work, and more. In her perception, her appearance crossed a subjectively defined boundary between the normal and the deviant, between what a woman should or should not have to endure. The fact that our evaluations did not match did not make her suffering any less tangible.

Moreover, I discovered that the medical profession was no more adept at determining which bodies were normal than I was. Despite attempts to develop objective criteria for appearance, my observations of the Inspector's difficulties in actually making decisions about who should have cosmetic surgery presented a different picture. In practice, he routinely complained that he was unable to see why the applicant wanted cosmetic surgery. He often tried, albeit unsuccessfully, to talk the patient out of having surgery, claiming that nothing was wrong with how she looked. By the same token, he sometimes refused coverage to applicants for reasons which had little to do with whether their appearance corresponded with his criteria for determining which problems warranted cosmetic surgery. But, most surprising of all, the Inspector seemed to be susceptible to the applicants' experience of suffering, even when he saw no "objective" reason for it. Although he was under considerable pressure from the national health insurance system to cut down expenditures on cosmetic surgery and was, therefore, expected to refuse coverage whenever possible, he granted coverage in the majority of the cases. During my field work, he awarded sixty-one percent of the applicants full coverage and another twenty-one percent partial coverage.

It would seem that standards for normal appearance are no less subjective than standards for beauty. Attempts to tackle the problem of when cosmetic surgery is needed cannot be resolved by developing aesthetic criteria or general guidelines for application. They neither enable medical practitioners to decide which bodies require surgical alteration nor do they shed light on why a particular individual is so determined to subject her own body to the rigors of surgical intervention. Understanding the puzzling discrepancy between public appearance and private suffering requires taking a closer look at what the recipients of cosmetic surgery have to say.

In this chapter, I begin to explore how women who have had their bodies altered through cosmetic surgery account for their decision. Drawing upon interviews with women who have undergone various kinds of cosmetic surgery, I will take a preliminary look at the kinds of explanations which are presented.[5] After providing an overview of the diversity of reasons, I draw together some of the common themes in these accounts in an attempt to make sense of the complicated relationship between physical appearance and bodily experience, between how a woman looks and how she feels about how she looks.

"I REALLY *HATED* THEM. . . ."

Unsurprisingly, women who had cosmetic surgery explained that dissatisfaction with their appearance was the reason for the operation. This was no routine beauty problem, however. For example, Julie, a thirty-four-year-old social worker, remembered years of terrible suffering because her face and neck were covered with dark moles. "I just *hated* those things, *really hated them*," she explained. She described looking in the mirror as a child and thinking that "deep down, I would give anything for another face." Sandra, a thirty-two-year-old artist who had recently had her breasts reduced, used similar language to describe her body. Prior to surgery, she saw her breasts as "this piece of your life that you just really hate," a "pair of sagging knockers" that just "hang there," an alien piece of flesh which "sticks to your body." Pamela, a thirty-four-year-old recipient of liposuction referred to her thighs as "these mountains of fat." As she put it, "Your ass shakes all over the place when you walk and you look totally unappetizing. It's all so *unaesthetic*, so completely unacceptable—*dirty*."

The problems were different—facial blemishes, sagging breasts, saddlebag thighs—but the language was remarkably similar. Each woman emphasized how ugly, awful, unaesthetic, or even dirty her particular bodily defect was. The vocabulary used vividly displayed the extent of her distress. Each depicted her body (or some part of it) as something which she could not possibly accept. Hated body parts were dissociated from the rest of her body as objects—"those things," "mountains of fat," "sagging knockers." They were described as pieces of flesh which had been imposed upon her—inanimate and yet acting against her. They became something which each woman wanted to, literally, cut out of her life.

Some women explained that they had suffered for as long as they could remember because of their appearance. They described their appearance as a negative force in their lives, influencing how they felt about themselves, their relationships, and their dealings with the world around them. For others, the anguish began later. Often puberty brought the onset of suffering. Several women remembered their horror at discovering that their breasts "were just never going to grow." Others described adolescence as a time of being mercilessly teased about their appearance. ("Hey, you with the big tits.") Pregnancy could also mark the starting point of a woman's difficulties as her breasts began to sag or stretch marks appeared. ("I looked just like my grandmother . . . just two flaps of skin.") Or a new job could transform a minor beauty problem into a full-fledged trauma. ("They don't like old women in corporations.") Whether a woman's problem was of relatively recent origin or of long-standing duration, the distress and pain were an ever present feature. Cosmetic surgery was presented as the final step in a trajectory of suffering—an attempt to alleviate a problem which had become unbearable.

"IT JUST MADE EVERYTHING ELSE WORSE. . . ."

For many women, their appearance began to represent "everything that was wrong" in their lives. It took on a symbolic character, becoming the focus of more general feelings of discontent or unhappiness. A bodily defect could exacerbate other difficulties. ("I was already shy, but my ears just made it that much worse.")

Elizabeth, a thirty-six-year-old former boutique owner, explained that she had always been unhappy with how she looked. ("I was too thin—just a bean pole with two meat balls.") After her second pregnancy, however, her breasts shrank, leaving her with, as she put it, "just two strings, hanging down." Under ordinary circumstances, she could have taken this change in her body in stride. However, she was at home with the children, feeling isolated, and her breasts became increasingly difficult to tolerate:

> You're dissatisfied with your life and so of course you keep sinking deeper and deeper into this hole. . . . When it came to being too thin, I could always tell myself not to make a fuss: "Quit complaining!" But *this*—it's something that you're confronted with *every* day. If you are already feeling depressed, it just takes so much longer to pull yourself out of it.

Caroline has a similar story about her breasts being the proverbial straw that broke the camel's back. She recounted having had a kidney stone removed when she was sixteen. The operation left a large, unsightly scar running across her entire torso. "It always bothered me, that I had smaller breasts but . . . then there was this additional scar." She might have coped with one defect, but two made her feel that fate had dealt with her unkindly:

> I see some girl with normal breasts walking down the beach and I can't help thinking: why her and not me? . . . It's just not *fair* . . . just because I *happen* to have two things wrong.

Many women acknowledged problems with appearance as part and parcel of the "feminine condition" ("every woman has something wrong"). At the same time, they presented their own problem as special, exceptional—of a different caliber altogether. They often described being disadvantaged vis-à-vis other members of their sex. "Sure, we all have our problems, but there are limits to how much suffering you should have to put up with." They regarded their particular problem as tipping the balance, however. Thus, cosmetic surgery became a legitimate way to reinstate a fair measure of pain—no less, but also no more, than any woman should have to suffer in the name of beauty.

"IT'S JUST THIS ONE PART. . . ."

Contrary to social scientific explanations which regard dissatisfaction with appearance as part of the female lot in life (Chapter Two), many of the women I spoke with were not particularly critical of their appearance in general. In fact, many assured me that they were quite satisfied with the way they looked. They could cite numerous features which they "wouldn't change for the world." ("I have great hair." "There's nothing wrong with my face.") It was only this one particular body part—this nose or these breasts—which was problematic—the culprit which, as they put it, "ruined the rest."

Moreover, many women did not seemed particularly concerned when other parts of their bodies began to show signs of wear and tear due to age, pregnancy, or loss of weight. Sagging breasts or crow's-feet were shrugged off with equanimity as "things that go along with getting older." Although such changes might evoke a momentary twinge of dismay, they belonged to the category of problems which could be dealt with. In the case of their present problem, however, it was inevitably one body part which was cited as being "something *completely different.*"

As if to underline the exceptional nature of their particular difficulty, many women would spontaneously compare their own operation with other forms of cosmetic surgery. Joyce, a business woman in her mid-forties, explains that her reasons for wanting a face lift are of an entirely different order than, say, someone else's need for a breast augmentation:

> For a long time, I thought that big breasts would be *great*, but I'd never be willing to have an operation for something like that—that would be going much too far. I don't have to be a Jane Mansfield or anything. . . . But this is something else altogether. . . . Your face, um, yes, it's just so important for first impressions—well, that's what I think. Look, big breasts, small breasts, in the long run, that just doesn't make that much difference. At least, not in the situations *I* have in mind.

Whereas a breast augmentation would "be going much too far," a face lift was crucial for her well-being and ability to get along in a man's world. For another woman, the priorities might be reversed: she wouldn't "dream of having anything done about her wrinkles," while her breasts were "another matter altogether." The body parts were different, but the feeling was the same. Each woman described one particular part of her body as being different than run-of-the-mill beauty problems. By presenting her own problem as exceptional, she could make a case for cosmetic surgery as exceptional solution.

"IT DIDN'T BELONG TO THE REST. . . ."

Many women explained that they had cosmetic surgery because one part of their body "didn't belong to the rest." Breasts could be too small or too large in comparison with hips and buttocks. ("I looked half man, half woman.") Saggy arms or faces might make them look older than they really were ("like a seventy-year-old woman.") Heavy hips or thighs were referred to as "this strange imperfection," marring an otherwise acceptable body. Puffy eyelids or a wrinkled neck could transform an energetic, middle-aged woman into "one of those dreary women you always see in the bus who look so tired and worn out." Although the details differed, the experience was similar; one body part "just didn't belong." It was perceived as an alien (and alienating) encumbrance which transformed her body so that it did not correspond to who she "really" was or would have been under different circumstances.

Sandra provided a particularly vivid description of the connection between her feelings about her body and her sense of who she was. Prior to having a breast reduction, she always felt that her breasts just "shouldn't be there." They made her seem like someone else—a different kind of person than she felt she was. "Big breasts are *supposed* to be sexy. So *you* get to be a sex bomb, whether you want to be or not." She recalled how other women were always jealous and men were continually staring at her, "only interested in one thing."

> After a while, I guess I just had the feeling that when Sandra turns the corner, the first thing you see are her tits and then you see Sandra.

To avoid being reduced to "just a pair of tits," Sandra recalled how she spent years keeping herself well hidden under bulky sweaters and jackets, or always leaving her shirt on during sex. Cosmetic surgery changed everything dramatically.

> Once I had the operation behind me, I was suddenly able to talk to everyone about it. And I was able to *show* them to people. (laughs) . . . They weren't really my breasts because you could still see the scars. They were someone else's work, not really mine because he had made them. But—I don't know how it works exactly—but suddenly I felt like I could show myself—it's like I've become some kind of *exhibitionist*—like I just want to show *everyone* my boobs. I'm so *happy* with them.

Appearance and identity go hand in hand. Before having cosmetic surgery, Sandra described her breasts as preventing people from seeing her as she really was. Although she continued to distance herself from her breasts after surgery, referring to them as the surgeon's "work" and complaining about the scars ("It looked like he wanted to *sign* them!"), she clearly seemed to feel more at home in her body. Not only did she delight in displaying her new breasts, but by showing them to other people, she felt that she was, for the first time, able to show herself. Paradoxically, cosmetic surgery enabled her to become the person she felt she could have been. ("I guess I just always was the small-breasted type.")

"YOU *JUST* WANT SOMETHING NICE TO WEAR. . . ."

Many women described not being able to buy clothes which fit as one of the main reasons for having cosmetic surgery. "I can never find one size which fits *both* top and bottom;" "Where can you get a triple A bra?" or just "Nothing *ever* looks good on me," were frequently heard complaints. Remembering the early days of second-wave feminism, I was often disconcerted to discover the importance which was placed upon not being able to buy a brassiere—that uncomfortable and demeaning harness which symbolizes the constraints of femininity.[6] However, I began to understand as I listened to accounts like the following.

> CHRIS: It's just nice to be able to go into a store and—like, you want to get a bra and it's for a party so you want something *nice* and so, um, I say that to the saleswoman. "I'd like to, um, have something that—so that I look like I have a little more than I have, something with padding or a little support," and—"Well, we *don't* have anything like *that* in your size. You have a double A, I'm sure." And then I think, oh god, why does this have to happen *every* time?

I: Yeah, it's like, "Why me?"

CHRIS: Yeah and when I go to buy a bathing suit and they give you another one, *naturally* nothing that is *low cut*, because they already see that on you, so then they just give you, you know, a tank suit, like something else just wouldn't be for *you*. I don't want to make a big deal of it, but I . . . you're just *always* confronted with it, every time.

For some women, buying clothes symbolized the pleasures of femininity. Women often enjoyed shopping in its own right and particularly looked forward to buying something nice for a special occasion. Many women lamented being denied this ordinary gratification and, like Chris, being relegated to the boring and unfeminine realm of the sporty tank suit and the high-necked, sensible dress. The department store with its racks of standardized clothes inevitably confronted them with the normal feminine body. One look at the available sizes was enough to remind them of the countless female bodies which were the right size, while theirs was different. Unsurprisingly, many women celebrated a breast correction by buying a bra—the lacier the better. It was the ritual of femininity *par excellence*.

Lucy, a thirty-three-year-old graduate student, also gave clothing a central role in her account of why she had her breasts reduced. Although she took issue with the idea that her operation was only about being able to buy fancy lingerie ("*I* buy all *my* underwear at Sears," or, "Spend all my time shopping for clothes? No, thanks. *I'd* rather spend *my* time in a book store."), she, too, described suffering because she couldn't buy the clothes she wanted. In addition to the physical discomfort of heavy breasts and the constant humiliation of being harassed on the street, she explained that "practically having to wear maternity clothes" was one of her main reasons for wanting to have cosmetic surgery. "Normal" clothes just never fit.

Most people now know me as someone who likes nice clothes and cares about how she looks, you know—but before the operation I was into hiding myself, trying not to be noticeable. I was a real mouse. No makeup, no nice dresses, just boring maternity clothes, anything as long as I wasn't noticeable. Yeah—you just can't imagine, you know? And, well, afterwards, I started to do that kind of thing . . . like just being able to wear nice clothes finally.

Clothing was a way for many of the women I spoke with to be ordinary, to establish that they were like everyone else. Other people (including me) were placed on the other side of the fence—as being unable to imagine how it might feel to be unable to partake in the mundane joys of femininity.

Cosmetic surgery became a way to join the club, to become "one of the girls." Recalling the terrible scars ("a real mess") and humiliations of her operation ("those doctors really treat you like a piece of meat"), Lucy explained calmly that she has never regretted having taken the step.

> You know, I spend most of my time dressed anyway . . . I figure that any one who is going to see me without clothes is just going to have to accept me the way I am. Otherwise they can just forget it.

"YOU JUST CAN'T STOP COMPARING. . . ."

Many of the women I talked to explained that they always felt that they looked different than other women. This sense of being different took the form of comparing their own appearance against other women's bodies. Once they started making comparisons, it rapidly became an obsession. A trip to the store, a day at the beach, or a party were automatically transformed into occasions marked by furtive glances and painful contrasts. Every other woman became a potential rival—to be sized up as thinner, more buxom, or younger.

Recalling her hesitation about going to a fitness center with a large group of friends ("Oh, God, now I have to wear a bathing suit."), Chris recounted the process:

> They all have fairly big breasts . . . and so, I guess you just start looking around you and . . . there's always someone who blurts out, "Gosh, I thought you had *more* than *that*." Of course, you can see that for yourself. You just have so much less.

She portrayed her ongoing struggle between going about life as usual ("You can't let something like that take over your whole life.") and the inevitable confrontation with her shortcomings as soon as she was with other women. Her attempts to shrug things off ("I guess I'm just a little jealous.") were invariably unsuccessful. Other women were quick to point out her deficiency. ("They don't mean to be nasty; they just mean it as a little joke .") Even if they exercised tact and refrained from making negative comments, Chris could, as she put it, "see for herself" that her body was different. Her conviction that her breasts were "just so much less than what other women have" was unshakable.

Self-consciousness often became a vicious cycle, leading to woman's sense that she was continually "on display." Caroline described the agonies of going dancing with her best friend:

> I just see these girls standing near me and they *all* have nice breasts. I'm *constantly* thinking: See, *she* looks great and look at me. I don't at all. I tell myself, "Don't make such a big deal out of it" and just go anyway . . . but when I'm at the discotheque, I crawl away into a corner so that no one can see me. I always feel like everyone is looking at me—I know, it's probably not true, but that's how I *feel*. And my girlfriend keeps telling me, too: "Do you really think they know whether or not you have breasts?" So, I go with her, but then I'm sitting there at the bar and then you hear the guys say "Look at that girl, look at those great tits," . . . like there goes all your self-confidence, you know what I mean. Then you start thinking, "See, they *do* notice beautiful breasts."

Like Chris, Caroline distanced herself at first from her tendency to compare herself with other women. She tried to talk herself out of it, take it in stride, or let herself be persuaded by her friend that she was exaggerating. Like Chris, however, she ultimately had no other recourse than to admit that her fears were, after all, valid. The experience of overhearing how men routinely size up women provided the support for her conviction that women's bodies are constantly subject to critical assessment.

Many women described the agony of feeling that everyone's eyes were glued to that one body part which did not meet the norms of how an acceptable female body should look. Even when they were alone, many women could not shake the feeling that they were being observed. One woman described it as though she were always looking at herself in the mirror, seeing herself critically through the eyes of others. She explained that she could no longer bear to undress in front of her husband because "I kept seeing myself in the mirror and seeing how *bad* I look." It was this experience of feeling permanently on display that turned even the most mundane experiences like going to the swimming pool or a social gathering into a source of perpetual discomfort and distress. In this context, cosmetic surgery became a way to become unnoticeable—to "be one of the crowd." As Sandra explained, remembering the aftermath of her surgery: "It was such freedom. I could finally just move around in my body. I felt *so free*. No one was looking at me."

"YOU NEVER KNOW WHEN SOMEONE IS GOING TO SAY SOMETHING. . . ."

For many women, the subjective sense of being on display was enhanced by remarks made by other people about their appearance. Small-breasted women were given tips on which exercises would increase bust size or would continually find themselves the object of ostensibly well-meant reassurances like, "Big breasts are *so-o-o* uncomfortable, dear. *I* wish I had yours." Several had experienced a tactless slip of the tongue when their appearance caught another person off guard.

Ellen, a forty-three-year-old housewife and mother of two daughters who had her breasts augmented gave a particularly poignant portrayal of how painful such remarks could be. She had just given birth to her first child and was lying in the hospital bed—"exhausted but on top of the world." She described how a nurse came in to give her a sponge bath.

> [A]nd she says, "So, Mrs. G., we're just going to freshen you up a bit." And she starts washing my face, and then she washes my breasts, and—"Gee, you're as flat as a *pancake*, aren't you?" (pause) It was (voice breaks) like being stabbed with a knife; it was (begins to cry), it was so awful, just really awful.

For Ellen, the remark disrupted what she experienced as her moment of glory. She had not only gone through the hours of strenuous labor, but was feeling "one hundred percent woman." The nurse's observation was a rude awakening, shattering Ellen's sense of self-satisfaction and well-being. It also reminded Ellen that she could expect to be judged and found wanting, even when she least expected it.

The nurse's remark falls under the category of tactless comments. However, many women described incidents which were even more harrowing. For examples, lovers suggested that they go in for a "boob job." First dates rejected them with a cursory "come back after you've grown some more." Others remembered being teased mercilessly as children. ("Rabbit face," "Dumbo.") A routine jog in the park for a heavy-breasted woman could become a veritable gauntlet, with boys yelling "Buttermilk, buttermilk," (Sandra : "like with all the shaking, the milk's going to go sour") or a stroll down the street an occasion for sexual harassment.

Diana, a school teacher in her mid-thirties, explained that being harassed by children was what ultimately made her decide to have her face rebuilt. She recounted the horrors of teaching her first class and having problems maintaining discipline:

> Kids tell it like it is . . . that you have a rabbit face, that you're Bugs Bunny. And they start imitating you all the time. . . . I had this really difficult class. It was just terrible. . . . If you have a good relationship with your class, it's not so bad, but when you have a bad relationship, then it's really awful. They naturally try to find your weak spots, kids sense them immediately. And I realized how awful it was for me to hear that, so terrible. It just really *hurt*. I remember how I used to spend hours crying about it.

Although many of the women could remember such incidents, these were, in most individual cases, few and far between. It often took them a long time to remember when someone had actually made a negative comment and then it was usually only a matter of one or two specific occurrences. The random and unexpected quality of the negative comments was what made them feel especially vulnerable. "You just never know when someone is going to say something."

As Diana put it: "I always felt as though I *were wide* open. It was as though anyone could just come right in. . . . Can you imagine? I was like a walking cash register with the drawer open."

Cosmetic surgery offered the promise of anonymity. Women did not expect to be beautiful, but to be able to move about in the world without being subjected to harassment because of some aspect of their appearance.

"I FELT SO ASHAMED. . . ."

Many women were ashamed of how they looked, experiencing their bodies as inherently deficient or faulty. The women I talked with often described their problems as a kind of disgraceful secret. Considerable effort was put into keeping them out of sight. Breasts and hips were concealed under bulky sweaters. Leather jackets were donned, even in the summer. Brassieres were stuffed with cotton. Hair was ironed to camouflage protruding ears or worn in the face to cover up blemishes or deflect attention from offending noses.

Other women told me that they avoided situations where they would have to get undressed in front of other people—from fitting rooms in department stores to sexual encounters with lovers or husbands. Many women complained about having to take their children to the swimming pool ("How can you avoid it when you have little kids?") and having to expose breasts, buttocks, or stretch marks in communal showers or dressing rooms. They told of stuffing their bathing suits and then worrying that their precautions would be noticed. ("I was always terrified every time I leaned over that it would fall out.") Others described how their feelings about their bodies interfered with their sexuality. They were afraid to get undressed in front of their lovers, left their nightgowns or a t-shirt on when having sex, or simply declared some part of their body off limits. ("My breasts were forbidden territory—no trespassing.") Still others avoided sex altogether in anticipation of negative reactions. In many cases, a husband or present boyfriend was cited as the first person who was allowed to see or touch a particular body part.

Elizabeth explained that one of her main reasons for having her breasts augmented was her sex life. She explained that her relationship with her husband had deteriorated since her last pregnancy left her with sagging breasts:

> I really noticed it when—all of a sudden it's like you're looking at yourself in a mirror and you see yourself doing things where you think, "Oh, is that *me* doing that?" . . . I don't even take my clothes off in front of my husband, I always keep something on. That's really awful, to see yourself doing that.

Shame became the mirror through which she experienced her body. She not only found her breasts so appalling that she couldn't bear to have anyone look at them; she was also humiliated for feeling that way. She became caught up in a vicious circle: estranged from her body and her feelings about her body, and, consequently, alienated from anyone else who wanted to look at or touch her. When I asked whether her husband shared her feelings, she looked a bit startled.

> He never actually said anything about my breasts and I can't say that he acts like they disgust him. He'll still try to caress them sometimes—but, well, as far as I'm concerned, they're just off limits.

She couldn't imagine actually talking to him about it and was quite certain that he had no idea how she felt before she announced her desire to have surgery. ("He didn't even know I wore falsies.")

> I guess I just didn't want to know what he had to say about my breasts . . . it was bad enough for me as it was . . . I just had enough problems with it myself without having to hear about *his problems*.

Shame is a private emotion. Many of the women I spoke with did not share their feelings with friends or relatives. They preferred to suffer in silence. Whereas cosmetic surgery did not eliminate shame altogether, it offered a degree of solace. Recalling how she felt before having her liposuction, Pamela explained:

> I always had this deep-rooted feeling of dissatisfaction, of *shame*. You look in the mirror . . . and it just confirms what you always knew. . . . You don't feel good to begin with and you look in the mirror and you feel so totally humiliated. And you start thinking, God, if only it could be a little less—just a little less—*shaming*.

For Pamela, a liposuction did not miraculously transform her. "I guess I'll always be an insecure person," she explained. However, it did seem to provide just a little less shame and, a little more self-acceptance.

"BUT I WAS TOO ASHAMED TO ADMIT IT. . . ."

Some women I talked with were not only ashamed of the way they looked, however. They were also ashamed for feeling ashamed in the first place. Margo, a forty-year-old artist, explained why she waited until she was in her late thirties to have her ears corrected. Although otoplasties have been performed routinely and without controversy on children for years in The Netherlands, it took her several decades just to be able to admit that she had a problem with how her ears looked. The middle child of a large family, she "wouldn't have dreamed of saying anything about something like ears." She had two seriously disabled sisters. In her family, she explained, "being healthy was the most important thing."

> You know, it was all really Calvinistic. Unless you had something really wrong with you, like a broken leg or something, you just weren't supposed to complain. To tell them that I wanted to have my *ears* fixed . . . they would have stamped something like that right into the ground (laughs). My father would have said, "Be happy that you have ears at all!"

Many of the women I spoke with were feminists.[7] This proved an additional hurdle—one more reason to feel ashamed about being so upset about one's appearance. They explained how infuriating it was for women to be constantly judged on the basis of appearance or to be "stuck with inferiority feelings." While they assured me that they were strongly against the pressures on women to be beautiful and advocated resistance to the norms of femininity, they also admitted that they were tortured by their own inability to put their political convictions into practice.

Julie explained how she wrestled with contradictory feelings—the dissatisfaction with her appearance (the moles on her face), the importance of feminism in her life, and her desire to have cosmetic surgery.

> [A]ll these contradictory feelings inside me. . . . I mean, feminism just didn't make the awful feeling go away. And deep in my heart I really wanted to get rid of them. But I was so ashamed to admit it. I felt like, no, you shouldn't be so upset about it and you should accept yourself as you are. And, well, all those things that I actually believe, too. . . . Yeah, you really want to take on these feminist norms, but you just miss the right feeling.

Julie's account showed how difficult it was to bring a normative commitment both to the feminist discourse of self-acceptance as the road to empowerment and to her own gut feeling that her face was something she just couldn't accept. Feeling different than how she feels she should was another source of shame—in many ways, more painful than her original sense of deficiency. It divided her against herself.

"THEY JUST DON'T KNOW HOW YOU FEEL. . . ."

Many of the women I spoke with complained about feeling entirely alone with their problem, unable to talk to anyone about it. For some, the interview was the first time they had actually explained how they felt about their appearance. Others recalled the occasional friend or family member—invariably, women—with whom they had discussed their difficulties. Even when they received a sympathetic listening, however, it appeared to do little to alleviate their sense of being alone. They often explained that other people simply couldn't understand what they were going through: "They just don't see how you really *feel*. They judge you and don't understand that it goes much deeper." Thus, while the possibility of sharing their experiences with someone else promised to relieve their isolation, in reality it often created more problems than it resolved. The problem became both more tangible for having been expressed and more shameful for having been discounted.

Sandra explained that she gave up bemoaning her breasts to her friends:

> If you talk about it . . . and, that's mostly to women—I guess it's jealousy, but they act like you are provoking all the cat-calls yourself. Or like "So what's the problem, big breasts are *nice*," or "Come on, just don't let it bother you."

Complaints about the offending body part elicited reactions ranging from blaming the sufferer for her own problem to more well-meaning attempts to minimize it. Her problem was reformulated as an advantage ("I wish *I* had your breasts.") or denied altogether ("*I* don't see anything wrong.") In some cases, her problem was acknowledged, but her suffering was discounted as exaggerated or irrelevant ("Don't let it bother you." "It's the inside that counts.")

Many women admitted that they had rarely been openly criticized about their appearance and, in fact, remembered receiving constant reassurances along the lines of "You're such a nice person," or "We like you just the way you are." For example, Julie recalled how her family and friends "always made a big point of telling me that I was worth a lot." Instead of making her feel better about her appearance, such remarks tended to backfire, confirming her sense that she was different. ("Why else would someone need to say something like that?") More seriously, reassurances and even compliments exacerbated her feeling that other people "just don't understand." Alone with her problem, it became increasingly difficult to voice how she felt.

> I needed a lot of time . . . before I could admit openly to myself that I just really hated my face and that I wanted to have those moles taken off. It was something that I had always felt, but just never could admit. And that whole business about how you are fine the way you are—that was like a *big, heavy blanket*, covering up how I really felt.

Cosmetic surgery was a way for some women to acknowledge their suffering—to admit they had a problem and do something about it. The fact that their decisions were often taken in opposition to family and friends only strengthened the sense that they were doing something for themselves. As Julie put it:

> It really did help to have those things taken off . . . it changed everything. . . . I think it has to do with my deciding to *do* something about the thing that I had always felt was the *worst* thing about myself.

In conclusion, the reasons women provided for having cosmetic surgery ranged from the seemingly mundane problem of being unable to find a bra that fit to a ruined sex life. In the remainder of this chapter, I shall discuss these explanations against the backdrop of the Western feminine beauty system and its dissatisfactions, which produce a need to engage in body improvement practices.

BEAUTY PROBLEMS?

One of the surprising features of women's explanations for their suffering was their unanimous reluctance to connect it with beauty. In fact, many went to great lengths to assure me that their particular problem had nothing to do with a desire to be beautiful. Since their problem was not about beauty, cosmetic surgery could not be regarded as part of the continuum of normal practices which women routinely undertake in order to beautify their bodies (makeup, diets, aerobics). This point was driven home in different ways.

Some women explained that they were not even particularly interested in how they looked. "It was never *my* ambition to be Miss World," or "*I* don't have to be some sex bomb" were frequently heard types of remarks. They would make disparaging comments about other women who were preoccupied with physical attractiveness. A woman who had her breasts lifted after her second pregnancy would assure me that face lifts were ridiculous because "wrinkles just go along with getting older." Or, a face lift candidate would express disapproval toward women who wanted to have their breasts augmented. "Breasts just don't make that much difference; it's not like your face. That's really important."

Other women would acknowledge that beauty did matter to them and that they, too, worried about how they looked. ("What woman doesn't?") This would be followed by long lists of physical features which fell under the category of beauty problems. A woman who had a breast augmentation might complain that she had "never liked the wrinkles on her face" or had always been much too thin ("a bean pole"). Or a face lift candidate would sigh that she "would give anything for bigger breasts" or "really hated having such hairy legs." They even admitted that they would love to have different bodies—bigger breasts, fewer wrinkles, slimmer thighs—only to exclaim that they would never consider cosmetic surgery "for something like that." They would then typically argue that the feature for which they had sought cosmetic surgery was in another class altogether—much uglier or more abnormal than such mundane beauty problems could ever be.

Although the women I spoke with varied in the importance they attributed to their looks in general, they were unanimous in their critical stance toward having cosmetic surgery strictly for reasons of beauty. Some scoffed at such operations as trivial: "Think of all the people who really have something wrong with them!" Others found cosmetic surgery for beauty problematic on ideological grounds: "It's terrible—women are always being told that there is something wrong with them." Or "We should be able to accept our bodies the way they are." Still others worried about the proliferation of medical technologies for beautifying the body, exclaiming, "It's all out of control," or "Where will it all end?"

These reservations having been presented, each woman drew the conclusion that her problem was different than the normal difficulties women have with their appearance—more serious, more limiting, or simply of a different order altogether. ("This is not about beauty; it's psychological.") Thus, whether beauty was something which mattered to them personally or just belonged to the normal problems most women endure, it had nothing to do with their reasons for having cosmetic surgery. Cosmetic surgery could, therefore, be presented as an extraordinary solution to an extraordinary problem.

At this point, a question could be raised concerning what the shared and rather vehement denial of beauty as a reason for having cosmetic surgery means. After all, both common sense and scientific interpretations of why women have their bodies altered tend to link cosmetic surgery to the female preoccupation with beauty. Why, then, do women who have cosmetic surgery reject this interpretation themselves so emphatically and with such surprising unanimity?

The most obvious explanation would be that women's accounts for why they had their bodies altered surgically are invariably made in a cultural context in which some discursive strategies are more likely than others to make their experience of suffering understandable and, therefore, the act of having cosmetic surgery defensible. It could be argued, for example, that their disclaimers merely reflect the prevailing discourses of Dutch Calvinism—discourses which make excessive vanity reprehensible, at best, and sinful, at worst. In The Netherlands, it is difficult to even admit to having cosmetic surgery at all. How, then, could a woman possibly justify going to such lengths for something as trivial and ignoble as beauty? While in the U.S. it might be easier for the potential cosmetic surgery candidate to claim straightforwardly that she just wants to look better or even that she has a right to look better, in The Netherlands, a woman cannot count on a sympathetic listening if she frames her suffering in terms of beauty.[8] However, the desire to be just ordinary is not only acceptable, but, indeed, a moral must.[9] As we have seen in Chapter One, in a welfare system individuals are, generally speaking, less likely to draw upon a discourse of rights to justify their actions than a discourse of need. If we conclude that in The Netherlands women who have cosmetic surgery have no other recourse than to explain their actions in terms of needing to be ordinary rather than having the right to be beautiful, the problem still remains of what being ordinary actually means to them.

BEING ORDINARY

To begin with, being ordinary seems to have little to do with standards of normalcy in physical appearance. The difficulties which the medical profession has in setting aesthetic criteria for determining which bodies fall outside the realm of the normal attest to the fact that beauty is, indeed, in the eye of the beholder. When scientific guidelines fail—as was frequently the case with Dr. Berg—medical professionals seek refuge in cultural norms concerning what constitutes an acceptable feminine appearance. Since a female body is rarely up to snuff in the context of the Western beauty system, it is not surprising that they, too, will cast an overly critical eye upon potential candidates for cosmetic surgery and too easily discover grounds for a breast augmentation or a tummy tuck. Such norms may enable individual practitioners to decide which patients should or should not have surgery, but they have little to offer concerning what makes one body ordinary and another not. Even the most enthusiastic plastic surgeon is likely to admit that appearance is hopelessly subjective. Women who are beautiful according to cultural standards can, nevertheless, decide to have their bodies changed, while individuals with more obvious bodily defects may be unbothered by their appearance and could not imagine having cosmetic surgery.

This discrepancy between public appearance and private suffering is not simply a problem for the medical profession, however. The women I talked with—much like the applicant who approached Dr. Berg for a breast augmentation—did not necessarily have bodies which, at first glance, seemed to require surgical alteration. In fact, when they showed me old photos before surgery, I was just as unable to see the problem and as amazed that they would have surgery for something so minor as I had been during Dr. Berg's consultations. Moreover, from their accounts, I could not help but notice that they were usually able to acquire jobs, find partners, produce families and, in general, lead fairly ordinary lives despite problems with their appearances. In short, women who have cosmetic surgery seem to be no less ordinary, appearance-wise than women who don't.

Ordinariness is, first and foremost, a matter of experience. The women I spoke with invariably told stories of terrible suffering which came about because they experienced their bodies as different or abnormal. They provided convincing accounts of how their appearances cast shadows over how they felt about themselves and their relationships and how, more generally, their appearances stood in the way of their happiness and well-being. Although the specific circumstances for deciding to have cosmetic surgery were different for each woman, the experience of suffering was the red thread running through their stories. It was this suffering which made their explanations ring true and their decisions to have cosmetic surgery understandable as a regrettable, but—at least in these particular cases—necessary step.

In the next chapter, I explore how the experience of being different is constructed in women's narratives about their appearance, showing how cosmetic surgery can be a strategy for becoming ordinary.

FOUR

FROM OBJECTIFIED BODY
TO EMBODIED SUBJECT

Diana is an attractive, vivacious high school teacher in her mid-thirties. Several years ago she had her entire face rebuilt surgically: her jaw shortened, her chin and nose altered, and her teeth fixed. The operation transformed her, as she put it, into a "totally different person."

She was referred to me by a mutual friend and agreed to an interview with me because "after going through such an ordeal, you really want to talk about it." I arrived at her home on a Saturday afternoon to find her living room all set up for the interview. On the coffee table I could see a pile of photographs, a family album, diaries, and brochures with information on the operation, all within easy reach. She brought in a steaming pot of tea and a plate of home-made cookies, switched on her answering machine, and assured me that we wouldn't be disturbed as her husband and daughter would be gone for several hours.

The interview began in the usual way. After a brief exchange of pleasantries, I explained how I got involved in this research about women's experiences with cosmetic surgery. I made of point of saying that despite all the attention currently being given to cosmetic surgery in the media, no one seemed particularly concerned about what the recipients themselves had to say about it. I was, therefore, especially interested in what made her decide to have cosmetic surgery, her experiences with the operation itself, and how she felt about it now that it was all over. I explained that I did not have a fixed set of questions and that she could talk about whatever she thought was relevant or wanted to tell me. I would only interrupt if I didn't understand what she was saying.

By explaining my agenda at length, I hoped to put her at ease and get her sufficiently interested to participate in the interview. This is fairly straightforward procedure for narrative interviews, the assumption being that the less the interviewer intervenes, the more likely the respondent is to talk about her experiences and rearrange them according to her own priorities and criteria of relevance.[1]

I soon realized, however, that things were not going to proceed according to the books. Diana launched into her story as though a starting shot had been fired. She raced through her account, scarcely pausing to catch her breath. She sat nervously perched on the edge of her seat. After going back to her situation prior to the operation and her experiences with the surgery and its aftermath, she leaned back, looking noticeably more relaxed, and announced: "So, I guess that's my story, more or less." Somewhat nonplussed, I began to consider turning off the tape recorder when, to my surprise, Diana leaned forward, picked up where she left off and went through the whole story again. In fact, she recycled her initial narrative in this way four more times during the interview, each time providing a little more detail. Most puzzling of all, however, was that she continuously interrupted her story to explain, justify, or defend her reasons for having cosmetic surgery. All my attempts to provide a sympathetic listening seemed to have been in vain. It was as if an invisible audience of critics were lurking in the shadows of her living room, just waiting to pounce, and she had to parry their attacks before continuing with her story.

My first reaction was to attribute Diana's narrative behavior to the sensitivity of the topic at hand. I began to worry that I had failed to establish rapport or that I had, unintentionally, showed signs of disapproval. After all, she was talking about experiences which had been painful and difficult to deal with in the past, often involving considerable embarrassment as well. I assumed that what I saw were "shame markers," that is, the telltale signs that accompany a person's anticipation that she could be negatively evaluated by another.[2] Perhaps there was something in my demeanor or my interview technique which was making Diana feel ill at ease, or eliciting defensive conversational behavior. Just as I concluded that I needed some additional interview training, however, our conversation took another turn, dispelling my fears and making me realize that something else was going on.

Midway through the interview, Diana suddenly seemed to relax and become more expansive, showing no signs of wanting to stop. She became increasingly forthcoming, bringing in more and more information about herself, her life history, and her relationships. She showed me pictures of her face before the surgery to illustrate her transformation. This was reinforced by the family photo album, with Diana laughing as she pointed out how she had looked at different intervals of her life. In an animated voice, she read excerpts from her diary before and after the operation. By the end of the interview, she not only appeared relieved, but excited. As I was getting ready to leave, she announced, smiling, that it had done her a world of good "to get it off my chest" and asked me to keep in touch with her about how my book was progressing.

The interview with Diana was not an exception. This discrepancy between the beginning and the end of the interview turned out to be a standard feature of how women talked about their experiences with cosmetic surgery. Women who began with hesitation or defensiveness surprised me later by announcing that this was the first time they had ever really talked about their experiences to another person. Women who told their stories with much blushing or hunched over with their eyes firmly fixed to the floor would make an abrupt about-face at the end of the interview and offer to show me their new breasts. My interviewer insecurities were further allayed when my respondents called me up weeks later to fill in things they had forgotten or when they sent me clippings about cosmetic surgery years after the interview.

I came to the conclusion that this transformation from shame to relief, from hiding behavior to unmistakable pride, were not artifacts of my conversational technique or narrative interview methodology, in general, but rather a reflection of the kinds of experiences involved. In other words, *how* women talk about their experiences with their appearance and the surgical alteration of their bodies is significant for *what* these experiences mean to them. Their stories allowed them to reenact and, retrospectively, make sense of the experience of having a body which was perceived as unacceptable—an experience which was often considered too shameful to be talked about with another person. Cosmetic surgery not only transformed this experience of embodiment, but it provided the occasion to express what had formerly been a carefully guarded secret. The relief and exhilaration were not only part of the experience of transformation; they were part of the activity of telling the story as well.

In this chapter, I show how a woman's experiences of embodiment change in the process of having her body altered through cosmetic surgery. Her narrative about this transformation process both reflects and constructs these experiences.[3] After providing a brief description of how cosmetic surgery narratives are organized in general, I return to Diana's story to explore in depth how she makes sense of cosmetic surgery as a way to become ordinary. By showing how it enabled her to renegotiate the "typical tension of feminine embodiment" (Young 1990b), I show how cosmetic surgery can be a strategy for becoming an embodied subject.

SURGICAL STORIES

Storytelling is the most common way for people to "package" their experiences (Sacks 1978). Stories about cosmetic surgery are no exception. They allow the narrators to define, elaborate, and give significance to their physical beings, and how this changes over a period of time.[4] Stories usually tell what led the individual to decide to have cosmetic surgery, what the operation was like, and how she felt about it after the fact. This entails more than a straightforward chronological rendition of what happened, however. Each narrative is itself a reflexive process by which the individual ongoingly deliberates and (re)constructs her relationship with her body. She draws upon her biography as a backdrop for understanding why she wanted to have her body altered surgically, to make sense of her decision and, in so doing, display the decision as making sense.

Women's stories about cosmetic surgery display several recurrent narrative features which give otherwise idiosyncratic experiences of embodiment and of deciding to have cosmetic surgery a recognizably similar pattern. These features show that women's experiences with their appearance are organized in such a way that cosmetic surgery can become an understandable and, indeed, unavoidable course of action in view of their particular biographical circumstances. These features include dividing their life histories into a before and after, establishing the suffering which makes surgery necessary, elaborating the problematic aspects of the transformation, and integrating the event in terms of their self-identities.

First, cosmetic surgery stories have a *before and after*.[5] The act of having one's body altered surgically becomes a biographical "turning point" (Denzin 1989a)—a crossroads in a woman's life which divides it into a before and after. It becomes the vantage point from which she looks backward at the past to make sense of her decision and forward in order to anticipate what it will mean for her future.

Second, cosmetic surgery stories are presented as a *trajectory of suffering*.[6] They begin with the woman's realization that something is seriously amiss with her appearance and follow her through a period of several years during which she comes to regard her body as an insurmountable constraint—a condition which leaves her "uprooted, at least to a certain degree, from the mundane common world and its normal course of affairs" (Riemann and Schütze 1993: 345). She describes her hopelessness and resignation as she discovers that there is nothing she can do about her problem. Her story takes on a quality of impending doom, becoming a "downhill path" or vicious circle (Riemann and Schütze 1991: 348–349). The stage is then set for cosmetic surgery as the event which interrupts the trajectory. It allows her to take action and regain a sense of control over her life.[7]

Third, cosmetic surgery stories are interspersed with *arguments and deliberations*. The women I spoke with would constantly break off their narrative, often mid-sentence, to explain or defend themselves. While this was sometimes precipitated by something I said, it seemed to be more frequently self-initiated. These sequences took on different forms. In some cases, they resembled a kind of private musing about a point which needed clarification. ("I was just thinking . . . .") On other occasions, possible objections or criticisms to the story would be anticipated and the individual telling it would take the other side for the moment, indicating that she understood that her action was problematic or controversial. ("I know I shouldn't be this concerned about my body, but . . . .") In some cases, an actual dialogue would ensue, whereby she would provide both the arguments for and the arguments against the decision to have cosmetic surgery. Such argumentative sequences were an ongoing feature of the interviews. They were part of women's attempts to make sense of their decision and indicated that they neither found their experiences self-explanatory nor their reasons for having cosmetic surgery unproblematic.[8]

Fourth, cosmetic surgery stories are stories about *identity*. The individual reconstructs her biography in terms of who she was before the surgery, who she hoped to become, and who she has, in fact, become. This entails going back over the narrative proper and doing some "biographical work." This is the activity of recalling, rehearsing, interpreting, and redefining which accompanies any event that disturbs, disorders or simply alters a person's sense of self (Riemann and Schütze 1991: 339). Various selves, both past and present, are brought together to create a "coherent sense of self-identity"—a narrative unity whereby the individual has integrated possible perspectives and versions about who she is into a meaningful life history (Benhabib 1992: 198).[9]

Taken together, these narrative features are typical for making biographical sense of the transformation of the body and self through cosmetic surgery. An individual woman's desire to have cosmetic surgery becomes comprehensible in light of her experience of suffering and the solution which it seems to offer in terms of taking control of a situation which she formerly felt powerless to change. By exploring these features, we can understand not only her elation at having taken the step, but her shame and reservations about it as well.

DIANA'S STORY

Having provided a brief look at the narrative structure of women's cosmetic surgery stories, I shall now take a look at one narrative in more depth. I have chosen Diana's story for several reasons. On the surface, her story resembles that of the other women I interviewed. It echoes many of the themes discussed in the last chapter: hating a particular part of her body, feeling that it didn't belong to the rest of her, experiencing herself as marked or different from other people, and so on. Upon closer examination, however, her case proves particularly good for exploring the relationship between women's experience of embodiment and their desire to have their bodies altered surgically.

First, and most prosaically, Diana had the most extreme form of cosmetic surgery of any of my respondents. The operation was not only the most extensive, requiring several hours under anesthesia, intensive care, a lengthy hospital stay, and a long and painful recovery period, but the transformation was the most dramatic. She had literally become unrecognizable to her friends, family, and even to herself. A physical transformation of such magnitude presumably required some getting used to, involving, at the very least, an integration of her new body with her old identity.

Second, Diana's face was the object of the surgery. Faces are particularly powerful cultural symbols of identity. The face is alternately regarded as representing who a person really is ("everyone has the face she deserves") or as distorting or disguising a person's true character. This mirror/mask dichotomy belongs to Western notions about the relationship between the face and the self (Strauss 1969; Synnott 1990; see also Goffman 1959). Thus, a major alteration of the face will presumably effect a person's sense of herself in dramatic ways as well.

Third, Diana was unusually articulate about her reasons for having her face altered. She used the interview as an opportunity to reflect on how she felt about her body, herself, and her relations with other people. Because she explicitly addressed the subject of how her operation transformed her feelings about her body and who she was, she provides a good example for an in depth analysis of how women experience their bodies and what ordinariness might mean for a woman's embodied identity and her decision to have cosmetic surgery.

The interview originally took several hours. I have divided it into several segments for analysis. I begin with a description of her initial narrative (the trajectory), showing what led up to her decision to have cosmetic surgery and her assessment of the outcome. In the second part, I show how she introduces the problem of identity through the biographical work which she does in order to make sense of the aftermath of cosmetic surgery. In the third part, I explore how Diana deliberates about the more problematic features of her decision, thereby bringing her story to a conclusion and establishing herself as—at long last—ordinary.

FROM "SUPER UGLY" TO "JUST A NICE FACE"

Diana's story begins with the statement that until the age of ten: "I just looked like a nice kid." She describes herself as an ordinary-looking child—neither especially pretty nor particularly unattractive. Her situation changes dramatically as her teeth start to protrude. Braces are of no avail and she finds herself transformed into someone who is "super ugly," different than everyone else. Although her other features contribute to her problematic appearance (glasses, unruly hair, skinniness), it is her "enormous front" which is the primary offender. It not only exacerbates all other physical imperfections, but turns her into a different person. ("I looked retarded.") She becomes the object of continual teasing and harassment from other children. ("Bugs Bunny, wanna carrot?") She has gone from ordinary child to social deviant in the space of just one year.

By the time she reaches adolescence, she is convinced that she has "somehow managed to get over it." She describes her resourcefulness in finding other ways to be attractive. ("Boys could always *talk* to me.") She has a flair for clothes, starts wearing makeup and gets herself a pair of contact lenses. She is good in school and starts making plans for attending the university. She even has a boyfriend. She explains that although she continues to think of herself as a "wallflower," as "someone who didn't belong" and "could be passed over easily," she also feels gradually better about herself and by the time she reaches her early twenties, she decides that she has "*finally really* gotten over it. Or, that's what I thought anyway."

Diana goes to considerable lengths to establish that she has done the most to make the best of a bad starting position and that her appearance is not going to interfere with how she lives her life. At the same time, however, she already intimates that this story will not have a happy ending. She constructs her adolescence and early adulthood as the proverbial calm before the storm.

Her conviction that she has her life under control is rudely shattered in her first teaching job. Confronted with the usual problems of disciplining a class, she describes her painful realization that she hasn't escaped her problematic appearance, after all. Her students tease her mercilessly about her face and she finds that she is back to square one. She is devastated ("I realized how *awful* it was for me to hear that . . . it just really really *hurt*.") Diana no longer believes that she will ever be able to "transcend" her body and move about in the world freely without being reminded of how she looks. What she has always "secretly known" is now confirmed: her body determines how her life will be. She realizes that she is a prisoner of her body and will never be able to escape its constraints. She is doomed to a life of misery.

However, Diana does not immediately turn to cosmetic surgery as the solution to her problems. As she explains, she would "never have dreamed of doing something like that." It would just make her more vulnerable—by showing the world how much appearance mattered to her. She even remembers going to a dentist to have a crown replaced and being thoroughly incensed at his suggestion that she might want to have some work done on her teeth ("Who asked *him*, anyway?").

It is only after talking to a friend who has had cosmetic dentistry herself that Diana decides to make an appointment with a plastic surgeon.

She presents this encounter as the turning point in her decision. Remembering her surprise at seeing photographs of other cosmetic surgery patients, she exclaims:

> It was amazing, all the different operations they can do there . . . all these people with really *major* problems like harelips or weird noses, and like I was just one out of all those people who came there. So what happens is that first you think you are this big awful exception. You feel that you're marked . You've covered it up all these years, but it keeps coming back. But when you go there, you realize, wow, here it's just normal, like just a real *normal* operation.

After years of experiencing herself as a kind of outcast from more ordinary-looking people, Diana discovers for the first time that she belongs, that she is not different than the others ("just an ordinary freak"). It is in this sense that cosmetic surgery loses some of its strangeness and becomes almost the normal thing to do.

Diana begins to prepare herself for the surgery. She gathers information about the procedure, talks with patients who have had the operation, and checks out the surgeon's credentials. Once she is sure that she wants to go through with it, she enlists her husband's support. He agrees to stand by her through the surgery and to take care of her during the long recovery period. They plan a long vacation so that she can get in shape for the surgery.

The operation is an ordeal. It involves sawing her jaw open in three places and wiring her teeth together. After being under anesthesia for several hours and a protracted stay in intensive care following surgery, Diana recalls waking up to excruciating pain. She is unable to communicate except by gesticulating with her hands. Later, she manages to scribble messages on a pad of paper. The nursing staff is unfriendly. ("I wasn't a serious patient in their eyes.")

After leaving the hospital, she embarks upon a long and arduous recovery period. Her jaws remain wired together for two more months. She can barely talk and is forced to take all her food through a straw. She is often nauseated and loses weight. During this time, Diana remembers avoiding all social contacts outside her husband and daughter. She is primarily concerned with getting enough to eat and keeping her strength up. After the wires are removed ("the most painful thing I

ever experienced"), she begins the final and, in many ways, most difficult part of the whole affair—"picking up my old life again."

She explains how difficult it is for her to return to work. She asks
her friends to help her by explaining to other colleagues what has
happened and to spare her the burden of having to tell her story over
and over again. In the beginning, she makes sure she doesn't go out in
public without having an escort. "Having your whole face redone is
not like having a breast reduction where no one notices afterwards
that you've had anything done." She remembers all the surreptitious
glances from her pupils and colleagues—unsure this was the same
teacher they had known before the summer break. ("Is that really
you?") While most people recognize her by her voice and movements, others walk right past her. Laughing, she recalls how one of
her colleagues entered the staff room and looked right at her, asking
"Where is Diana?"

Having covered the operation and its aftermath, Diana begins to
take stock of the outcome:

> What I noticed right away was that no one noticed me. Now,
> *that* was a great feeling, let me tell you. I realize that more and
> more. Finally, nobody is there looking at me. Not a single kid
> who yells something at me. That was the first thing I noticed
> after the surgery and I was really glad.

Since the experience of being harassed and made to feel different is
what initiated Diana's desire for surgery, it is fitting that the experience
of not being harassed and of feeling ordinary becomes the measuring
stick which allows her to assess the outcome of her surgery. As she puts
it, the operation does not make her especially beautiful and, in fact, she
expected to look better than she does. However, as she puts it:

> I don't *have* to look like a movie star or anything. It's just . . . well,
> it's a *nice* face now . . . that's the main thing, I'm just *ordinary*.

In addition to her relief at having an ordinary face, Diana cannot
suppress a certain amount of pride that she took the step at all.

> It also gave me a kick, like, I'll be damned, but *I really did it*. You
> know? I got it together. I dared to do it. And I still feel that way.

Like I made the decision, I did it and no one can take that away from me, even if it doesn't look as nice as I had hoped.

She concludes her initial narrative with an episode which illustrates her feelings about the outcome of her surgery. She is asked to participate in an educational film for high school students about racism. It is a major production involving activists and politicians. Although she enjoys working on the film, she recalls going to the premiere "with sweaty hands":

I had never seen myself in a film before and suddenly—you can imagine (laughs)—there I was, *bigger than life* (laughs). And I kind of liked seeing myself—like, that's not a bad-looking woman (laughs). Not gorgeous or anything, just nice looking. Yeah. (pause) I *approved* of the way I looked. And, well, since that film really, and afterwards when I saw myself in pictures or in the mirror, I was just really *satisfied*. I'm really glad I did it. (pause) So, I guess that's about all there is to my story.

This episode is both catharsis and coming-out. It is the moment when Diana no longer feels estranged from her body and seems to have accepted her new face as belonging to her sense of who she is. With much laughter and hand movement, she expresses her delight at having taken the step and her satisfaction with the outcome.

In short, Diana's narrative has all the makings of a surgical success story. After years of suffering, cosmetic surgery enables her to extricate herself from the downward spiral. By having her face remade, she has not only obtained an acceptable appearance ("just a nice face"), but she can enjoy the kick which accompanies the experience of taking a step which alters her life. She portrays herself as an agent who acts upon the world rather than an object to be acted upon by others.

There is a shadow side, however, to Diana's story. Just as she seems to be bringing her tale to a triumphant conclusion, she picks it up again—this time, however, on a more contemplative note.

"IT JUST GOES VERY DEEP. . . IT HAS SO MUCH TO DO WITH YOUR IDENTITY"

Diana now begins to retrace her steps, going back over her narrative and unraveling the implications of the operation for her feelings about her body, her sense of self, and her relationships. Rather than providing a panacea for all her problems, cosmetic surgery seems to have introduced some new ones as well.

> This face in the mirror, you just don't recognize it any more. It's like . . . it's very *strange* . . . especially when you see the first picture of yourself, it's just such a complete shock. It's something about . . . how you see yourself, how the way you experience yourself has to do with seeing yourself in pictures and in the mirror—And I just couldn't (pause) yeah, couldn't bring it *together.* It—it wasn't a whole any more . . . it took at least a year before I could see myself in a photograph and see that it was me.

This segment elaborates a previously mentioned theme, namely, the difficulties of not being recognizable. Whereas Diana seems able to cope with colleagues and friends, it proves much more problematic not being able to recognize her own face. It is, indeed, "shocking" to be unable to match her new face to her old sense of who she was before the operation.[10]

Whereas Diana's primary problem before the operation was that her face didn't belong to her body or to her image of herself, she begins to present her experience with her body in a different way. The problem of perceiving herself "as a unity" still exists, but it is no longer presented as a statement of fact, but rather as a task to be accomplished. Confronted with the difficulty of integrating her body with her sense of self, she shows that identity is something which she can actively negotiate rather than a matter of fate to be passively accepted.

She begins by going back over her biography, returning to her experiences in her family in order to make sense of herself in relation to her body. Slowly and with much hesitation, she explains that her childhood wasn't "all that great" and that her mother "wasn't exactly a pro when it came to encouraging her kids." She remembers being constantly "played off" against her sisters who were all "*much* more beautiful than I was, of course." Her mother's reminder that she wasn't pretty went hand in hand with Diana's sense of belonging to her family. By recalling this criticism, Diana picks up on the experience of being singled out as different which has been a familiar ingredient of her story up until now. This time, however, her loneliness seems to be even more dramatic than it was in random interactions with strangers or with her pupils.

I don't know. (pause) I don't know. Like I'm still just as depressed as I used to be, I can feel just as insecure as ever, on the inside . . . I can get really depressed because of the way it was at home, always being alone, just left to yourself. (pause) My mother was frustrated herself, always projecting it on her kids. (pause) Yeah, I guess it's a kind of *emptiness* inside which you— well, you just don't get rid of it that easily. And you can't do it with an operation either.

Diana appears to be struggling to make sense of her experiences with her appearance against the backdrop of her personal history. She places her dissatisfaction with her body in a broader context of lack of validation. Unable to see herself positively through the eyes of another (her mother), she has difficulties developing a sense of herself in her body; she experiences herself, literally, as empty. This loss of identity, while directly related to her experiences with her body, is far too profound to be eliminated through cosmetic surgery. Diana begins to temper her earlier exuberance concerning the changes wrought by cosmetic surgery and wonders whether it can ever be a solution to a damaged sense of self. Thus, she uses her experience of bodily transformation as an occasion to explore her alienation—from her mother and, more generally, from earlier parts of her own life history.

DIANA: I tried to get control over my life by saying "I'm me and I had this surgery and this was what I had to do." And, you know, I thought it was wonderful *not to tell* my mother about the operation (laughs). Just like that. It helped me loosen my ties with her, with my past. . . . I guess it also played a role in why I got so much pleasure out of it, secretly, that she didn't know about it, that she had to hear about what I had done from someone else. And that I—well, I became *unrecognizable* for her, too.

Well, O.K., I guess I'm still dependent on my mother to a certain extent, I *still* am. Ultimately, of course, I did go see her. I hadn't been to visit her for five or six years . . . and when I did finally visit her . . . well, she hardly even reacted. Like . . .

I: (surprised) Like she couldn't *see* that you had had it done?

DIANA: No. She looked like—umm—Oh, well, yeah, those are just her tactics for getting back at someone. Look, I actually didn't think it was such a big deal. But, yeah, I was in the phase then that I wasn't all that secure about my appearance. My *new* appearance.

In this segment, Diana confronts her difficult relationship with her mother in the aftermath of her operation. She moves from a stance of gleeful defiance to a more reasoned deliberation about her dependence upon her mother's opinion of her. In a manner reminiscent of Fay Weldon's heroine in *The Lives & Loves of a She-Devil*, she resorts to cosmetic surgery as a means to shift the balance of power in her relationships. Whereas her mother's lack of validation is described by Diana as part of her long-term difficulties with her identity, she now uses the operation to provoke a response from her mother. By taking the step to alter her face, she kills two birds with one stone. She takes an independent action ("I'm me and I had the surgery") and forces her mother to acknowledge her.

To be sure, Diana's act of rebellion is not entirely successful and her mother continues to maintain the upper hand by refusing to recognize the change. Nevertheless, the change is unmistakable. Diana now redefines their relationship in terms of power, referring to "tactics" for gaining control on both sides. She admits being dependent on her mother, while, at the same time, minimizing the significance of the dependency ("not such a big deal," "I was in a phase.") While Diana does not come out on top in this particular skirmish, she assesses the conditions under which it has been waged with a certain amount of "discursive penetration"[11] and is able to cut her losses with a degree of equanimity. In short, she presents herself as a knowledgeable and active subject engaged in an interaction of power rather than as a helplessly dependent child.

Having reformulated her relationship to her mother, Diana begins to renegotiate her relationships with the rest of her family as well.

I guess this was the most difficult thing for me, that people who had the most trouble in accepting my new face were my sisters. Because, of course, I had the family face. My father had the same mouth and the buck teeth and even my mother a little bit, too. In my case, it just got to be really irritating . . . But it was a family characteristic.

And, so, suddenly, it's gone. My sister still has it and she didn't like what I had done. She had a hard time with it, yeah, like "You don't look like me any more"—and so did I because, well, I'm pretty close to her and so, I felt bad about it, too.

And I actually never heard one word from them, like "Don't you look great." Not since the operation, never. That's what I find really difficult, it's really hard, not nice at all, you know? But, O.K., I guess that for them it meant that I just didn't belong to the family any more. I guess it's a kind of consequence.

So, it really does interfere with part of your identity. It just goes very deep. It's something I couldn't have foreseen, that it would go that deep . . . that your appearance would have so much to do with your identity.

Diana unravels both the positive and negative ramifications of her surgery for her position in her family, grappling with the theme of identity. She still suffers under the onus of being different because of her face. Ironically, Diana's new face seems to have made her an outsider again by evoking a critical response from her family. She now takes a more analytic stance, however. While she still bemoans the lack of validation she receives from her family, she is also able to understand their point of view. The outcome of these deliberations is that she can accept responsibility for her action, taking their reaction as a consequence of her decision. Despite her sadness at this visible loosening of family ties, she is able to make sense of her contradictory relationship with her family in a way which maintains her position as agent.

Having come to the end of this family story, Diana appears noticeably relieved. She smiles and asks whether I would like to see some pictures. When I nod, she opens one of the albums lying on the coffee table and proceeds to leaf through it, pointing to snapshots of herself as little girl swinging in her backyard, playing with girlfriends, or posed with the family at a birthday party. As we look at the pictures, I return to the topic of identity again, inviting her to elaborate on it:

I: That's interesting, what you said before, about it having to do with your identity, your feeling about yourself and who you are.

DIANA: Well, I notice that I like this face better, that it fits me better than the other one. I feel that now it looks like, uhm, like I was as a child. (She points to one of the snap shots in the album.) See, as a child I was nice looking and was also— well, being petted and hugged. You know, like this is our little Diana, the youngest, kind of heart warming, you know. But that just disappeared when I turned ten, *completely*. That's how it felt to me, at least. You can see it in the pictures, too (She points to another snapshot.) See? There. I look like this miserable teenager—all angles and not knowing how to behave, not belonging with the adults, but no longer a child either. I was in that stage for a long, long time and it had a lot to do with how my appearance had changed.

Yeah, and well, I just feel like now I belong—like now I'm almost—back to the way I was before, before my face changed.

I: Back to the beginning.

DIANA: Yes, back to beginning. Yes.

Like the episode about the film which brought Diana's initial narrative to a close, this excerpt seems to provide a kind of happy end to the problem posed at the outset—namely, how to reconcile her new face with her old identity. It follows a painful and intensive struggle to integrate her body with her sense of self, both past and present. It is by no means a perfect resolution, however. Cosmetic surgery may have transformed her into "just a nice face," but she retains the emptiness and sense that she will never be "completely one" with herself. Having worked through the difficulties, she seems to have achieved a kind of workable identity—for the time being at least. With considerable ingenuity, Diana manages to construct a temporal continuity between her past and present selves. By comparing her ten-year-old self ("just a nice-looking kid," "our Diana," the one who is "petted and hugged") with the person she has become since her operation, she transforms the years of unhappiness prior to the operation to a mere interlude in her life story. Cosmetic surgery has not only changed her face, but has restored her to who she really was all along.

Thus, cosmetic surgery proves to be more than an intervention in a person's body; it is an intervention in her identity as well. By going back to the beginning, she begins a process of integrating her body with her sense of self, and of establishing a line of continuity between who she was and who she has become.

"I'M REALLY NOT CHANGED AT ALL"

Having worked through her family history and integrated her new body into her life story, Diana takes a different stance. While she continues to explore the problem of identity, she adopts an argumentative style of speech. The final part of the interview moves from a straight-forward narrative to a series of debates, sometimes in private dialogue and at other times in interaction with me. These argumentative sequences provide clues to what makes cosmetic surgery a problematic intervention in identity for Diana. Becoming ordinary seems to require more than having her body altered and reconstructing her biography. It also entails finding a way to put the transformation itself behind her and return to business as usual.[12]

Diana begins with the rhetorical question, "You know, I was think-ing—doing this interview with you—about what makes you do something like this?" and proceeds to supply the answer in the form of another anecdote about being tormented by children. This time, how-ever, she constructs the anecdote as a defense for her decision to have cosmetic surgery.

> I remember coming out of the building where I worked and there were two kids standing there shouting insults about my face. You know, there you are, tired and depressed, and that is *so-o-o* awful.
>
> It's probably what Blacks hear all the time, too, like "dirty nig-ger." And when you don't feel particularly strong at a particular moment anyway, you just feel like sinking into the ground. With racism, it's different. At least, you can be proud of your color, of your community. There are people like you. It's such a difference compared to something like this—when you don't belong *any-where*. You don't fit the norms for white people or for people of color either. Then you can't empower yourself *through* the group—something which, I guess, *is* possible for people of color. Like the "black is beautiful" discussion as a way for Blacks to develop pride in themselves, in how they look. I think that's a good reaction to racism, like, you can be beautiful *in* your being different. But that's being different and also being part of a *group*. Well, of course, that just wasn't possible in my case.

This story paves the way for an interpretation of cosmetic surgery as a remedy for social practices of exclusion and derogation. Diana describes her body as different than the dominant norms for physical beauty. Like people of color, she runs the risk of being subjected to public humiliation on the basis of how her body looks. By highlighting the shared features of racism and her own experience of harassment, the reactions to her appearance can be presented as oppressive. While this rhetorical strategy is part of her justification for having cosmetic surgery, it can also backfire.[13] Diana seems to anticipate the objection that these experiences are different by pointing out herself how they are not alike: while people of color have the option of celebrating "difference," she is merely stigmatized by it.

Having drawn upon the arguments of difference and exclusion as a defense for her decision to have cosmetic surgery, Diana then proceeds to deconstruct these same arguments. In other words, she argues against her previous position that her appearance had made her different from other people and had accounted for her being subjected to special forms of oppression. In so doing, she seems to be building a case for why cosmetic surgery was not strictly necessary in her case, and, more generally, should not be regarded as an acceptable solution for people's difficulties with their appearance.

At first glance, Diana seems to be oddly self-contradictory. However, taken together, these reversals in opinion strengthen rather than weaken her case. Let us take a closer look.

Reflecting on the problem of harassment, Diana explains that while "people's reactions can be really harsh" and that it "can be pretty awful," she also knows that "if I had been someone else, I wouldn't have found me attractive either." While she finds it offensive that "you're always supposed to toe the line," she is quick to amend that it is "not so much about being a victim." Hesitating, she reasons:

> You know, people just get *irritated* when you deviate from the norm. (pause) And, well, I notice myself that when I look at other people who—you know—have something different, that I'm just as harsh. I'm not one bit better, even though I've gone through it all myself.

Diana gradually modifies her original assessment of being tormented by children about her appearance. While she does not condone harassment, she redefines it as normal, just the way people are. Her suffering is no longer dramatic, but simply a matter of irritation. Rather than situating herself on the other side of the fence as the victim of exclusion, she takes up the perspective of her former oppressor by showing that she is, after all, no different than they are.

In a similar vein, Diana undermines the significance which her appearance has had for her other interactions with people.

You tend to think that people react to you *because* of your appearance. Well, I guess it does play a role in what goes on in your relationships, but basically I think appearance is really pretty relative. (pause) Because in my case it just didn't make any difference. No difference at all. I mean, whether people liked me or didn't like me. Or whether I liked them. That all just stayed the same. *Absolutely nothing* changed. The only thing that changed were the superficial contacts. In the train, in the bus, on the street. That's all.

At the beginning of the interview, Diana repeatedly stressed appearance as the source of her suffering. Now, she does an about face and concludes that it made no difference at all. The suffering which was so devastating before is now limited to superficial contacts, hardly relevant to the more important things in life. With the operation behind her, she can take a different position on the significance of appearance. It is no longer a matter of concern for her.

Recalling how the doctors warned her that she could expect a "complete personality change" after an operation like this, she laughs:

DIANA: Well, not that I noticed. In that respect, I'm really not changed at all . . . I guess I hoped that because of everything I went through I would be calmer, mentally. After all that suffering, you know. After that terrible pain. (pause) But that's not what happened. Can you imagine if you were in a convent for several months? You would be a different person, right? Mentally. That's actually like what I did. A few months of complete isolation. And—in a way—I expected that. But it had very little effect on how I was later. (laughs)

I: Yeah, like all this must have *some* effect.

DIANA: Yeah, that's what you hope, right? Yeah, I find that disappointing. Like maybe it will change more than just my appearance. Because now I do think the way I look is great. But, well, I haven't—well—become more calm or happier or more in harmony with myself. . . .

Diana deconstructs the common-sense notion that cosmetic surgery is a dramatic transformation, drawing upon the powerful metaphor of the spiritual purification which follows a religious retreat. While her surgical ordeal had the same ingredients of discomfort and protracted isolation, the effect was different. Diana has emerged just as she was before. In contrast to her insistence at the beginning of the interview that cosmetic surgery had transformed her into a "completely different person," she now concludes that, after all, the only thing which has changed is her looks.

These instances do more than contradict Diana's original narrative. Taken together, they work to eliminate the dramatic dimensions of cosmetic surgery as an intervention in identity. By minimizing her original problem as well as the outcome of the surgery, Diana relativizes a step which might otherwise set her apart from others who have not taken such drastic measures to deal with their appearances.

This process is completed as she begins to distance herself from the practice of cosmetic surgery in general. For example, she embarks upon a debate with me about the importance of beauty for women. "Hairy legs—now that's a problem, let me tell you," she explains, and regales me with stories about the indignities of having legs waxed or brave attempts to "just let it grow."

> I'd love to have bigger breasts or a different nose. But I'm not going to do anything about that. . . . Look, maybe if there was some easy way, take a pill or something that wasn't dangerous, then I would do it. But, sometimes I just think, like where do you draw the line? With all that manipulation of your body . . . there's a limit . . . ; it's not like just taking an aspirin or something. You know, like "let's just lengthen this little bone here or lets move this one up or push this one a little closer." That's just crossing the line. I think, no. (pause) No, not *that*. No.

Thus, Diane's narrative comes to a close. What began as a defense of cosmetic surgery as the only solution for the suffering and victimization of being different has become a critique of cosmetic surgery from the vantage point of someone who has nothing more than the usual beauty problems. She now can acknowledge the limitations of her own transformation and, like any other woman, is free to explore the illusory and controversial features of cosmetic surgery as a means for altering one's body and/or one's self. She has reentered the fold of the ordinary looking.

BECOMING AN EMBODIED SUBJECT

Diana's narrative is about the relationship between embodied experience and identity. By altering her body, cosmetic surgery opened the possibility of alleviating a sense of being caught in a body which is different. It intervenes in a process of suffering and provides the possibility of becoming ordinary. Cosmetic surgery is not a magical solution: a new body, a new life. Looking at Diana's narrative in depth, it becomes clear that the surgical intervention is only the beginning. It displays how cosmetic surgery necessitates renegotiating her relationship to her new body, integrating the transformation into her biography, and finding a way to return to life as usual. It shows that becoming ordinary is a formidable endeavor, indeed.

The first part of her narrative establishes her body as different and her sense of self as irrevocably disordered. Her experience of embodiment is organized as a trajectory which provides the narrative framework for understanding cosmetic surgery as a plausible and, indeed, necessary course of action—the only way to interrupt the downward spiral of her suffering. Her story is about *being different*: the raison d'être for the intervention.

The second part of the narrative involves retelling the story, this time from another angle. The intervention having been established as necessary, she now begins to reflect on what her bodily transformation means for her sense of self. Cosmetic surgery entails biographical work, compelling her to bring together past and present identities into a coherent story of self. Her story is about establishing *continuity*—integrating who she used to be with who she has become.

The third part of the interview shows that it is not enough to integrate past and present. Cosmetic surgery remains a dramatic and unsettling action. It sets her apart from others who—for whatever reasons—do not take such drastic measures. This entails another reconstruction of identity—this time, as someone who has to deal with disappointing outcomes and take a critical distance from her own cosmetic surgery. Her initial position is abandoned and she becomes, after all, just like everyone else. Her final story is about the process of returning to *life as usual*—normalizing the seemingly dramatic dimensions of the transformation.

In conclusion, cosmetic surgery is an intervention in identity. It does not definitively resolve the problems of feminine embodiment, enabling a woman to transcend the constraints of her body; nor is it an unproblematic act of liberation. However, by providing a woman with a different starting position, cosmetic surgery can open up the possibility to renegotiate her relationship to her body and construct a different sense of self. In this way, it intervenes in the disempowering tension of Western feminine embodiment—the entrapment of objectification. Cosmetic surgery can provide the impetus for an individual women to move from a passive acceptance of herself as nothing but a body to the position of a subject who acts upon the world in and through her body. It is in this sense that cosmetic surgery can, paradoxically, provide an avenue toward becoming an embodied subject rather than an objectified body.

Obviously, many women suffer because of their appearance and do not turn to the plastic surgeon. An individual woman's desire to have her body altered does not mean that she will actually decide to have cosmetic surgery. In the next chapter, I take a closer look at the process by which this decision is actually taken.

FIVE

DECISIONS AND DELIBERATIONS

On March 17, 1992, BBC television broadcast a program in the series *Forty Minutes* about the new and highly controversial practice of stomach-stapling ("So Much to Loose").[1] It was about two women who had been unable to control their weight through dieting or exercise and had opted for the surgical fix. The documentary follows both women through the decision process, the operation itself, and its aftermath. They are shown weeping, in consultation with a kindly, gray-haired male surgeon in white coat, who explains the advantages of the procedure for "women who nibble too much." He provides a "scientific" demonstration of how the procedure works, using a small plush cushion which is presumably meant to represent a stomach but looks like a cross between a pin cushion and a child's toy. He draws a line to show where the staples will come and then holds up a syringe, indicating how few deciliters the stomach will hold after the operation. The patients are left nodding their heads, apparently reassured.

The next scene is a hospital bed, where the first woman lies with an unsightly incision running vertically down the length of her abdomen. She is in obvious pain, but smiles bravely. Although she now suffers from flatulence as a permanent side effect of the surgery and later develops a stomach ulcer, she still has no reservations. The operation has completely transformed her—from a housewife with no interests outside her family ("just a fat frump") to an active and attractive woman with a new permanent, contact lenses, and a brand new wardrobe. She announces that she is no longer prepared to devote herself to her family ("I was stuck in the same old rut"), but has her own life and is going to "put herself first from now on."

The second woman is less successful. While she initially enjoys a weight loss, she gains it all back because her staples keep bursting and, later, the silicone ring which is used to close off part of her stomach erodes. We see her sitting in a hospital waiting room with a friend who asks her in disbelief, "Surely you're not going to put yourself through all that again?" She nods, worried only that the surgeon may refuse another operation. She explains that she "can't go back to being fat." The program ends with her propped up in a hospital bed, ready for her fifth operation.

This program is not exceptional. The media is full of similar stories about women who seem determined to go through terrible surgical ordeals to have their appearance altered.[2] Their desire for surgery seems almost pathological. In spite of the side effects and less-than-satisfactory outcomes, they are unstoppable, prepared to go to any length for the sake of beauty. As a feminist viewer, such programs invariably leave me with several contradictory responses.

The first response is anger at the misrepresentation and downplaying of the hazards of the surgery. I cannot help but suspect that, had these women known in advance what they were getting into—that is, been properly informed about the risks and side effects of the surgery, they never would have gone through with it.

The second response is mystification at the apparent irrationality of their insistence on having such dangerous surgery and at their willingness to not only put themselves through repeated operations, but to take the—often major—side effects in stride. I find myself wondering how they can engage in behavior which seems so manifestly against their own welfare.

While both responses contradict my heartfelt belief that women who have cosmetic surgery are competent decision makers and that cosmetic surgery can be a reasonable choice in some circumstances, they also show how difficult it can be—even for a self-acclaimed proponent of women's agency like myself—to reconcile this particular conviction with the more pernicious surgical practices like stomach stapling. The dissident, but nagging worry remains that there may be some cases where women have so little information or where the pressures are so overwhelming, that their agency may be less relevant to the situation at hand than their lack of choice.

This contradiction between agency and the circumstances which constrain it lies at the heart of understanding women's involvement in cosmetic surgery. It is implicated in the issues of choice and informed consent which are invariably raised in conjunction with cosmetic surgery. Choice presupposes that the individual has viable options to choose from. Informed consent assumes that she has been given sufficient information to understand and evaluate the intervention and that her consent has been freely given; i.e. not coerced. Questions which often arise concerning cosmetic surgery are, for example: to what extent does an individual's suffering eliminate her ability to rationally assess the advantages and disadvantages of the surgery? Given the enormous pressures on women to meet the prevailing standards of beauty, can we ever speak of consent which is freely given? If cosmetic surgery is the action of choice, what have women had to choose from in the first place? In other words, to what extent can women choose to have cosmetic surgery and can they receive sufficient information to make their decision an informed one?[3]

Lisa Parker (1993) tackles these questions, using the controversies surrounding breast implants as a case in point. In 1992, the FDA announced its decision to restrict the availability of silicone implants to "urgent-need patients" due to health risks (ibid., 58). While the implants would remain available to all reconstruction candidates, only a "very limited" number of augmentation candidates would be allowed to have them and only if they were enrolled in clinical studies. Parker launches an attack upon this policy, showing that it is paternalistic and tramples upon women's right to informed consent. The medical profession has a long and checkered history of making decisions on women's health "for their own good," while simultaneously restricting their access to information or excluding them from decision making which would enable them to exercise control over their own bodies.[4] Surgeons tend to view women who have augmentation surgery as neurotic—at best, overly narcissistic and, at worse, addicted or hysterical. The standard example of the "typical" breast augmentation candidate is the middle-aged woman who "hopes to save her marriage by having her breasts done." Her decision seems to be motivated less by a rational assessment of the benefits and costs of the surgery than by her neurotic anxieties or unrealistic hopes (Gifford 1980).[5] The paternalistic argument against choice rests on the assumption that women who want cosmetic surgery need to be protected—from themselves (their narcissistic desire for beauty) or from undue influence from others. This ostensibly benevolent concern with women's supposed inability to make their own choices is used to keep information about medical procedures and technology firmly in the hands of the medical profession.

Parker, like most feminists, finds the medical paternalism which undermines a woman's right to make decisions about her body generally objectionable. By deciding in advance which women "really" need surgery (i.e., reconstruction candidates) and limiting its availability for augmentation candidates, the FDA ruling denies that women are competent to make their own risk/benefit analysis. Parker points out that while any woman's desire for augmentation surgery is undoubtedly shaped by cultural definitions of female beauty, the decision to have a breast augmentation cannot be chalked up to a woman's blindly acting out some "cultural script."[6]

Moreover, information about the safety of silicone implants is not only inadequate, but it is inconclusive (Parker 1993: 63–64). Research indicates that the majority of augmentation candidates regard the surgery as beneficial and are satisfied with the results. The FDA ruling does not take the positive experiences of women who have had breast augmentation surgery into account (ibid., 64–69). For these reasons, breast augmentation candidates should be given the prerogative of making an informed choice—that is, they should be treated as competent to weigh the dangers of the procedure against their subjective perception of need and of the possible benefits of the operation.

I agree with Parker that decisions concerning cosmetic surgery should not be left to the medical profession. It is the individual woman rather than medical experts who should decide what happens or does not happen to her body. As the person who has to live "within" her body, she, rather than the medical expert or anyone else for that matter, is the one who should be the final judge whether a particular procedure is in her best interests or not. She is the only one, ultimately, who can determine whether the level of pain is acceptable, the risks worth taking, or the procedure excessively invasive. The refusal to respect this right is a violation of her personhood.

Moreover, Parker's argument for women's competency in making their own risk/benefit analysis concerning augmentation surgery is well taken. This is not only because the risks of the surgery are inconclusive and the outcome often beneficial. In an uncertain and hazardous world, most individuals have to negotiate their actions by assessing risks and evaluating benefits. More often than not, these decisions are made on the basis of less than perfect information and in the face of limited options.[7] While this does not make risk a strictly individual matter or absolve us from placing risk in a broader social and political context, it does suggest that women who have cosmetic surgery are no less able than anyone else to assess risks and calculate benefits on the basis of the information available.

In short, Parker's position makes it possible to take the subjective experience of the individual seriously—as the only one who can know how unbearable her suffering is or how beneficial surgery might be. While it allows cosmetic surgery to be linked to the cultural pressures on women to meet the norms of feminine beauty, women who have augmentations do not have to be regarded as more culturally determined than any other woman.

While Parker's plea for choice and informed consent are well argued and sympathetic, it raises issues which cannot be resolved theoretically, either as women's abstract right to make decisions about their own body or as a respect for their competence as decision makers. Cosmetic surgery can only be a choice under circumstances where options are limited. It is never undertaken under conditions of perfect knowledge. Given the ubiquitous pressures upon women to meet the cultural definitions of beauty, it is hardly feasible to speak of an absence of constraint. Thus, to talk about choice and informed consent requires an understanding of the conditions under which the decisions are taken and the concrete context which gives choices their meaning. They cannot be dealt with adequately unless we take a look at how women actually decide to have cosmetic surgery, how they assess the advantages and disadvantages of the operations, and how they regard their decision in light of the outcome.

In the next two chapters, I propose to do just that, using breast augmentation surgery as a case in point.[8] Drawing upon interviews with women who are in the process of having breast augmentations, I trace their decision-making process from the moment that they first considered surgery through their deliberations and conversations with friends and relatives and their encounters with various representatives of the medical profession. Although the interviews were conducted before the FDA hearings placed the safety of silicone breast implants so dramatically on the agenda, I show how the women I spoke with made (or did not make) allowances for the side effects or drawbacks of implant surgery in their own decisions and to what extent they considered their decisions a matter of choice. In the next chapter, I return to these same women a year after the operation in order to see how they viewed their decisions in the light of negative side effects and failed operations. To what extent did they feel duped? Given what they had learned, would they do the same thing again? On the basis of these interviews as well as of recent controversies about the safety of breast implant surgery, I will argue that cosmetic surgery is a choice—albeit a choice taken under conditions which are not of women's own making.

JUSTIFYING COSMETIC SURGERY

The interviews were conducted in a clinical setting and the women I spoke with had been waiting to have breast surgery for nearly a year—the usual period for this particular form of cosmetic surgery. Unlike the women I had interviewed initially, these women were not primarily professionals or academics. Most of them lived in small towns and came from working-class backgrounds.

The clinical setting posed special problems for both the women I talked with and for me as interviewer. It gave the interviews a more formal character than the earlier ones, which had been conducted at my home or in the respondents' homes. The secretary of the plastic surgery department at the university arranged each interview by telephone and I would go to the reception desk in the outpatient clinic at the appointed time to meet the woman in question. The receptionist would call out her name and, after she had come up to the desk, we would retreat to the interview room which was, in fact, an examination room, replete with an examining table covered in white paper and a glass-doored cabinet full of medical paraphernalia.

Many of the women assumed that I was a physician and were anxious to find out more about the surgery. They asked questions which they had forgotten or not dared to ask during the consultation with the plastic surgeon. Several wondered whether I had any pictures of what "it would look like afterwards." When I explained that I was "only a psychologist," they often framed their accounts in psychological terms, explaining, for example, that their problem with their appearance was "definitely psychological" or explaining that they had always had a "complex" about their appearance. Others were more defensive. One woman announced at the outset of the interview that "you people probably think we're all crazy to be doing this" and proceeded to assure me that she really didn't know what she could tell me that would be helpful for my research.[9]

Although each of the women had volunteered to participate in the study, nearly all admitted that they felt nervous about coming to the clinic to talk with me. They were often accompanied by friends, mothers, or husbands. One woman was so worried that the receptionist would mention the reason for her visit when she called her name that she came up to me herself, tapping me on the shoulder and whispering "Are you the one doing the interviews?" Several described wanting to turn around and go home and, in fact, one respondent did just that. When I called her later, assuming that something unexpected had come up, she explained that she was in the waiting room when her name was called, but got "cold feet." Somewhat sheepishly, she admitted that she had even been sitting in the waiting room when I went around asking various women whether they were "Ms. L." and had denied being that person to my face. Despite having taken off from work and driven two hours for the interview, she "just couldn't go through with it." After a long telephone conversation, she did finally agree to talk with me—this time, in her home.

Whereas my earlier interviews had been with women who had already had cosmetic surgery, these were not. While I knew that once these women had gotten this far in their decision process, they would be unlikely to turn back, I often found myself secretly hoping that they would reconsider. For this reason, I was not adverse to supplying information about breast implants or statistics about their side effects. I often encouraged them to take a more assertive stance with the surgeon in order to get answers to their questions. In some cases, I found the interviews upsetting and was confronted with some moral dilemmas of my own. This was the case with the younger respondents—one of whom had just turned seventeen—whose breasts were, literally, still developing. I was horrified that they had been able to obtain cosmetic surgery at all and had gotten through a whole series of medical practitioners without anyone interceding.

While the information I provided about potential drawbacks of augmentation was welcomed, it did not serve as a deterrent. The women I spoke to were apprehensive about the surgery, but they were, without exception, determined to go ahead. Having come this far, they seemed to be ready to get on with it. This did not mean that the decision to have cosmetic surgery was unproblematic, however. Just as the desire to have one's body altered requires some explanation, so does the actual decision to undergo cosmetic surgery.

FROM FANTASY TO REALITY

Cosmetic surgery was not a sudden or unpremeditated step. The women I spoke with invariably described years of terrible suffering interspersed with more-or-less successful attempts to come to terms with their appearance, before even considering an operation. Once they began to entertain the possibility of having their breasts augmented, it often took many more years before they actually saw a plastic surgeon about it. The decision was presented as a long and often painful process, involving various steps. It took considerable deliberation and struggle before their desire to have a different body moved from the realm of fantasy to reality.

Ellen remembers the exact moment that she thought about having a breast augmentation. After years of suffering because of her small breasts, she describes her delight when her breasts filled out during pregnancy. ("I never felt so feminine.") Her joy was short-lived, however. As soon as she stopped nursing, her breasts shrank to "even less than what I had before."

> Well, I guess that was the first time that I thought: if they told me tomorrow that there was a way to make them bigger, you better believe that I'd be lying in that operation room in two seconds flat!

The experience of having larger breasts during pregnancy and the effect that had on her feelings about herself provided a glimpse of how different life would be in another body. Although the transformation was temporary, she could then imagine actually having larger breasts. Wanting to alter her body was not the same as doing it, however. It took another twenty years before Ellen seriously considered having a breast augmentation.

The catalyst was a magazine article which belonged to her then nineteen-year-old daughter. She remembers paging through the magazine and seeing a piece about breast corrections, augmentations and reductions.

[A]nd there it was in black and white: "Dissatisfied with your breasts? Then do something about it!" It was supposed to be for young women. I said to my daughter: "If I were just ten years younger, then I'd just go and do it." Then she said: "Why don't you do it *now*?" I said: "Oh, yeah, I can see it all now, here's this old bag and still so concerned about her figure . . . she's still trying to mix with the younger crowd." "No," she said, "That's not how I see it at all. You've felt bad about this for such a long time," she said, "and you just have to do something to make yourself feel better." She said: "You have thirty, maybe even forty more years to go, so why not have thirty or forty years of pleasure?"

So, well . . . because you've been thinking about it for years anyway and then someone talks about it to you in such a positive way . . . I started thinking: you know what? I'm going to *do* it, too!

This episode shows how an old desire, long buried, becomes reactivated. The difference with the earlier occasion is that Ellen now has a chance to talk to someone about actually doing it. She reenacts the conversation with her daughter, who provides the counterarguments which assuage Ellen's doubts. This dialogue enables Ellen to ventilate her own reservations and shows that she needed to be persuaded into taking the step.

Ellen's story is not unique. Most of the women I talked with had known about cosmetic surgery for years. They had read about it in women's magazines or seen documentaries on television. Some had even considered it for themselves ("if only I could . . ."). Although for some women financial difficulties stood in the way ("You have to have money for something like that and I sure didn't."), the majority did not seem to be, first and foremost, concerned about whether or not they could afford an operation.[10] Instead they initially discarded cosmetic surgery as something they couldn't imagine themselves doing. A middle-aged woman might regard it as something for younger women, while a teenager would wonder whether she didn't need to be older in order to have surgery. Many simply saw cosmetic surgery as something for "movie stars or Michael Jackson, but not for me." Once they began to contemplate a breast augmentation as a possible course of action, they still needed some convincing.

Susan, my youngest respondent, is a seventeen-year-old florist's apprentice. She comes from "a long line of flat-chested women" (aunts, sisters, her mother), all of whom have had breast augmentations. She remembers being taken by her mother to the family doctor when she was only nine because her breasts began to swell and hearing her mother say hopefully that "maybe you are going to get breasts after all." The swelling disappears to Susan's dismay, however, and the breasts are not forthcoming. The turning point in her decision to have a breast augmentation occurs several years later, when she is at the swimming pool with her mother. She recalls noticing scars running along the sides of her mother's breasts.

> So I asked: "Where did those scars come from?" And she said: "Well, I guess the time has come to tell you. I had my breasts enlarged." "Oh," I said. "Can I have it done, too?" I had already been thinking about it for awhile anyway, like whether something could be done for me. And . . . from then on, we just never stopped talking about it.

While Susan's mother is willing to discuss the possibility, she warns her daughter that the operation is not a perfect solution. Susan is sent to an aunt who has had five breast corrections, all unsuccessful. The aunt advises against surgery, but Susan now seems determined to go through with it. ("I'm a different person and maybe it will work with me.") Once she has decided that she "really wants to do it," her mother becomes encouraging. ("'Do it,' she said, so I did.") She not only provides information about the logistics of the surgery and what to expect, but she accompanies Susan to the family doctor, and, later, to the plastic surgeon and to the medical inspector for the national health insurance system to request coverage for the operation.

Susan justifies her operation by situating herself in a family of women "whose breasts just never grew." Her operation becomes legit-imate, almost a way of following in the footsteps of her mother. She describes her "luck" at having a mother who supports her decision, recalling a girlfriend who had to get a breast augmentation on her own. ("That must have been really hard.") At the same time, she appears to be aware that her age might be construed as problematic ("I know I'm a little young, but . . . "). She goes to considerable length to explain that she has not been influenced by her mother, but has decided to have the operation on her own.

> Before I talked to my mother I just thought it would be a lot more difficult, I had no idea how it went. And I thought, yeah, it wouldn't be possible, especially at my age. When I found out

about her operation, that's when I started asking around. . . . But I would have taken the step anyway. It just would have been a few years later. I'm sure glad I can do it now, though.

GETTING HELP

Taking the step turns out to be no easy matter and generally requires some assistance. Each woman refers to a particular person—an acquaintance, friend or family member—who helped her make the decision. It may be an aunt who, after seeing a television program on breast corrections, calls her up, saying "it's just the thing for you." Sometimes the other person has had a breast augmentation herself and suggests that she should try it, too. For some women, cosmetic surgery is almost a family affair. They describe a whole network of women in their immediate circle who have had some form of cosmetic surgery—an aunt with a tummy tuck, a sister-in-law with a breast reduction, or a mother with breast implants. By sharing their experiences, cosmetic surgery seems more acceptable—literally, closer to home. They gain practical information about the operation and what can be expected from it.[11] With the exception of one woman who is encouraged by a man—a male plastic surgeon who she just happened to meet at a party—in most cases, it is another woman who persuades them to take the step.

Taking the decision seems to require some outside encouragement. However, it has to be given by a particular kind of person. The person is always presented as being wholeheartedly in favor of cosmetic surgery. This is contrasted with the doubts and reservations which each woman has about taking the step. The person has to actively persuade her to have cosmetic surgery. This process often is described in the form of a blow-by-blow account—like Ellen's conversation with her daughter— where the other person supplies the arguments and information to take away her qualms and uncertainties about the operation. It is only after her reservations have been eliminated, one by one, that she is convinced that cosmetic surgery is an appropriate course of action for her. Finally, the person has to be both objective and sympathetic, possessing a credibility which allows her to make cosmetic surgery acceptable. Husbands and lovers, for example, are rarely cited as helpmeets in making the decision. Their enthusiasm can easily be misconstrued as dissatisfaction ("I know my husband hates my breasts, too."), making their support a mixed blessing, while a friend or female relative can be supportive without raising doubts about her motives. A feminist woman seems to require reassurance from a feminist friend, while a woman from a traditional or religious family background decides to have cosmetic surgery when her cousin supports her. Thus, she is reassured that having her body altered surgically does not mean that she will become a different person altogether.

In short, each woman has a person who helps her work through her doubts about cosmetic surgery and gives her the needed push toward making the decision. While such reassurance appears to be an essential ingredient to being able to take the step, it also seems to be limited to one or two encouraging others.

OVERCOMING OPPOSITION

Nearly all the women I spoke with recounted being strongly discouraged from having the surgery by friends, colleagues, or family members. They often had to face an endless battery of comments like "is this *really* necessary?" or "are you *sure* you want to do this?" Many began to avoid situations where they would have to talk about their decision. Some women put off having the operation until their vacation or periods when they were unemployed so they wouldn't have to explain their reasons to other people.

Betty describes these negative reactions as the most difficult part of the whole decision. She lives in a small town where everyone knows everyone. By her own admission, she is "not a brave person" and cares a lot about what other people think. ("I want everyone to be my friend.") Although she receives encouragement from her favorite aunt to have a breast augmentation, the rest of her family is skeptical. She finds herself having to constantly defend her decision against their criticisms.

> A lot of people just can't understand it . . . they say, "You're married, you have a husband, children, why do you want something like that now? You don't have to look good any more."

She describes her painful struggle to come to terms with this opposition—a struggle which is reflected in the interview itself. She ongoingly interrupts her account to justify her decision.

> It's ridiculous. I mean, I want it for myself, for my own feeling that I look good. . . . It's important for me because I'm the one

who has to see me every day and I don't like the way it looks and I hate myself when I look at it. . . . I don't want to live like that . . . I don't feel that old . . . I'm just thirty-one and I'm the one who has to spend the rest of my life looking at it. Well, that's how I see it. . . . I guess I think you have to think of yourself some-times. I have thought about other people often enough.

The women I spoke with were not only compelled to reassure family members, but their partners seemed to be far from pleased about their decision. While some partners shrugged it off with a neutral "if that's what you really want . . . ," others tried to actively persuade their wives or lovers to abandon the project. "You don't have to do this for *me*" or "*I* like you the way you are" revealed thinly veiled anxieties about why a woman wanted to have a breast augmentation.[12] Several women con-cealed their wish to have surgery from their husband because they were afraid he would try to dissuade them . It was only when they were sure about the decision, that they broke the news. Some women described having to actively console apprehensive husbands. "He didn't like the idea of my having something foreign in my body," or "He was more worried than I was," were frequently heard remarks. Whereas the women I spoke with differed in their willingness to engage with their partner's anxieties ("I have enough problems of my own."), they invariably admitted that such reactions, ultimately, had little effect on the decision itself.

Many of the women expressed indignation about the assumption that they have been pressured into having their breasts augmented. Caroline, for example, recalls being infuriated when the first thing the plastic surgeon wanted to know was "what my boyfriend thought about my having a breast augmentation."

It's just not about what *he* thinks. He says that he's satisfied with my breasts . . . and, well, it's probably true, too. But *I'm* not. *I'm* the one who wants it done, and what does it matter what he says? I'm doing it for myself and not for someone else.

It is not surprising that women portray cosmetic surgery as a coura-geous act. The opposition to their decision places them in the position of having to disregard the wishes and opinions of others in order to "do something for myself." For many, this is a new experience. Betty, who, as she puts it, "always puts everybody else's needs before my own," remarks, laughing:

> I guess it *was* pretty brave of me to take this step. I guess that's how
> I see it. And, now, I'm really glad I did it, I'm glad I took this step.

Thus, in order to make the decision to have cosmetic surgery, a woman not only needs time to convince herself and some support from a friend. She also needs courage.

MEDICAL HURDLES

Most cosmetic surgery is performed in private clinics, both in The Netherlands and in the U.S. Such clinics are advertised in the newspapers, women's magazines, and even in movie theaters. A woman who wants to have cosmetic surgery only has to look up the clinic in the telephone directory and make an appointment for a free consultation. While such consultations are conducted in luxurious offices with wall-to-wall carpeting, expensive furniture, smiling receptionists, and helpful surgeons, they can often be extremely humiliating. The potential candidate not only has to describe her problems to the surgeon as he appraises her appearance, murmuring "I see what you mean," but will probably be informed that she has other defects which could do with a little surgical improvement as well. ("Have you ever thought about having your thighs lifted, too?" or "What about a little face lift, while we're at it?").[13]

For women who have cosmetic surgery in a hospital setting and who manage to get it covered by medical insurance—as was the case with the women I spoke with—the process is no less humiliating and the operations are considerably more difficult to obtain. They have to run a veritable gamut of medical professionals, from the family physician to the plastic surgeon to the medical inspector for the national health insurance system.

Many women put off going to see a doctor or even go in several times before they manage to bring up the subject of wanting to have a breast augmentation. Betty, for example, remembers going to her general practitioner:

> At first I just couldn't mention it. I just couldn't bring myself to
> say it. I was so ashamed. Finally, I did and the doctor said: "It's
> not like you've got nothing there now, is it?" I said, "No, I don't
> have anything." "Oh, yeah, come on. You do, too!"

It was not unusual for physicians to have to be convinced that a woman had valid reasons for wanting cosmetic surgery. In countries with national health insurance, general practitioners are frequently reluctant to refer a patient to a medical specialist for what they see as an unnecessary medical intervention. A common response is to belittle the problem or to talk the woman out of surgery. This leaves her with the humiliating task of having to persuade the doctor that her breasts were "really small enough" to be considered a problem.

Such paternalistic techniques are rarely successful in side-tracking women who have come this far in their decision. It often simply fuels their determination to go through with the plan. If they can't convince their own doctor, they shop around until they find someone who is willing to refer them to a plastic surgeon.

Plastic surgeons are less likely to discourage the prospective patient from taking the step. None of the women I spoke with seemed to encounter difficulties in finding a surgeon willing to perform a breast augmentation. The consultations were anything but pleasant, however. Already apprehensive, many women described the consultation as a painful ordeal. It involved having to wait, bare-breasted and shivering, until the surgeon arrived and then enduring the embarrassment of having their breasts scrutinized and commented upon. Many remembered feeling like "a number" or "just a piece of meat." The worst part of the consultation, however, was being made to feel that their problem was trivial. Many of the women felt that the surgeons were willing to do the surgery, but disapproving of them as people ("just another silly woman, worried about her looks"). Surgeons often made tactless or flippant remarks. ("Breasts today, thighs tomorrow," or "Where will it end?") While some women reacted with anger ("It's not like I'm here to buy a hamburger or something."), others described feeling ashamed about wanting surgery "for something like this." ("He's probably used to dealing with people who are really sick.")

Consultations were short—usually less than five minutes and confined to a brief rundown of what to expect after the operation. Unlike the clients of private clinics, where before and after photographs and high-tech computer imaging is used to sell the surgery and eliminate the patient's anxieties, none of the women I interviewed received much information.[14]

Surgeons did not provide pictures or even diagrams, and most of the women were at a loss as to what to expect after a breast augmentation. While the women expressed the desire to receive enough information to assess whether the results were going to be worth the trouble, the surgeons seemed most concerned with medical criteria like function or discomfort. Aesthetic criteria—that is, how the breasts were actually going to look—were of secondary importance.[15] However, even when they did deal with the issue of appearance, surgeons seemed to speak a different language than their patients.

Caroline remembers her amazement when her surgeon answered her query about how big her new breasts would be by dumping a slippery, gel-filled bag into her hand with the mystifying query: "So, how many cc's do you want?"

> I mean, just imagine. You have no idea what this guy is talking about. Like how am I supposed to know how many cc's I want. I just want a B cup, that's all.

Many of the women I spoke with complained that they were not given a say in the way their breasts would look. The surgeons appeared to have their own ideas about the desired outcome and were not to be deterred by the particular wishes of the recipient. For example, Elizabeth explains that her surgeon refused to take into consideration that despite her slender figure she had always had big breasts. She wanted a breast augmentation to restore her breasts to the way they had been before her pregnancy. However, when she asked for a larger cup size, the surgeon immediately brushed her request aside with an "Impossible, that doesn't match your build." She remarks, indignantly:

> That's *not* such a strange request—I think it does fit, but, "No, (mimicking the surgeon) that's impossible, that doesn't fit you." That gave me a bad feeling, to have it just shoved under the table like that. They just don't listen to you.

On the whole, most women seemed to fare better when it came to getting information about the side effects of the surgery, although the risks were frequently minimized. For example, they were usually warned that their breasts might be "a little sensitive" after surgery or to expect some swelling. The surgeons invariably mentioned that there was "some chance" of encapsulation, but that it could generally be remedied by daily massaging of the breasts. No mention was made of the common intervention by which the surgeon breaks down the fibroid tissue surrounding an implant through vigorous and—for the women—excruciatingly painful palpitation. The possibility that the implant might have to be removed was rarely mentioned and, if it was, it was treated as something which could be alleviated with further surgery. None of the women were informed that the implants would have to be replaced as a matter of course within fifteen years, although some did discover this after the operation. The surgeons did not tell the recipients that implants could leak ("gel bleed") or even rupture, and no mention was made of recent controversies concerning cancer or connective tissue and autoimmune disease.

In short, the surgeons seemed to have spent more time ridiculing women's reasons for wanting surgery than in providing them with information which would enable them to evaluate the risks against the benefits of the operation. If they were advised against having a breast augmentation, it was because their problem was not considered important rather than because the intervention itself was problematic.

The consultation with the surgeon did not mark the end of the ordeal of getting cosmetic surgery, however. Most women had to visit the medical inspector for the national health insurance system in order to get coverage for their operation.[16] In order for the expert to decide whether the recipient's breasts were smaller than "normal," she had, once again, to undress and subject herself to a stranger's judgement. Since this was invariably a highly subjective undertaking, there was usually some need to negotiate. As we saw in Chapter Three, it was not unusual for the medical inspector to contribute his personal opinion while assessing a woman's breasts. ("*I'm* a man and *I* like the way they look," or, "Yeah, you *don't* have much to show for it.")

Caroline remembers this humiliating encounter all too clearly:

> I had to raise my arms and he says, "Well, if it was my decision, I wouldn't do it." I thought: "What's going on?" and I said: "What do you mean?" So he says, "With your build and your breasts, it just belongs together." It was weird. I mean, how can he judge? He's not even my friend, he's a complete stranger . . . just because he's a man and thinks he wouldn't have problems if he saw me walking down the beach. . . .

She ended up getting her full coverage for psychological reasons (she was in therapy at the time of the consultation), but was left with the message that the operation "wasn't really necessary."

For women who were less successful in their negotiations with the medical inspector, there was the option of appeal. They could take their case to a special board of review. This meant another trip and another examination—this time, however, with five medical experts, all male, who would confer about her breasts while she sat on the examining table before them, naked to the waist. While for many women this was undoubtedly a stumbling block, for those who were willing to go through with it, their chances of getting coverage increased by another fifty percent. This hurdle having been taken, they would then return to their plastic surgeons and have their names put on a waiting list. For breast augmentation candidates, as we have seen, this meant at least another year and sometimes up to one and a half years.

In short, the decision to have cosmetic surgery is not taken suddenly or without deliberation. It is not only proceeded by years of terrible suffering and by unsuccessful attempts to accept the problem, but, once the decision is made, it still may be followed by many more years of procrastination before the step to the surgeon's office is actually taken. Moreover, this step is only the beginning. The would-be recipient has to run a time consuming and often humiliating obstacle course from the general practitioner, who has to be convinced that the problem is serious enough to require that kind of help, to the surgeon, who does not take the time to consider her wishes and address her fears, to the medical inspector, who has the power to deny her coverage. Despite this ordeal, the women I talked with had become more rather than less determined to see their decision through. Whatever doubts and hesitations they may have entertained originally about having surgery, once the decision had been taken, there was no turning back. How can we make sense of this?

HEROIC TALES

The process of deciding to have cosmetic surgery has all the ingredients of a classic heroic tale: a plucky protagonist who valiantly conquers opposition and bravely overcomes all obstacles in her path, until she finally emerges, victorious and triumphant, with her goal accomplished. While the women I spoke with often described themselves prior to the decision as passively suffering victims of fate, taking the decision gives their life stories a dramatic turn. From the moment that they first contemplate doing something about their appearance, they position themselves as agents, underlining their own role in bringing the event from the realm of fantasy to reality. At long last, they are able to take the reins in hand.

Their involvement in cosmetic surgery is presented as a valiant struggle for one's self rather than capitulation to the norms or wishes of others. Each woman portrays her decision to have surgery as an act through which she initiates an important change in her life. It requires stamina, decisiveness and, last but not least, a substantial dose of courage. By deciding to have cosmetic surgery, she overcomes her shame and dares to do something to alleviate her suffering. While she may need a little support at the outset, cosmetic surgery becomes more and more something for herself. This is not surprising, given the ongoing opposition to her decision from critical relatives, worried husbands, or disapproving friends. Cosmetic surgery can feel like an oppositional act—often the first of her life.

Heroism is also part of the process of obtaining the surgery. The woman who has it has to repeatedly place her most hated body part on display and suffer the indignity of having her problem discounted as trivial or neurotic. However, this experience—while not in itself new—no longer locks her into the silence of shame and despair. While she becomes the object of critical scrutiny, she does so at her own instigation. Instead of fearing that she will be found deficient, she now hopes for that finding as the legitimation of her past suffering and the precondition for its alleviation. While the process is an ordeal, this time it is an ordeal which is voluntarily undertaken.

It is in this context that the exhilaration expressed by each of the women begins to make sense. It is an expression of relief at altering a situation which is experienced as unendurable. It is the pride at overcoming fear and doing something which is difficult. It is the joy which accompanies being able to alter a situation which seemed to be immutable. It is the excitement of taking a step. Or, as the heroine of Weldon's *The Lives & Loves of a She-Devil* would say, "since I cannot change the world, I will change myself" (p. 56).

Whereas the newly found capacity for taking action may account for presenting the decision to have a breast augmentation as a heroic deed, in view of the recent controversies about the safety of silicone implants, the line between heroism and foolhardiness becomes a thin one. Heroic tales may be—and, indeed, often are—produced in a context where the teller feels especially powerless or out of control and wants to discursively reinstate her battered sense that she is, after all, an agent in the making of her life.[17] Thus, it is easy to wonder whether these women may not have gotten just a bit carried away, after all.

Aren't they allowing hope to interfere with a reasoned assessment of the risks? Are they closing their eyes to the possibility that a breast augmentation may be their undoing rather than their chance to do something for themselves?

DELIBERATIONS: THE DIALECTICS OF RISK AND HOPE

Breast augmentations are not only performed on otherwise healthy bodies, but they are themselves potentially health threatening. As we have seen, the critics of cosmetic surgery, in general, and of silicone breast implants, in particular, have rightly attacked the medical profession and the pharmaceutical industry for withholding information from recipients. This disguises the dangers and makes it impossible for women to make an informed decision. What about the women in my study? Should they be viewed as the victims of medical manipulation, too?

On the one hand, all the women I spoke with indicated that they knew that breast augmentations had side effects. In addition to the information they obtained from the surgeon, they had invariably read articles in newspapers or magazines or watched documentaries on television. Without exception, they indicated that they knew that the implants could become hard. Many had heard horror stories about implants slipping during gymnastics, bursting, or "wandering." Each woman mentioned the possibility that the implant might be rejected by her body and have to be removed.

For example, Ellen, an avid reader of women's magazines, provides a knowledgeable account of the dangers of breast surgery, including statistics about the rate of failure. She explains:

> Yes, those are points—yeah, you would really like to just ignore all the negative things. I would, anyway. When you read about it, you like to kind of skip over all that and just read about the positive things. But it does sink in, that's for sure. You start thinking, gosh, there's *that* side of it, too.

Every woman indicated that she was anxious: about the pain, the surgery ("I hate the thought of having to have anesthesia."), the side effects, and, most importantly, the chance that she might be left in worse shape than she was before the operation. Although many admitted, like

Ellen, that they preferred not to think about what might happen, they did, in fact, continue to worry about the risks. They deliberated about the advantages and disadvantages of the operation as best they could with the information they had at hand. This involved navigating a course between their perceived need plus their assessment of the benefits of a breast augmentation and their knowledge of the chances of failure.

For example, Susan comes to terms with the possibility of failure by drawing upon the notion of "luck":

> I know that some people are lucky and if it doesn't work with me, I will have been unlucky. You just have to resign yourself. That's the only way you are able to do it.

Betty, on the other hand, tends to approach the risks of surgery more fatalistically:

> I don't know what the percentage is—maybe fifty-fifty—the same percentage that it will turn out as that it won't. O.K. (pause) Well, I guess I'll just have to cross that bridge when I come to it.

Whereas these two women's methods for balancing the risks and confronting the possibility of failure differ, their conclusions are remarkably similar. While the risks are acknowledged—either as statistical probability or mysterious fortune—they are situated against the conviction that each has little to loose. "It can't be worse than it already is" or "anything is better than what I have now" provided the refrain which explained how their subjective perception of their suffering ultimately tips the scales and makes the risks worth taking.

Finally, the dangers of the surgery are measured against a newly found sense of agency. The choice is passively accepting the status quo and continuing to suffer or taking action under the motto "at least, I will have tried to do something about it."

Remembering her struggle to come to terms with the dangers of the operation, Ellen explains that it's a matter of "doing it and seeing where your ship runs aground."

> If I don't do this now, then maybe I'll regret it all the rest of my life. I don't know how it will turn out. I realize that. I'll just have to wait and see. (laughs) But of course I *hope* that they'll make me look better.

The women I spoke with did choose to have cosmetic surgery. They were not compelled to have their breasts augmented and, indeed, encountered considerable resistance to their decision. They invariably knew that the operations were risky and made every attempt to inform themselves. While they invariably admitted to being susceptible to hope, they did not appear to be blinded by it. Worse case scenarios were ongoingly played out and each woman tried to imagine how she would cope when the time came. However, when all was said and done, cosmetic surgery seemed to be worth trying.

While the women I spoke with were competent decision makers who, as Parker (1993) puts it, weighed their subjective experience with their bodies against a rational assessment of the risks and benefits, it was also clear that they did not have all the information. This was not only because the information was unavailable or actively withheld. It was also because the information was—under the best of circumstances— quite simply inconclusive. In short, women did not and, indeed, could not have all the "facts" at their disposal.

In the next chapter, I return to the same women a year after their surgery. Given their experiences with the operation and its outcome as well as the increased availability of information resulting from the FDA hearings in the U.S., do they still insist that cosmetic surgery is something they did for themselves? In other words, knowing what they know now, would they still choose to have their breasts augmented? Or, if they had it to do over again, would they opt for something other than the surgical fix?

S I X

CHOICE AND INFORMED CONSENT REVISITED

Just as I was about to begin this chapter, I received a phone call from Irene. She had read an interview with me in a local newspaper where I had been quoted—somewhat out of context—as having said that women who have cosmetic surgery often feel "that they are finally taking their lives in their own hands." She was angry. She explained without further ado that the dangers of cosmetic surgery were constantly being downplayed. "Who is listening to the women who actually have to live with the failures?" Before I could get a word in edgewise, she informed me that she had had breast implant surgery herself more than fifteen years ago and had had no less than eighteen operations since then—all to no avail. Cosmetic surgery had not only ruined her appearance, but left her with severe damage to her health as well. "Do you really think that if I had known about all *this*, I would have done it?" she demanded.

My initial reaction to this was to defend myself, explaining that I, too, was upset about the way the media covered cosmetic surgery and that I was on the side of the recipients, not the plastic surgeons or the pharmaceutical companies. I attempted to establish my feminist credentials and sooth my caller's ruffled feathers by situating us on the same side of the fence. Our conversation came to an amicable close.

I might have concluded that this was simply another example of being quoted out of context and that caution was in order when giving out interviews to journalists eager to stir up some controversy. However, the telephone conversation left me feeling troubled. I began to worry whether I wasn't letting myself off the hook too easily. In my zeal to wrest cosmetic surgery recipients from the position of cultural dopes of the beauty system, had I, inadvertently, downplayed their lack of control and level of victimization? Perhaps the telephone call was a timely warning that my theoretical convictions were not adequately grounded, after all. Had I failed to hear what women were telling me about the shadow side of cosmetic surgery?

It is often tempting to run away from phenomena which do not seem to fit one's theoretical or political perspective and, I must admit, I was tempted. On the other hand, as a qualitative researcher, I also have learned to appreciate the value of the exception—the unruly or recalcitrant case which evades explanation. Such examples are not only intriguing in their own right, but provide a valuable opportunity to interrogate theoretical starting points and fill in the missing pieces.[1] I, therefore, decided to embrace this troubling conversation as an opportunity to be explored. In other words, if my theoretical perspective with its emphasis on the knowledgeable female actor, the embodied subject who takes her life in hand, excludes the victims of failed operations, medical malpractice, or the systematic withholding of information, then it is not the women, but the perspective which needs to be discarded.

This chapter is about cosmetic surgery and its aftermath. I explore the narratives of the same women who in the last chapter had just decided to have their breasts augmented, from the vantage point of one year after they have had their operations. How do they regard their step in the light of the outcome of the operation? Are they still convinced that cosmetic surgery has enabled them to take control over their lives? Do they continue to regard it as their best option under the circumstances or do they, like my irate caller, feel that they have been had and that cosmetic surgery is anything but a choice? After taking a look at their accounts, I return to the story of the caller and draw conclusions concerning the problem of choice and the possibility or impossibility of informed consent in the case of cosmetic surgery.

SURGICAL SUCCESS STORIES

I was not only curious, but also somewhat apprehensive about how my respondents had fared in the year following their operations. I had visions of encapsulated breasts, gel bleed, ruptured or wandering implants. These images of disaster were immediately dispelled, however. Women who I had remembered as sitting hunched up in their chairs, swathed in heavy sweaters, nervous and hesitant just one year before, arrived for the follow-up interview in low-cut t-shirts, glowing with vitality, and grinning from ear to ear. Their body language expressed the transformation. One woman who had continually plucked at her blouse during the first interview, as if to say "see, nothing there," now expansively gestured toward her breasts as she talked, drawing attention to them with circular hand movements.

For the most part, they seemed satisfied with the outcome of the surgery. Some were unreservedly enthusiastic, describing their breasts as "really beautiful," or "just gorgeous." Others were more reticent, yet still pleased ("it's much better than I had expected," "one hundred percent better than it was"). They continually contrasted their previous suffering with examples which illustrated how improved their lives had become.

Betty recalls how modest she used to feel about her body. She couldn't "have imagined getting undressed in front of someone else." Her biggest problem prior to surgery was not being able to find a bra which fit and worrying that people could see her nipples through her blouse. ("That's just not how I was brought up; you have to keep it covered up.") Now, with a twinkle in her eye, she recounts going to a family reunion and taking off her blouse to show off her breasts to her brothers, sisters and their families.

> I don't mind getting undressed in front of other people now. I just don't find it difficult any more . . . in fact, I am really *proud* . . . yeah, really. . . . When I walk down the beach in a bikini or when I look in the mirror, I think: "Yes! That's more like it. Yes." It's amazing, isn't it, what a pair of breasts can do for a woman?

Many women explained that it was wonderful not to be preoccupied with their breasts any more. "I can walk around freely now" or "I just forget about them being there" were frequently heard comments. Others remarked that it was wonderful to be "in proportion" or to "look like a woman." "I like to feel feminine and breasts just go along with that, I guess." Several women were exuberant about the changes in their sex lives. Their relations with their partners had changed enormously.

Ellen recalls how anxious her husband had been about her having the surgery. ("You don't need to do this for me, you know.") Having seen the result, he has changed his mind completely. When Ellen asked him several months ago what he would like for his birthday, he announced that "the best present would be that you stay the way you are now." Her husband is not the only man to notice the change. Ellen's favorite story took place when she went to the country fair with her husband.

> We were sitting around talking and drinking beer with some people and there's this one man who keeps *looking* at me and then all of a sudden he says: "I really like the way you look. You look *great*." Just like that. Then he says: "I just can't stop looking at you—you have such *beautiful breasts*." (laughs) Well, I loved it! I mean, my breasts were completely covered up, but my dress was tight so they showed a lot. And I just really loved it. He says: "I like to look at you, you're so beautiful and you have such beautiful breasts." I thought: "Now, that is a real compliment, just like that, from a complete stranger, some man you've never seen before." It was just great . . . like I felt about ten-feet tall, I'm not kidding.

In the first interview, Ellen recounted several humiliating experiences of people making comments about her breasts (a boyfriend who told her to come back after she had "grown some more," a nurse who blurted out that she was "as flat as a pancake"). In the second interview, the potentially embarrassing experience of having a drunken stranger make a remark, albeit a positive one, about her breasts is presented as not only highly pleasurable, but an instance where Ellen feels affirmed, self-confident, and at one with her body. There is no hint in her account that she finds it offensive that a drunken stranger takes it upon himself to comment on her body. She transforms an event which could easily be taken as ambivalent, at best, and insulting or enraging, at worst, into a moment of glory. She seems to feel free to enjoy her new body and to experience the scrutiny of another person as self-affirming rather than diminishing.[2]

The most ecstatic of all my respondents was Susan. She arrived for her follow-up interview with her mother—just as she had for the previous interview. I didn't recognize her immediately, as she was wearing a heavy leather jacket and helmet. As Susan explained to me later, she and her mother had joined a motorcycle club. She didn't have her license yet, so her mother had to bring her. Since our last interview, Susan had put on about fifteen pounds, which made her fairly hefty. She seemed, if anything, more awkward and shy than she had been before—the same self-conscious teenager who kept her eyes averted and had to be drawn out before she could talk about herself. However, my first impression was belied, once the ice was broken, by Susan's announcement that she had "become a completely different person."

In a series of contrasts between how she was before and how she was now, she described the transformation as a radical one, indeed. Before the operation, she had presented herself as miserable, self-conscious, and too shy to make friends. Her only real friend seemed to be her mother—the one person who understood what she was going through. She now explained that she had not only become "really beautiful," but had changed in other ways as well.

> I used to be really shy and now I'm not at all. I stand up for myself now and I never used to do that. People would call me names and I'd just look at them and not say a word. But now—now I jump all over them and I never did that before. . . . I never used to say anything and now, there I am, talking a blue streak. It's amazing that things can change so much!

Cosmetic surgery appears to have dramatically changed not only Susan's feelings about her body, but her relationships and the way she moves about in the world. She has no difficulty mobilizing evidence to support her case, namely, that by remaking her body, she has literally remade herself. These changes are not apparent to me and, indeed, I continue to see the ungainly adolescent trying to emulate her mother in everything from breast augmentations to motorcycle driving. However, Susan's exhilaration and conviction that she has become another person altogether are unmistakable.[3]

Unfortunately, not every woman I talked with was as satisfied with the outcome of surgery as Susan.

SURGICAL FAILURES

Caroline's story is a dramatic one.[4] When I first spoke with her, she was twenty-six—a pretty blond woman who worked in a grocery store, had her own apartment in a small town, and was engaged to an auto mechanic. At the time of our second interview a year later, she had already undergone three operations and her right breast was massively scarred. More importantly, it was uncertain whether her body would accept the latest silicone implant or, for that matter, any implant. She began her story with an account of how her right breast became painful and swollen immediately following surgery. A painful abscess developed, culminating in a traumatic experience three months later when "this slippery white thing poked its way through the infected hole in my breast right before my eyes." The breast implant had to be removed until the infection subsided, leaving Caroline with "one good breast and this gaping *hole*." In the meantime, Caroline had gone on sick leave, become severely depressed, was seeing a psychiatrist, and had broken up with her fiancé.

After six months, the wound was sufficiently healed for a second operation. However, the abscess had left so much scar tissue that there was no room for the implant and it remained too high on her chest ("leaving a bulge with a flat place underneath.") Caroline had to wear heavy elastic pressure bands around her chest in an attempt to coax the recalcitrant implant into place. This, too, proved unsuccessful and, one year after her first operation, Caroline returned for her third breast correction. The surgeon moved the implant into place and "corrected" the incision, which had been "a bit sloppy" the first time around.[5] At the time of our interview, Caroline was hopeful that this operation might have been successful. However, she still had to wait and see whether her body accepted the new implant.

Caroline's story provides an opportunity to explore the nightmare of every cosmetic surgery recipient—the failed operation and the possibility that she will be left in worse shape than she was before. I expected Caroline to have a rather different perspective than the women whose surgery had been more successful. However, upon being asked how she feels about her decision to have surgery, Caroline replies without hesitation that she is "very proud" that she didn't give up and that she is glad to have had the surgery. I must have looked a bit startled, because she begins to laugh, explaining:

> You know, in spite of *everything*, the way I feel about my breasts now is just that they *belong* to me. You don't even notice that the implants are there. You just remember the operations and you see the scars as a reminder, but I'm not always thinking—what I used to worry about—"These things are in there, they don't belong to me." I *could* have felt that way, but luckily I didn't. My immediate reaction was: "This is me." At least, for sure, my left breast, but it's even the way I feel about the other one now, too. It's just *me*.

It is difficult to understand Caroline's reaction in light of what she has been through and the—at best—uncertain fate which lies in store for her. She seems to be nearly as satisfied with the outcome as the women who had successful operations. This is even more perplexing considering her reason for having cosmetic surgery. She had decided to have cosmetic surgery not only because she disliked her breasts, but because she already had a scar from a previous operation and felt that "two things wrong is too much." It is ironic that she takes the massive scarring on her breasts in stride and, indeed, has no difficulty incorporating it into an acceptable body image. The difference seems to be less a matter of how her body looks than of agency. Whereas she previously presents herself as the hapless victim of fate, she now portrays herself as an agent in interaction with her circumstances. ("You have to keep going," "You just can't just stop and forget about it.")

Caroline is an exception and, perhaps, she is just trying to avoid feelings of regret that might reasonably accompany the negative outcome of surgery which she had voluntarily agreed to have.[6] However, before we draw this conclusion, let us take a closer look at how the women I spoke with reconciled their satisfactions with the discomforts and side effects of the breast augmentations.

LIVING WITH THE AFTERMATH

Nearly every woman I spoke with complained about some discomfort or side effects following her breast augmentation. This ranged from numbness in the nipples to a cold sensation in the breasts. Sometimes implants shifted during strenuous activity like jogging or aerobics. Several women complained that the implants looked a bit unnatural, particularly when they were lying down ("like two mountains"). One woman remembered that she couldn't hug her children for months after the surgery because her breasts were so hard that she was afraid they would notice. Almost half of the women experienced some encapsulation, often in both implants.

They responded differently to these negative aspects of the surgery. Some shrugged side effects off as a minor inconvenience. For example, Ellen remembers feeling as though her breasts were stuck to her body and that they felt "just like ice cubes" when she went running or for a bike ride. Although discomfort continued for several months, she dismisses it.

> I guess that my body just had to adjust to them at first. Some-times I felt like they were *protesting*, like my body temperature just didn't quite fit and especially when you go into a warm room after being out in the cold, they would suddenly become com-pletely stiff. You really knew that they were there, but then I'd just remind myself: "Oh yeah, that's just the way it is," and it did-n't bother me any more.

Interestingly, Ellen doesn't seem to regard her implants as foreign objects in her body, but rather as welcome newcomers who have to get used to her. She seems to have no difficulties accommodating these difficulties as something which goes along with the surgery.

Other women find ways to minimize problems. This might mean describing scars euphemistically as "just a kind of groove"—or as "something a lot of people have anyway." Or they might try to look at the brighter side, searching for additional factors which make a prob-lematic operation more bearable—"at least the stitches are nice," or "it doesn't look like I've had a breast augmentation; it could be anything."

Betty is a case in point. One of her breasts became infected after surgery when the drains were taken out too early. It became so inflamed and painful that she had to go back to the hospital ("on Easter weekend, too!") where she was informed by the surgeon that the implant would have to be removed. After several weeks of taking antibiotics and wearing an ice pack in her bra, the infection finally subsided and another implant was inserted. She continued to have problems with encapsulation which made it painful for her to raise her arms and left her breasts "as hard as tennis balls." She returned to the surgeon four more times to have the tissue palpitated until it became supple again—an excruciatingly painful process. At the outset of our second interview, Betty explains that her breast is already starting to harden again and she has made another appointment with the surgeon.

> The idea that I might have one big breast and one small one is a pretty terrible thought, I have to admit. I didn't expect *that*, even though I was pretty well informed—at least about everything but the infection. But, well, look, these implants just get hard sometimes, it can happen. . . . But, at least my other breast is completely O.K. It's really just what I always wanted.

Although the outcome of her operation is worse than she had expected and her future remains uncertain, Betty takes a surprisingly optimistic stance. "One good breast is better than nothing." She repeatedly assures me that "in spite of everything" she has no regrets about having the operation and "would do it again for sure." Rather than dwelling on the problems, she seems to be looking for ways to make her less-than-perfect situation more bearable. She alternately portrays herself as an unlucky statistical exception ("It almost never happens this way . . . but I just had bad luck, I guess.") and a person who is willing to take a risk.[7]

> I just figured, that's the risk I have to take, then. Look, if it does-n't work, then it's my bad luck. But at least I will have tried.

Although she could not have foreseen that her breast would become infected, Betty admits that she knew the surgery could be risky. She was aware of the possibility of encapsulation, silicone leakage, or the possibility that the implants might have to be removed and the operation done all over again. Throughout the interview, Betty goes to great length to explain why the *outcome* of the surgery doesn't change how she feels about her *decision*:

> BETTY: You have to stand behind the decision. You have to know for sure that you want to take the risk . . . because just imagine if there had been encapsulation in both breasts and that they both had to be removed and then you don't have anything, then you would have had less than you had before the surgery. That's the risk that's involved and that's what you have to think about real carefully. (pause) Well, I guess

> I didn't have to think about it for very long because I had already had the problem for so many years and I just wanted it, no matter what the risks.

I: You were willing to take any risk?

BETTY: Yes. Yes, that's right. . . . You know, my husband warned me before I did it, "Should you be doing this? You don't know how it will turn out," but I said: "Well, I'll just cross that bridge when I come to it. At least, then I'll know that I tried and that there's nothing else I can do about it. Because there just isn't anything else to do after this."

Betty seems almost overly willing to shoulder responsibility for the outcome of the surgery. And yet her explanation shows the importance which she attaches to the decision and her competence in making it. Her disappointment at the results of the surgery does nothing to alter this. At the same time, however, she presents her decision as an ambivalent one. Although she was prepared to take on all the risks associated with breast augmentation surgery, she also felt that she had little other recourse. Her explanation reflexively constructs her action as a matter of both choice and constraint, as being freely chosen and as being unable to do otherwise. By going back over the process of making the decision, Betty explains and transforms the outcome into an acceptable one—as less than she had hoped for, but better than what she had.

But can the recipient of the even more completely failed operation adopt such a stance? Can she, too, take the view that her complications are something "which can happen" and stand behind her decision, despite its consequences? Let us take another look at what Caroline has to say about her decision against the backdrop of repeated surgical failure:

> It was just a series of coincidences, that's all . . . Sure, the first operation shouldn't have happened like it did, but it's also a matter of how your own body heals itself. . . . [I]t's easy to say later, you should have gone to another surgeon, but, yeah, the hospital does so many breast augmentations and breast reductions every year, so, well, I guess I'm just one of the unlucky ones.

Caroline differentiates between what is a matter of bad luck (her propensity to develop scar tissue; the statistical possibility of failure) and what is a matter of medical malpractice (the first operation). She takes a fatalistic stance towards her misfortune, describing herself as one of the unfortunate few ("just one of the twenty percent"). At the same time, she does not present herself as a victim. She stresses her competence in calculating the risks and distinguishing between what she could control and what she could not have foreseen or influenced. While she laments the way her operation turned out, she does not present herself as the victim of deception or evil intent. ("It can happen to anyone.")

When I ask her if she sometimes wonders where this is all going to end, Caroline laughs:

CAROLINE: You just can't stop in the middle of things and say: "I'm not going to do this any more." Your left breast is fine, so you just can't say, "I'm not going to go through with it." And to have that thing taken out of my other breast when it's just fine, that would only mean another scar. So, I guess, you really have to go through with it.

I: You can't go back.

CAROLINE: No. You can't go back. You just can't say after an implant has been taken out, "I'm not going to do this." Of course, you think about it, but it's impossible because then there you'd be with one big breast and one small one. That would be a real life sentence. So you just have to keep going.

Caroline refuses to dwell upon the past, attempting instead to make the best of a bad situation. Whereas prior to the operation she presented her life as a downward spiral over which she had no control, she now emphasizes her determination to keep going.

Although many of the women I spoke with seemed, like Caroline, prepared to shoulder even very negative outcomes with a surprisingly philosophical attitude, this does not mean they were uncritical about the way they had been informed of what to expect or about their treatment at the hands of various medical professionals.

COMPLAINTS AND CRITICISMS

Without exception, the women I spoke with were critical of the conditions under which they had to make their decisions. Regardless of the outcome of the surgery, many women indicated that they were angry at not having been consulted about what they wanted from the operation.

For example, Elizabeth, who is "generally pretty happy" with the way she looks now, is "still really bothered" that her surgeon was unwilling to give her larger implants. "They just don't pay any attention to how you feel, don't even listen to what you say." She is still convinced that she should have been able to have the size she had before her pregnancy and that the surgeon hadn't taken her seriously. She blames herself for not having "made a bigger fuss about it at the time." ("I should have pounded my fist on the table.") Her frustration is exacerbated by the fact that her nipples now droop and one of the implants is becoming increasingly hard. Somewhat apologetically, she explains:

> I just feel a little disappointed, I guess. I'm not giving the hospital one hundred percent of the blame. That's nonsense. I was there myself. But I can't help feeling that, well, if you go through all this to have the operation, you should be more satisfied than I am.

As the interview draws to a close, she tells me that she is thinking of going to another surgeon to get a second opinion. If there is any chance of improvement, she is prepared to go through the whole procedure again. As she puts it, "I guess I feel you just have to keep going until you're really satisfied."

In retrospect, several women complained that they had been poorly informed about the discomfort and side effects which often accompany breast implant surgery. They did not know until several weeks after the operation, for example, that massaging the breasts could help prevent the implants from becoming hard. Others explained that, while they had heard about the risk of encapsulation, they had no idea what to expect. They were completely unprepared for the spectacle of a hardened implant. ("If I'd seen a picture, I might have had second thoughts.") Nor did they know what to expect when they came in to have the encapsulated implants palpitated. ("I thought I would die, it was so painful.") Several were furious that no one had mentioned until after the operation that the implants would have to be replaced at a certain point.

Interestingly, most of the women explained that knowing more about the risks would not have altered their decision. In fact, the majority of the women I spoke with indicated that, given the chance to do it again, they would probably have done the same thing. However, as Elizabeth put it:

> You know it's a risk and I would have taken it, even if I had known what I know now. But I would have liked to have known exactly what I was getting into. That's all.

In conclusion, most of the women I spoke with seemed to want to take responsibility for their decision. They seemed—often surprisingly—able to deal with side effects and even permanent damage. What they couldn't accept, however, was not being treated as competent to make decisions about their own bodies. They reiterated that they had a right to have their wishes taken seriously and to have adequate information about the operation and its aftermath. While this information might not have made them act differently, it would have facilitated their ability to come to terms with the outcome of the operation.[8]

Not every woman who has cosmetic surgery is as prepared to take side effects and failed operations in stride, however.[9] While the women I spoke with seemed—often surprisingly—willing to accept disappointing results and take on more than their share of the responsibility, I could not help but wonder about women who were less compliant. What about the recipient who feels that she is the victim of medical malpractice? How does the woman who is quite sure that cosmetic surgery is not something she would ever consider doing again look back upon her decision to have it?

I will now return to Irene—the telephone caller I mentioned at the beginning of this chapter—and take a look at what she has to say about choice and informed consent in the light of what is anything but a surgical success story.

FROM SURGICAL CASUALTY TO POLITICAL ACTIVIST

Irene is a small, lively, attractive woman in her early fifties. For years, she was "just a housewife," living with her husband and three children in a provincial town. The children have long left home and she now heads an organization which provides support and information for women who have problems with silicone breast implants. When I asked Irene for an interview, she agreed readily, warning me that it "might take a few hours." And, indeed, it turned out to be a six-hour interview, which included a run down on the workings of the organization, a lecture on the drawbacks of silicone implants, and her own personal history of augmentation surgery.

The interview takes place in Irene's living room. She has laid out four different kinds of breast implants on the end table in the living room, including a jar containing one of her own former implants, slightly the worse for wear. She has already installed her latest television interview in the VCR to play for me. Before we start our interview, she shows me her office and her impressive archive with newspaper clippings and scientific articles on breast augmentation surgery and silicone implants. She points proudly to a hefty file of her ongoing correspondence with various plastic surgeons. Since the FDA hearings in the U.S., silicone implants have become controversial and Irene estimates that she receives phone calls from at least five women a day who are contemplating having augmentation surgery and want more information or who already have implants and are worried. In addition to providing support and information, she sends out photocopies of articles upon request—often at her own expense or with the help of an occasional donation.

Irene's own story begins nearly twenty years ago when her breasts became infected after her first pregnancy. The infection got worse after her second pregnancy, leaving her with "two, puss-filled flaps of skin." She remembers going into the hospital so that her doctor could "take a look" and coming out of anesthesia to discover that most of her breasts had been amputated. The surgeon explained that she didn't need to worry as "it wasn't cancer" and "we'll fix you up as good as new." Since her right breast was still very infected, she received an implant in her left breast. ("A C cup, with my slender body!") The other breast was operated on later, but the implant was rejected by her body. Since then, Irene has undergone no less than fifteen operations on her breasts. The overly large implant in her left breast was successfully replaced with a smaller one. However, her right breast was a constant source of problems. Despite repeated surgery with implants of various types, the results were disappointing—constant infection, encapsulation, and, finally, rejection. By this time, Irene was desperate. "It was a real mess, all craters, just like on the moon." She had resigned herself to the fact that her breast was so disfigured that it couldn't be fixed. While this continued to be upsetting, it was, ultimately, her health which became her main concern. After the sixth operation, she began having rheumatic symptoms: pain, fatigue, difficulties walking. The "reconstruction work," as she put it, continued, but, in the meantime, she felt that she was becoming "a vegetable—just a burden to everyone." She closeted herself in her home and her life seemed to center around interaction with various doctors and unsuccessful attempts with new implants. "And I just let it all happen," she explains sadly. "Twenty years of my life, right down the drain."

The turning point came when she received a "slow bleeding silicone prosthesis"—the latest in a long series of failed operations. The surgeon assured her that this one was "completely safe," but Irene was no longer as gullible as she had been before. ("I really thought these doctors were the next best thing to God himself.") Whereas she had always allowed herself to be talked into operations which would later prove disastrous, she now decided that "it's time to take my place at the helm." With some trepidation ("I never got past high school."), she went to the library and began to wade through encyclopedias and medical journals in order to find out about the effects of silicone.

> I read everything I could find; I really learned an enormous amount about it. And I can't help thinking if I—just a little housewife—can do this, where in the hell are all those scientists?

Irene has mixed feelings. On the one hand, she is infuriated by what she reads. The more she discovers, the more horrified she is: the side effects, the contradictory findings, and the cover-ups. She realized that she hadn't been "just some hysterical complainer" all those years, but that the doctors hadn't been taking her symptoms seriously. She recalled asking a surgeon several years after he had put in a silicone implant whether he knew about the possibility of damage to the immune system. He said that he did, but that "it just didn't *occur* to him and that he *thought* I seemed better."

While Irene is angry, she is also proud of her struggles to make sense of the unfamiliar medical terminology and understand how silicone effects the body. She recalled a phone call with a medical professor who asked her if she is "a colleague." She laughs:

> I can put on quite a show with the medical jargon now—almost as though I were brought up with it. I mean, I use these words in my letters now, too, but, believe me, I always look them up to see if they really are the right words. So, he says: "How do you know this, can you read that, do you understand it?" "Yeah, of course, why not?" Of course, I didn't mention that it takes me hours, I figure he doesn't need to know that!

As she educated herself about the effects of silicone and the history of its use in breast implants, Irene became politicized. She describes herself as a survivor, as someone who has overcome her pain and managed to pull herself up by her bootstraps. The experience has made her a stronger person. She has not only learned a lot, but now has a mission in life: "to spread the word to women who are in the same boat as I am." She explains that she has always been "a bit ashamed" of her lack of education and having wasted most of her life and she is now determined to make up for it. Her problems have become hurdles to be overcome rather than reasons for despair. As an example, she cited her difficulties in setting up a system of documentation for her archive on breast augmentation surgery.

> I had no experience doing administration. You know, I'm really a terrible slob, chaotic and messy—that's me. But now I can immediately find what I'm looking for, just home right in on the right file. You know, I'm still amazed at what I'm able to do. If you had told me I'd be doing this five years ago, I never would have believed it.

Irene is proud of her new accomplishments even though she continues to feel depressed about the way her breasts look. She explains that she feels "one hundred percent better" since she had both implants taken out, but can still understand only too well why women are willing to put up with health problems rather than having to face life without their breast implants. "We all need a straw to hold onto." She is still learning to accept her body. She illustrates this with her current approach to sunbathing in public:

> I force myself to lie still when people walk by—sometimes with clenched fists, but O.K., I am going to learn to live with this and I'm not going to hide any more. If people who see me are shocked, well, then let them be shocked. As long as *I* get over it. I *have* to get over it, I have to accept that this is the way it's going to be for the rest of my life. There's no other way. This is just better for me than to keep denying it.

Having come to the end of her story, Irene concludes that her pain goes hand in hand with the joy of having a new life.

Despite all those awful years, those awful, completely negative years—well, I have managed to free myself. I turned it around in a positive way and I can mean something for other people. All those times that it was so terrible—when I really hit rock bottom—it will *never* be that bad again.

Irene's story is about what can happen when cosmetic surgery fails. She personifies the nightmare of having an operation which leaves one in worse shape than before surgery. However, she is not just the survivor of the worst case surgical scenario. Irene's story is also a success story. It is about a self-made woman who, through her struggles to come to terms with the terrible aftermath of her surgery, made the journey from full-time patient to productive activist, from oppressed victim of the surgical fix to champion of women's struggle for informed consent over their bodies. Paradoxically, cosmetic surgery disrupted her life, but in so doing also provided an opportunity for her to renegotiate her identity; after it her life took a turn for the better. For Irene, cosmetic surgery has been profoundly disempowering and a road to empowerment at the same time.

DIFFICULT CHOICES

Several months after the interview with Irene, I receive another phone call from her. She explains that she has been invited to give a workshop on silicone implants at a seminar for women who have had mastoplasty (a condition involving benign lumps in the breast and continual infection which can become so aggravated that breast amputation and implant surgery is recommended), but is apprehensive about doing it alone. She wonders whether I would be willing to facilitate the group and I agree to.

The workshop is part of a large conference held in Amsterdam. Our group consists of ten women between the ages of thirty-five and fifty. All have a history of benign breast tumors and four have had mastectomies following breast cancer. One woman is facing another operation because her implants have become encapsulated. Each looks to the workshop for help in deciding whether or not to have implant surgery.

Irene begins with a well-documented history of silicone breast implants, followed by a dramatic rendition of the dangers associated with silicone. She finishes with her own story and concludes with the message: be careful before having a breast implant.

The participants listen with rapt attention and nod affirmatively. They shake their heads in disbelief or gasp with astonishment at some of the more horrific episodes in Irene's story. At the end of her presentation, I open the floor for discussion.

A tiny, middle-aged, Indonesian woman begins. "I just don't know, I don't know what to do." She tells the group that she has always had benign lumps in her breasts. After years of constant infections, she developed breast cancer and has recently had a full mastectomy. Her hair is nearly gone from the radiation treatments and she has massive scars on her chest which she shows the group, calmly pulling down her sweater. She seems surprisingly cheerful and jokes about going to the beach after the operation with her nine-year-old daughter, who consoles her by saying "Mom, look, we're just the same."

She says that she's glad to have the information about silicone implants and she believes that they are risky. Then, she shakes her head and says that she'll probably have it done anyway. "What can I do? I guess it's just how you feel about yourself, isn't it? I don't know, I just don't feel like I'm really a woman now." She thanks Irene for her presentation and as she leans back in her chair, the woman next to her turns to her and compliments her on the sweater she is wearing ("What a lovely color!")

A tall, red-haired woman with glasses takes the floor, explaining that she, too, has been struggling with the decision to have an implant put in since she had her left breast amputated a year before. She explains how important it was for her that her son—and not just her daughter—asked to see how she looked after the mastectomy and reacted with a "Oh, Ma, it's not so bad." Another woman laughs, appreciatively. "*My* daughter didn't want to know anything about it." The red-haired woman admits that she is concerned about the side effects, but doesn't know whether she can live with just having one breast. The group discusses how difficult it is to choose something when "you *know* what you're getting into." By the end of the session, she concludes that she is still uncertain about what she will do, but that she is thinking more in the direction of "training myself not to find breasts so important."

The workshop ends with profuse expressions of thanks and we all retire to another room for drinks, entertainment, and closing statements by the conference organizers. The room is packed with women—all of whom, like the participants in our workshop—have serious health problems, and many of whom have had mastectomies. It is difficult to imagine that these women who, just minutes before, had been discussing tumors, surgery, and medical malpractice are the same women who are so obviously enjoying themselves now. The atmosphere is animated with women conversing in small groups, exchanging addresses, or passing out pamphlets.

This experience is instructive for several reasons. First, it shows that suffering does not necessarily go together with disempowerment. The women at the workshop seemed able to face often severe damage to their appearance and their health without losing their ability to enjoy life. Their suffering did not automatically lead to resignation, but rather became an opportunity for action.

Second, it illustrates the importance of being able to deliberate about the advantages and disadvantages of cosmetic surgery before deciding to have it. This means more than receiving adequate information, although that is certainly necessary for making a decision. The supportive context of the workshop enabled them to evaluate and—in some cases—reconsider their options.

Third, it highlights the significance for the individual of being able to make her own decision. While the participants were not all as critical as Irene about cosmetic surgery and came to different conclusions about whether it was worth the risks, they all agreed that, ultimately, the decision could and, indeed, should only be made by the individual herself.

The workshop which I just described obviously does not represent a solution to the problem of informed consent and choice as applied to cosmetic surgery. It does, however, provide a glimpse of how we might begin to think about women's decisions to have cosmetic surgery. It shows why taking the decision out of the recipient's hands is not only paternalistic, but misrepresents women's competence to make a choice on the basis of the information available. More seriously, by denying women the power to decide to have cosmetic surgery, it also forecloses the opportunity for them to decide not to have it. Rather than encroaching upon women's rights to making decisions about their bodies, it is my contention that we need to think about ways to effectuate their decision making: by providing information, support, and opportunities for reflection and deliberation.

THE PROBLEM OF CHOICE AND INFORMED CONSENT REVISITED

At the outset of Chapter Five, the question was raised whether a woman can choose to have cosmetic surgery in a context where her options are limited. While the issues of choice and informed consent are central to understanding women's decisions to have cosmetic surgery, it is impossible to come out strongly for or against a belief in the possibility of informed consent unless attention is paid to how women actually decide to have cosmetic surgery and how they reflect on these decisions afterwards.

Before surgery, the women I interviewed referred to cosmetic surgery as a matter of choice. However, they left no doubts about seeing an operation as their only option—a last ditch attempt to remedy a situation which is experienced as unbearable. The decision was not lightly taken and they had their doubts about the operation. However, once they had decided, they seemed first and foremost ready to get on with it—or, as they put it, to "do something about it." This was the state of affairs before the operation. How did they regard their actions following the surgery, however? Having had the opportunity to reflect on their decisions in the light of the outcome, did they still regard cosmetic surgery as a matter of choice?

One year later, the women I interviewed had more mixed reactions. While those with successful operations were unreservedly enthusiastic, others took a more reflective stance. They considered the early information they had received and their previous expectations against the backdrop of the aftermath of the operation. Remembering how they had earlier calculated the risks of surgery against its benefits, they tended to stand behind their decisions. They took responsibility for these decisions despite serious side effects and often permanent disfigurement. In other words, they seemed prepared to live with unforeseen consequences (idiosyncratic bodily responses, failed operations) as a part of the game, provided they had been given the opportunity to make their own decisions. They continued to regard cosmetic surgery as a choice, but as a choice in a context where they had no other recourse.

They were considerably less prepared to accept the context in which their decisions were taken, however. They were more, not less, vocal about their right to receive adequate information and to be treated as competent in making their own decisions. This is not to say that more complete information would have automatically compelled them to decide differently. While in some cases this might have made a difference, other women admitted that they probably would have done the same thing anyway. Either way, however, the fact that information was withheld before the operation exacerbated their problems in dealing with the aftermath. In short, both before and after the operation, women regarded cosmetic surgery as something they chose as competent decision makers. They emphasized their right to make their decisions under conditions where their wishes were respected and they were provided with adequate information.

Agency—or the capacity of the individual to act upon her circumstances—is central to understanding both *why* women decide to have cosmetic surgery and *how* they experience its outcome. It explains why the decision is both exhilarating and anxiety ridden as well as why a woman can be glad she had the operation, even when the results are disappointing. The decision to have cosmetic surgery is more than assembling the available information or rationally assessing the chance of success or failure. It is about how the individual makes sense of and gives shape to her life. Even under the bleakest of conditions, individual women can discover resources which they did not know they had, as they manage to survive or, in some cases, to even give their lives a surprising turn for the better. This does not deny the constraints under which their decisions have been taken. Nor does it minimize the tragedy of the disfigurement or damage which accompanies many cosmetic surgery operations. However, it confirms the significance of agency. It means that women who have cosmetic surgery are also agents who creatively and knowledgeably negotiate their lives, even under circumstances which are not of their own making.

The interviews also show that the constraints and restrictions are essential to understanding women's decisions to have cosmetic surgery as well as their reflections about their actions afterwards. The choice to have cosmetic surgery may be genuine, but it is also bounded. Women's relation to their appearance is constrained by cultural definitions of feminine beauty. Cosmetic surgery can only be a viable option in a context where medical technology makes the surgical alteration of the body both a readily available and a socially acceptable solution to women's problems with their appearance. Women's willingness to calculate the risks of surgery against its benefits can only make sense in a context where a person is able to view her body as a commodity, as a possible object for intervention—a business venture of sorts.

The conditions for informed consent are rarely adequate. Most women decide to have cosmetic surgery without being able to discuss their problems and their options with others who are sympathetic to their situation. They do not have the opportunity to make an optimal assessment of the operation and its drawbacks. This is not only because the available information is inconclusive or because there is always a certain amount of risk involved in surgery. Physicians systematically withhold information or downplay the risks of surgery. As the FDA hearings on silicone implants dramatically demonstrated, medical research is often inadequate and the dangers of procedures or devices are frequently kept hidden from the public.

In conclusion, women's decisions to have cosmetic surgery are rarely taken under conditions of perfect knowledge or absolute freedom. However, in a social order which is organized by gender and power hierarchies, it seems fair to say that very few choices which women make are truly genuine—that is, taken in a context untainted by coercion, manipulation or simply lack of better alternatives.

Women routinely make decisions under conditions over which they are only partially aware and over which they have, at best, only limited control. If we account for the unacknowledged conditions and unintended consequences which constrain all social action, then women do choose to have cosmetic surgery. These choices, however, are bounded by a broader context of lack of choice, where women's options are invariably limited and usually more than a little ambivalent.

By the same token, informed consent cannot be regarded as an abstract right, to be respected without considering the context in which it is made. Nor is it simply a matter of the individual making the most rational decision in light of the information available. Instead it should be viewed as the process by which a person draws upon the information she has and deliberates about her options. The result is a decision which is, at best, viable for the time being and under the present circumstances.

Up until now, I have focussed on how cosmetic surgery can be a way for individual women to alleviate their suffering and take their lives in hand. However, even if cosmetic surgery is regarded as a viable course of action for some women, it remains a problematic one. Women's involvement in it evokes—and, indeed, *should* evoke—the wish that circumstances might be otherwise and that women might chose a different course of action. In the next chapter, I turn to what has proved to be the most difficult dilemma of all concerning cosmetic surgery.

SEVEN

FACING THE DILEMMA

In this chapter, I return to the two issues raised
at the beginning of the book. The first concerns
the problem of understanding why women are willing
to undergo a painful, risky, and often demeaning
intervention like cosmetic surgery. The second concerns
the problem of finding a way to be critical of cultural
discourses and practices which inferiorize the female
body and—literally—cut women down to size—without
treating the recipients themselves as the misguided victims
of false consciousness. Drawing together the themes which
have emerged in the course of this inquiry, an attempt will
be made now to elaborate the feminist critique of femininity
and of the cultural discourses and practices of the beauty system

in such a way that it is possible to have the best of both worlds—that is, to be critical of cosmetic surgery without uncritically undermining the women who see it as a solution to their suffering. As a concluding note, some proposals will be made for a feminist response to cosmetic surgery which takes ambivalence and empathy rather than political correctness as a starting point.

TAKING WOMEN AT THEIR WORD

The focus of this inquiry was why women have cosmetic surgery. What kinds of experiences with appearance could compel them to have their bodies altered surgically? And, how did they explain their willingness and even eagerness to undergo an intervention which was often dangerous, painful, humiliating, or even left them in worse shape afterwards than they were before?

Interpretative sociology has a long-standing interest in everyday accounts as a good place to begin understanding people's actions (Schwartz and Jacobs 1979). Particularly when individuals engage in behavior which is considered problematic or relevant for some social problem—i.e. suicide, schizophrenia, criminality, or deviant behavior, the "member's perspective"—that is, her or his subjective interpretation about what is going on—is deemed essential for a sociological reconstruction of the life world.[1] Taking the member's point of view is supposed to help the sociologist avoid the professional trap of insisting that she or he knows better than the person in question what is really going on. This "policy of credulousness" means finding a way to

> believe statements and stories which one's college training, the professional literature, good common sense, and all else that is held sacred and holy say are dead wrong (if not crazy), and that one treat the problem as lying with the sacred and holy, not the beliefs of the respondent (Schwartz and Jacobs 1979: 72–73).

I adopted this policy in my attempts to understand how the recipients made sense of cosmetic surgery. Without forgetting feminist critical perspectives on women's involvement in the feminine beauty system, I bracketed the notion that women and their bodies are determined or colonized by this system in order to see if (and how) I might find a way to believe the explanations they themselves had.[2] And, indeed, this policy of credulousness helped me to elicit extensive and open-hearted personal stories from women who have had cosmetic surgery—stories which not only confirmed what I already knew about cosmetic surgery but produced some surprises as well. These biographical accounts of how individual women came to have surgery and their experiences with its aftermath were not only quite different from the explanations provided in the medical (Chapter One) and social scientific (Chapter Two) literature on the subject, but they upset some of my previously held feminist notions about women's involvement in cosmetic surgery as well.

First, the women I spoke with explained that they did not have cosmetic surgery because they wanted to be more beautiful. Although they insisted that they were just as interested in their appearance as the next woman, this had nothing to do with their desire to have it. It was not about beauty, but about wanting to become ordinary, normal, or just like everyone else. (Chapter Three). They provided convincing accounts of how it felt to live in a body which was experienced as different and of the destruction it wrought upon their relationships and their capacity to move about in the world. They showed how a problem with appearance could generate a biographical trajectory of suffering which was no less devastating to their sense of self than, say, the experience of having a chronic illness or of coming to terms with a debilitating accident (Chapter Four). Caught in a downward spiral from which there appeared to be no escape, they viewed cosmetic surgery as a solution of sorts—a way to alleviate suffering beyond endurance. It opened up the possibility for the individual to renegotiate her relationship to her body and through her body to the world around her. Cosmetic surgery was presented as part of a woman's struggle to feel at home in her body—a subject with a body rather than just a body.[3] Paradoxically, cosmetic surgery enabled these women to become embodied subjects rather than objectified bodies.

Second, the women I spoke with unfailingly insisted that cosmetic surgery was something that they had done for themselves. Contrary to popular belief, they had not been pressured into the operation by husbands with a fetish for voluptuous breasts or knife-happy male surgeons in search of female victims. Instead most women had to overcome considerable opposition in order to have cosmetic surgery. They described their decision as a kind of heroic tale, presenting themselves as courageous protagonists who not only faced their own fears head on, but tackled the reservations of others as well (Chapter Five). They displayed an unmistakable elation at having acted by themselves and for themselves—often for the first time.

Cosmetic surgery was, of course, not without its shadow side. Most women were considerably less enthusiastic about the actual process of getting surgery, once the decision had been taken. Visits to family physicians for referrals, consultations with plastic surgeons, or negotiations about national health insurance coverage were routinely described as humiliating and degrading ordeals. Having gone to considerable effort to inform themselves about potential risks and side effects prior to having surgery, many expressed anger at the cursory and often disrespectful treatment they received from surgeons and were outraged upon discovering afterwards that information had been withheld or procedures improperly tested (Chapter Six). They were adamant about their right to be allowed to make an informed decision—as competent decision makers who are able to weigh the risks against the possible benefits of the surgery.

The overwhelming majority of the women claimed that they were pleased with the outcome and glad they had taken the step. Interestingly, their satisfaction did not necessarily correspond with the actual outcome of the surgery which was, in many cases, disappointing. Many women had side effects and even permanent disfigurement to contend with following the operation. Nevertheless, looking back on their decision, they often claimed to have no regrets and, given a second chance, would probably do it again. They seemed to be prepared to accept responsibility—within reason—for their decisions, including the often less-than-fortuitous consequences (Chapter Six).

Third, the women I spoke with treated cosmetic surgery as something which was morally problematic for them and had to be justified. They were ongoingly oriented to possible objections which could be levelled at cosmetic surgery, in general, and their own decision, in particular. Contrary to the popular stereotypes of the scalpel slave and the female with a predilection for the surgical fix, these women seemed highly critical of the beauty norms which compelled them to take such a drastic step. They were invariably skeptical about cosmetic surgery as a general remedy for women's dissatisfaction with their appearance. Instead it was presented as the lesser of two evils rather than as an answer to all their problems.

Justifying cosmetic surgery proved a complicated business. It not only entailed explaining why an operation was legitimate in their particular case, but also why it was not acceptable in general. They drew upon available cultural discourses to make their claim—discourses concerning femininity (equality and difference), freedom and social determinism, justice (rights and needs), and more. The same discourses could be used interchangeably—with a little creativity—to explain why cosmetic surgery was justifiable for them as well as why it was indefensible in general. Cosmetic surgery was defended in terms of justice (the need to intervene in suffering which had passed the limits of what a woman should normally have to endure). They often explained their actions in terms of rights—the right not to suffer, the right to a reasonable degree of happiness or well-being, or the right to take advantage of available services and technologies. Cosmetic surgery was, however, also criticized in terms of justice—as a symptom of an unjust social order in which women are forced to go to extremes to have an acceptable body. The ubiquitous primacy of a morality based on rights—for example, every individual should have the right to do with her body as she will—was invariably countered by claims that cosmetic surgery should not be universally available, but rather limited to those who really needed it.

In conclusion, these accounts showed how cosmetic surgery can be an understandable step in the context of an individual woman's experiences of embodiment and of her possibilities for taking action to alter her circumstances. They show that while the decision is not taken lightly and, indeed, remains problematic, it can be the best course of action for some women. They provide an answer to the perplexing question raised at the outset of this inquiry; namely, why do women desire and decide to undergo a practice which is both dangerous and oppressive.

Cosmetic surgery is not about beauty, but about identity. For a woman who feels trapped in a body which does not fit her sense of who she is, cosmetic surgery becomes a way to renegotiate identity through her body. Cosmetic surgery is about exercising power under conditions which are not of one's own making. In a context of limited possibilities for action, cosmetic surgery can be a way for an individual woman to give shape to her life by reshaping her body. Cosmetic surgery is about morality. For a woman whose suffering has gone beyond a certain point, cosmetic surgery can become a matter of justice—the only fair thing to do.

Thus, by listening to women's narratives as an instance of the member's perspective and by attempting to believe them, an interpretation of cosmetic surgery can be made which treats it as a lamentable and problematic, but, nevertheless, understandable course of action. Women who have cosmetic surgery do not appear to be blindly driven by forces over which they have no control or comprehension. They do not seem more duped by the feminine beauty system than women who do not see cosmetic surgery as a remedy to their problems with their appearance.

But can we really take women at their word like this? The objection might be made that by taking the member's perspective, I have lost the analytic distance necessary for explaining their involvement in a practice like cosmetic surgery. Perhaps in my eagerness to understand women who have cosmetic surgery, I have fallen into the trap so familiar to anthropologists of "going native." This raises the question of whether it would be possible to listen to the same stories and yet come up with a very different reading.

MISPLACED WORDS AND PARADOXICAL CHOICES

In a recent article, Kathryn Morgan (1991) poses the same question which I have asked: why do "actual, live women . . . choose to participate in anatomizing and fetishizing their bodies as they buy 'contoured bodies,' 'restored youth,' and 'permanent beauty'" by undergoing cosmetic surgery (ibid., 28). As a feminist, she finds women's apparent willingness to engage in this phenomenon troubling and argues that it is essential to listen to what women who have undergone surgery have to say about it. To this end, she has developed a "feminist hermeneutics" which will enable her to interpret women's "words and choices" against the backdrop of the production of femininity in patriarchal culture, the normalization of women's bodies through technology, and contemporary debates in mainstream and feminist bioethics (ibid., 26). In this way, she hopes to make sense of her "genuine epistemic and political bewilderment" when confronted with women's willingness to undergo surgery (ibid.). Although Morgan and I seem to have similar aims, she comes to a conclusion which is very different from mine.

Morgan argues that women's words are mistaken, deceptive and inaccurate—indeed, little more than the misguided mumblings of a RoboWoman (ibid., 30). They cannot be heard as an accurate representation of women's experiences with their bodies. Their decision to have cosmetic surgery is taken under circumstances which preclude genuine choice. In the final analysis, women's accounts are just more evidence for what we already know; namely, that cosmetic surgery is bad news for women and that no woman in her right mind could possibly choose to do it. Therefore, the only appropriate response to the dilemma of cosmetic surgery is not to do it and, more generally, to denounce that it is done at all.

Morgan's argument is threefold: First, women who believe that they are creating a new identity are "at a deeper level" choosing to conform to the norms of femininity. What appears to be the desire for a more beautiful body "turns out to be" compliance to "white, western, Anglo-Saxon bodies in a racist, anti-Semitic context" (ibid., 36). Cosmetic surgery is the public display of the male-identified woman to the hypothetical male viewer and, more generally, to the norms of compulsory heterosexuality. In view of cultural ideologies which pathologize the female body, perfectly ordinary-looking women are tricked into believing that their bodies are abnormal and that cosmetic surgery is the normal step to take toward remedying the problem. In short, cosmetic surgery is not about self-creation, but about conformity.

Second, women who believe that cosmetic surgery enables them to exercise power over their lives by transcending hated bodies are "in reality" the victims of exploitation. They have been coerced by lovers, husbands, or family members who "taunt" or "harass" them into improving their bodies (ibid., 37). They have been tricked by the false promises of male cosmetic surgeons whose coercive practices are disguised as "benevolent, therapeutic and voluntaristic" (ibid., 37). The normalizing power of femininity has not only "colonized" the outer surface of the female body through a host of disciplinary and normalizing practices, but it has taken over the consciousness of the individual woman, dominating her from within as well (ibid., 37). "In seeking independence, they . . . become even more dependent on male assessment and on the services of all those experts they initially bought to render them independent (ibid., 38)." The belief that cosmetic surgery enables a woman to do something for herself is thus little more than "ideological camouflage" which masks the actual absence of choice (ibid., 38). In actual fact, the power is on the other side of the fence—the medical profession, mainstream bioethics, and the patriarchal social order. The cultural colonization of the female body and the technological imperative are the reality behind the rhetoric of freedom and choice. In short, cosmetic surgery is not about liberation, but about domination.

Third, women who believe that their decision to have cosmetic surgery can ever be defended as an acceptable course of action are mistaken. They have failed to confront their individual choices with the normative and political implications the practice of cosmetic surgery inevitably raises. Cosmetic surgery belongs to a set of practices and technologies which are oppressive for women. It can never be ethical to support a practice which contributes to this deplorable state of affairs, no matter how much a particular woman may feel that she needs it. Under conditions of oppression, the only truly moral—that is, "politically correct feminist response to cosmetic surgery" is refusal and the development of (feminist) alternatives which do not feed into relations of subordination and domination (ibid., 41). This includes anything from individual resistance to the collective refusal of women as consumers to the more "utopian" response of revalorizing the "domain of the ugly" by reappropriating the techniques of cosmetic surgery and putting them to a different use: for example, freeze-dried fat cells for fat implantation, wrinkle-inducing creams, or having breasts pulled down rather than lifted (ibid., 41–46). Given that Morgan's feminist utopia would be just as dangerous to women's health as the contemporary surgical culture she abhors, it is not surprising that this "ghoulish array" is mainly meant to "shock" the reader into appreciating the gravity of the problem (ibid., 46–47). In short, cosmetic surgery is never morally acceptable; it is morally reprehensible and politically incorrect.

Thus, Morgan concludes that women's insistence on referring to cosmetic surgery in terms of self-creation, freedom, and individual choice is off course. The reality is something else altogether. Cosmetic surgery is about women being coerced into conformity, lured into normalization, and misled into believing that an operation is an acceptable response to their problems.

Morgan's case against cosmetic surgery raises the question of how the same objective that I have—understanding women's own reasons for having cosmetic surgery—can lead to such diametrically opposed conclusions. In order to understand the discrepancy between what Morgan and I have heard and how we have attempted to come to terms with our feminist unease concerning women's desire to have their bodies altered surgically, I shall now take a closer—and more critical—look at her arguments. I show how both the *methodological* and *theoretical* assumptions which shape her critique of cosmetic surgery make it impossible to do what she sets out to do.

LISTENING TO WOMEN'S VOICES

The first problem with Morgan's approach concerns her claim to have listened to women who desire the surgical fix. Whereas she explicitly claims that a feminist approach to cosmetic surgery requires that we listen to women's "voices" (ibid., 33), there is no evidence in her article that she actually spoke with any women who have had surgery. Instead of interviewing women with firsthand experience, she provides quotations from articles in women's magazines and newspapers with titles like "Changing Faces," "Cosmetic Surgery for the Holidays," "Retouching Nature's Way: Is Cosmetic Surgery Worth It?" Thus, the media is Morgan's sole source of evidence for understanding women's "words and choices." As we all know, the media do abound with personal testimonies about women's surgical experiences, and such accounts can be a rich source of analytic material for a feminist critique of the practice.[4] However, the media are hardly an unmediated source for women's voices. Whatever a cosmetic surgery recipient might originally say, her experience is invariably reworked by the journalist who selects, condenses, translates, and polishes her words, and then reassembles them into a narrative which fits his or her interests as well as the editorial policy of the magazine or newspaper. Both personal stories and accounts which appear in the media are embedded in broader cultural discourses which provide typical discursive formats for both spoken and written texts about cosmetic surgery: the Before and After Story (Dull 1989; Smith 1990b), the Success Story ("How Changing My Nose Changed My Life"), the Atrocity Story ("I'll Never Listen to Another Doctor Again"), the Celebrity Story which is of interest because of who the recipient is (Cher, Michael Jackson, movie stars, former Miss Americas), or the Deviant Story ("Scalpel Slaves" or "Women Who Don't Know When To Stop").[5]

Morgan does not reflect on the textual practices and discursive formats which construct women's voices in the media. More seriously, she ignores and, indeed, obscures her own textual practices—practices which construct her analysis in a particular direction. For example, she makes no mention of how she happened to select particular instances from all the possible examples available in the media. She does not explain anything about the women, but presents a series of quotes as a collection of "voices" which ostensibly represent women's reasons for having cosmetic surgery. The label "voice" is, of course a familiar metaphor in feminist scholarship, a metaphor which has been used—and abused (Davis, 1994)—to represent what women really feel and know as opposed to what they are supposed to feel and know under patriarchal relations of power (Gilligan 1982; Belenky et al., 1986). By drawing upon this metaphor, Morgan constructs a text which can be read as representing how women "really" feel about cosmetic surgery, thereby supporting her claim to have taken women's reasons for wanting cosmetic surgery into account.

Morgan not only neglects to provide the reader with an opportunity to understand the reasons women might actually put forth or how they would explain them, but she obscures the fact that she has not listened to women's experiences herself. Her presentation authorizes a particular reading of why women have surgery as representative, but, at the same time, misguided and lacking credibility. Rather than using her reaction of puzzlement as an interpretative resource in her hermeneutic analysis of women's involvement of cosmetic surgery, Morgan seems to be primarily concerned in showing why cosmetic surgery is antithetical to choice. In short, Morgan's methodology makes it impossible for her do to what she set out to do—namely, understand women's reasons for having surgery. For that, she would need a hermeneutics which allows her to interpret the ambiguities and complexities of women's explanations, while critically acknowledging her own reflexivity and partisan stance as part of these interpretations.[6]

However, even if Morgan had spoken with the same women I spoke with or employed a methodology which was conducive to understanding a member's perspective, she would still have come to the same conclusion. The reason for this is theoretical rather than methodological. Morgan makes certain theoretical assumptions which are central to her critique and yet lead to a restrictive and overly simplified interpretation of women's involvement in cosmetic surgery. They prevent her from treating women's reasons as credible or as having anything of relevance to add to her analysis. Instead these reasons can be dismissed without further ado or else marshalled as evidence to confirm the standpoint which Morgan already holds. These assumptions concern identity, power, and morality.[7]

INTERPRETING WOMEN'S CHOICES

Morgan conceptualizes women's *identity* as emerging through conformity (or resistance) to the norms of femininity and, more specifically, of feminine beauty.[8] This assumes a notion of self as overdetermined—as a cultural straightjacket which forces women to alter their bodies in order to meet the constraints of conventional femininity. Identity seems to be little more than a collection of prescriptions which are blindly followed without improvisation. The process by which individual women appropriate, interpret and assemble these prescriptions to create an acceptable sense of self is noticeably absent. The complex realities of women are ignored as, for example, women of color who may not only be "trying to become white."[9] In Morgan's analysis, white, Western, heterosexual femininity seems to attach itself mysteriously to the passive female body as ready-made creation, without a female subject who actively makes sense of herself vis-á-vis her body.

Such a conception of identity is inadequate for an empathetic understanding of how it might actually feel to have a body which is perceived as different or alien to an individual's sense of self and of the suffering which this perception might entail. It provides no way of exploring how individual women make sense of such embodied experience as a problem of identity. Consequently, it offers no help in coming to terms with their desire for cosmetic surgery as an intervention in their identity—as a way to reinstate a damaged sense of self and become who they feel they really are or should have been.

In order to understand women's involvement in cosmetic surgery, identity needs to be treated as embodied—that is, the outcome of an individual's interaction with her body and through her body with the world around her. It would have to be regarded as situated in culture rather than statically determined by it. And, finally, identity would need to be explored as a negotiated process rather than as a set of prescriptions, a process whereby the individual actively and creatively draws upon cultural resources for making sense of who she is, who she was, and who she might become.[10]

Morgan seems to assume that *power*—whether at the level of social practices or cultural discourses—is primarily a matter of oppression, coercion, or control. In her conception of power, women are victims of individual male lovers, husbands, or surgeons. They are the objects of normalizing power practices which colonize their bodies and infuse their consciousness. And, they are the dupes of ideologies which confuse and mystify them with the rhetoric of freedom and individual choice.[11] The myriad ways in which women—often quite resourcefully—negotiate some degrees of freedom for themselves tend to be ignored or regarded as irrelevant in view of the broader context of their oppression. Social practices which are oppressive and disempowering seem automatically devoid of any enabling or even empowering dimensions. By the same token, dominant ideologies like liberal individualism with its discourse of choice appear to be imposed upon obedient and uncritical individuals who are blissfully unaware of their true interests or real lack of choice. It is impossible to entertain the notion that ideologies might provide the common symbolic resources for legitimating both liberatory *and* oppressive social practices.

This conception of power precludes viewing cosmetic surgery as both a means for controlling women through their bodies and as a strategy for women to exercise control over their lives. Their exhilaration at having taken a step—albeit a step with serious drawbacks and dangers—remains an enigma. They appear to be incompetent at making decisions about their own lives. Their claim that cosmetic surgery was the best choice for them under the circumstances has to be attributed to the fact that the ideological wool has been pulled over their eyes.

Understanding why women decide to have cosmetic surgery requires a conception of power which focusses on the relationship between social structures and cultural discourses and the activities and practices of individuals. It needs a conception of power which neither denies systemic patterns of domination, nor treats individuals as free to shape the world in accordance with their own desires. Instead, individuals would have to be reinstated as active and knowledgeable agents who negotiate their lives in a context where their awareness is partial and the options limited by circumstances which are not of their making.[12] Rather than treating ideology as a web of cultural discourses which ensnares the unwitting individual, we need a conception of ideology-in-action. This would mean showing how people draw upon both shared and contradictory cultural discourses in order to make sense of and legitimate their actions.[13]

Morgan assumes in advance that there is no moral defense for cosmetic surgery and that it can never be an acceptable solution to women's suffering. Her conception of morality separates the discussion of the normative dimensions of morally problematic practices from the everyday moral deliberations of the individuals involved. Their doubts and reservations are treated as having nothing of relevance to contribute to a feminist ethics.[14] For Morgan, morality seems to be a matter of demarcating the good from the bad in accordance with an ostensibly universal feminist standard of moral truth rather than exploring issues which are, in most cases, not only complex and contradictory, but more often than not essentially contested. It is a conception of morality which precludes ambiguity, making it impossible to understand how arguments formulated under the same moral banner (for example, social justice) might be used to both reject as well as to accept problematic practices. (For example, cosmetic surgery is unjust for women in general, but just in special cases to reduce pain that has gone beyond an acceptable limit.) It is a morality which advocates simplistic solutions to complicated issues rather than contextual or particularistic resolutions of the for-the-time-being variety.[15] Morgan's normative position results in a call for a politically correct response to moral dilemmas—a response which, by definition, assumes that there is a clear and unequivocal position for the feminist critic to take.

A conception of morality which discards cosmetic surgery as straightforwardly objectionable assumes incorrectly that women who have it are necessarily in favor of the practice. This assumption ignores their struggles to come to terms with the normative dimensions of what is often a problematic decision, thereby obscuring what makes cosmetic surgery both morally acceptable and unacceptable to them. Both their arguments in defense of their right to be considered special cases and their critiques of the options available to women in general seem to have no relevance to Morgan for the project of developing feminist normative standpoints concerning cosmetic surgery. Since there can be no doubt concerning which side of the fence the feminist critic should be on, her own arguments do not have to be considered as either partial or situated and are, therefore, not amenable to self-critical reflection, let alone revision.

A more adequate conception of morality than Morgan's would take women's situated moral practices as a starting point for analyzing their involvement in dangerous or demeaning practices like cosmetic surgery. It would explore the normative grounds of their defense—that is, how they discursively construct their action as acceptable—as well as their critique—that is, under which circumstances cosmetic surgery would or should be unacceptable. Developing a properly normative stance toward cosmetic surgery would require an approach to morality which explores the arguments for and against the practice—that is, its existence as a practice which is controversial—rather than one which searches for a resolution that eliminates controversy once and for all. It would be a conception of morality as self-reflexive and communicative rather than as elitist and correct.[16]

In conclusion, Morgan's theoretical assumptions about identity, power, and morality enable her to censure the cultural pathologization of the female body, to attack the technological imperative which forces women to have surgery, and to dismiss cosmetic surgery once and for all. These same assumptions, however, tend to result in an overhasty and far too easy rejection of women's reasons for having cosmetic surgery. Her theoretical framework makes it almost impossible to understand women's suffering, to account for their decisions, and to appreciate under which circumstances cosmetic surgery might be an acceptable choice. Contrary to her own claims, she seems to have avoided engaging with women's ambiguous and contradictory reasons for having cosmetic surgery, as well as her own puzzlement as a feminist concerning their involvement in the practice.

Morgan is, however, not alone in this. In Chapter Two, I discussed several contemporary feminist perspectives which are available for analyzing women's involvement in the practices and discourses of the feminine beauty system—perspectives which provide the ingredients for both a critical and convincing analysis of cosmetic surgery. Despite their merits, these perspectives often share Morgan's tendency to treat women who engage in cosmetic surgery as culturally scripted, oppressed, and ideologically manipulated; i.e., as the cultural dopes of the feminine beauty system.

It is possible to reconcile a feminist critique of cosmetic surgery with a respectful view of its recipients. This would require some theoretical revisions, however. A framework is needed which enables us *both* to take a member's perspective *and* to explore the social pressures upon women to meet the norms of feminine beauty.

COMBINING A MEMBER'S PERSPECTIVE WITH THE FEMINIST CRITICAL EDGE, OR: THE "HAVING-YOUR-CAKE-AND-EATING-IT-TOO" STRATEGY

In Chapter Two, I concluded my foray into current feminist perspectives on beauty with the work of Iris Young, Dorothy Smith, and Sandra Bartky. Like Morgan, these theorists are unanimously critical of the beauty system, decrying it as nothing less than the "major articulation of capitalist patriarchy," of a kind with the "military–industrial complex" (Bartky 1990: 39). They, too, situate women's concerns with their appearances in the context of the production and reproduction of femininity (Smith 1990b), and of the "aesthetic scaling" of the bodies of subordinate groups (Young 1990a). What makes these writers of particular interest here, however, is that they provide the theoretical ingredients for combining a member's perspective with a critique of women's involvement in cosmetic surgery. While they do not apply these insights themselves to this particular topic, their insights have enabled me to do just that.

For Young (1990b), identity is always the outcome of women's active negotiation of the contradictions of feminine embodiment. The sine qua non of feminine embodiment for her is the condition of being caught between existence as just a body and the desire to transcend that body and become a subject who acts upon the world in and through it. Although the objectification of the female body is part and parcel of the situation of most Western women and accounts for a shared sense of bodily alienation, women are also invariably subjects who attempt to overcome their alienation, to act upon the world instead of being acted upon. By focussing on this tension, it becomes possible to explore how women's interactions with their bodies offer possibilities for them to become subjects even though they put constraints upon their person-hood. The suffering of the woman who has cosmetic surgery becomes part of a shared continuum of feminine embodied experience—cultur-ally shaped, but no more scripted than the next woman's. The desire for cosmetic surgery can be situated in women's struggle to become embodied female subjects in a context of objectification.

For Smith (1990b), agency is central to all social practices, includ-ing women's attempts to beautify or improve their bodies. Beauty is part of femininity, but women are not simply passively normalized or coerced into beautifying their bodies. Femininity requires knowing what needs to be done to remedy one's body, assessing the possibilities, and acting upon them. It becomes possible to imagine how an activity like cosmetic surgery could be a way for a woman who has tried everything else to engage in the activity of doing femininity along with the rest of her sex. She can be viewed as a competent and knowledge-able subject even when she acts under conditions which are not of her own making.

For Bartky (1990), morality and correct-line thinking are antitheti-cal when it comes to analyzing women's involvement in the practices of femininity. Femininity is, by definition, both seductive and humiliating, gratifying and oppressive. Women's everyday experience of femininity entails an ongoing struggle with contradictions, between gut-level desires and discursively held conviction that these same desires are rep-rehensible; between sensings of inadequacy or shame and the feelings created by moral precepts which condemn a sense of inadequacy as unjust and unacceptable. Using her method, cosmetic surgery can be explored as a dilemmatic situation for the recipients themselves—some-thing which is both morally problematic and, at the same time, desirable and necessary.

Taken together, these theoretical insights allow a respectful explo-ration of women's reasons for having cosmetic surgery, while permitting a critique of their decision to embark upon this particular course of action. In other words, an approach to cosmetic surgery can be of the "having-one's-cake-and-eating-it,-too" variety, thereby pro-viding a solution to the feminist dilemma which informed this inquiry (see Introduction).

Ironically, the very theorists who provided such welcome assistance for my own endeavor, seemed to show a marked reluctance to use their own theories for tackling the problem of women's involvement in cosmetic surgery. While they were willing to entertain the notion of agency in women's use of makeup (Smith) or in their playful encounters with fashion (Young), or to consider the moral contradictions in feminine sexuality (Bartky), cosmetic surgery was rather quickly discarded as a straightforward case of normalization or oppression—as a practice to be criticized rather than understood from the recipient's vantage point. Even Young (1990b), who explicitly discusses breast augmentation surgery, admits that she believes that "much of it must be frivolous and unnecessary, like diamonds or furs" (ibid., 202). She does not seem to regard cosmetic surgery as an opportunity for women to (re)negotiate the typical tensions in feminine embodiment or as a strategy which might—at least, hypothetically—have empowering as well as disempowering effects.[17] Apparently, having the theoretical tools to take seriously women's reasons for undergoing such surgery does not guarantee that the tools will actually be put to use. Whatever their theoretical orientation, feminist scholars seem to balk at the thought of exploring how surgery might be desirable, empowering, or even just contradictory, preferring instead a critique which strongly and definitively dismisses the practice as bad news for women.

This condemnation of cosmetic surgery among feminist theorists of beauty puzzled me at the outset of my inquiry. It became a preoccupation, however, in the wake of the responses I began to encounter as I gave presentations and wrote papers on the subject. Somewhat to my dismay, I found myself being asked whether I wasn't worried about "being too liberal." Concern was expressed that I was not sufficiently aware of the dangers of cosmetic surgery ("I do hope you are going to write about silicone implants.") While my postmodern feminist colleagues tended to appreciate my theoretical stance, they often found my choice of subject matter slightly off-putting. ("Why don't you do something about female bodybuilders or cross dressing?") Those more skeptical of postmodernism tended to regard my approach as misguided or insufficiently concerned with the structural constraints upon women.[18] While I was invariably given credit for good intentions ("Of course, you can't *blame* those women"), the suspicion remained that I had gone too far. By not coming out strongly enough against cosmetic surgery, I put my feminist credentials in danger. In some cases, I was even accused as being an advocate for cosmetic surgery as a solution to women's problems with their appearance.[19]

These experiences were troubling and often unpleasant. However, they also aroused my curiosity about why feminists are reluctant to take a more nuanced look at the phenomenon. The answer began to take shape for me at a conference where I found myself once again being placed on the wrong side of the fence. Ironically, just as this book began with my experience of confusion as a feminist at a conference on cosmetic surgery, it will end with a similar experience at another conference. While the first conference produced an uneasiness which was the impetus for the inquiry, the second provided one which enabled me to bring the inquiry to an end.

STEPFORD WIVES AND FEMINIST CRITICS

The conference was on feminist ethics and included a panel on cosmetic surgery. The participants were Kathryn Morgan and Lisa Parker—both of whose work has been discussed here—and myself; the audience consisted of primarily North American feminist philosophers.

In my talk, I discussed some of the consequences of a welfare system of health care for cosmetic surgery and then the recent expulsion of cosmetic surgery from the basic health care package in The Netherlands. While this decision has made cosmetic surgery less available (good news for feminists), it was taken in such a way that the needs of recipients were ignored (bad news for feminists). I argued—typically—for an approach to health care policy which would take the needs of individuals into account while tackling the necessary business of choosing which services should or should not be covered by national health insurance.

As I spoke, I scanned the audience for a sign of recognition, but saw, to my dismay, rows and rows of faces with blank expressions and heard the low rumble of whispered comments. When the floor was finally opened for discussion, the questions displayed barely concealed irritation. Comments seemed to be aimed at what I had *not* said (but should have). My position was characterized as "problematic," not "radical" enough, or—the final clincher—"too liberal." Once again, I watched my plea for a feminist approach which took the needs of the recipients into consideration disappear unheeded and unheralded and there I stood, transformed into a member of the liberal establishment and academic mainstream—a feminist scholar of tarnished alloy.

The response to my talk—and, parenthetically, to Parker's as well—was unpleasant, but it was also familiar.[20] It seemed to confirm what I already knew—namely, that my approach to cosmetic surgery evokes discomfort or protest among feminist scholars. The next speaker, Kathryn Morgan, presented the analysis of cosmetic surgery discussed above with a rather unusual introduction and received a very different response from the audience. It was ultimately this discrepancy in the reception of our presentations which supplied the missing piece in the puzzle of why I continually seemed to find myself with the "wrong" approach to cosmetic surgery.

Morgan began with an anecdote in which she described going to a meeting attended by wealthy, middle-aged women who had clearly been the recipients of repeated cosmetic surgeries. To underscore her horror at these suburban surgical junkies, she compared them to the "Stepford Wives": the beautiful but mindless inhabitants of the New England town of Stepford (in Ira Levin's 1972 bestselling novel) who have been diabolically transformed into robots by husbands in search of perfect wives. The meaning was plain: the cosmetic surgery recipient has not only traded in her real self for a more perfect body, but she has become the obedient victim of the patriarchal order.

The audience reaction was notably unlike it had been to Parker's and my presentations. To begin with, the Stepford Wife analogy evoked a ripple of laughter. Morgan's description of the dangers of cosmetic surgery and her analysis of women's participation in it as part of the normalization of the female body produced approving nods of assent and there was a palpable sense of *this-is-more-like-it* in the air. At the end of the day, she was heralded as having provided the "more radical" analysis of cosmetic surgery.

My own response to Morgan's anecdote as well as to the audience's reaction were mixed. Initially, I was reminded of watching numerous Oprah Winfrey or Phil Donahue programs on T.V. ("Addicted to Surgery," "Plastic Makes Perfect," "A Woman Who's Spent Thousands to Look Like Barbie," "Plastic Surgeons Turn Old Wives into New Women") where cosmetic surgery recipients would walk stiffly across the stage and face the camera with zombie-like smiles. They did, indeed, bear some resemblance to the ghostly and ghastly female inhabitants of Stepford. My initial response to them was horror, disapproval, and a nervous laughter which affirmed how alien and other they were—nothing like my friends, nothing like me.

My initial sense of *déjà vu* was quickly dispelled at the conference, however, as I remembered the women who were the subject of the present inquiry. I found myself jumping to their defense: *their* faces had not been empty or vacuous; *they* had not been placid robots, merely complying with their husbands' desires for a servant with big breasts. In short, *they* were nothing like Stepford Wives. I became increasingly irritated at this image, which erased their suffering, their struggles, their protest against circumstances which made cosmetic surgery their only viable course of action. The laughter of the audience seemed to be a collective process of distancing which marked and even celebrated the gap between us and them, between feminists who openly disapprove of cosmetic surgery and those women who either desire it or are willing to support those who do so.

My experience at this conference provided me with the missing clue to the problem of how we can understand cosmetic surgery without undermining the recipients *and* without loosing our "critical edge" as feminists (Bordo, 1993:32). While I had discovered methodologies and theoretical frameworks which enabled me to explore this problem as a dilemma, I had overlooked one crucial aspect. No matter how sophisticated our methodological and theoretical tools are, they are of no help unless we are prepared to use them. This raises the final question, then, of whether we as feminists can afford to face the dilemma of cosmetic surgery at all.

THE PROBLEM OF POLITICAL CORRECTNESS

The conference made clear to me that cosmetic surgery belongs to a set of social practices which evoke strong reactions and heated debates about what constitutes an appropriate or adequate feminist response. These practices, ranging from in vitro fertilization to self-starvation or pornography or compulsory heterosexuality, are controversial for feminists because they are both dangerous and/or demeaning and yet fervently desired by large numbers of women. Such things inevitably present us with the thorny and uncomfortable dilemma of having to take a stand against the practice without blaming the women who take part, and therefore they often elicit reactions like those of the women at the conference. These reactions lie at the heart of what I—for want of a better word—will call (feminist) political correctness.[21]

Political correctness is a concept which emerged in the late '70s in the U.S. and has since blossomed into a full-fledged cultural phenomenon which is specific to the American social landscape at this particular historical moment.[22] It refers to an ensemble of beliefs and causes, ranging from a rejection of the traditions of the West—the so-called canon—to a critique of dogmatic intolerance on the part of the Left. The term is employed, somewhat confusingly, to refer to a—more or less—desirable phenomenon as well as to actual positions in specific debates. To add to the chaos, it is employed by both radicals and traditionalists to criticize positions taken by the other. Traditionalists discredit the arguments of left-wing intellectuals—"the race-class-gender faction" (Wolfe 1993: 730)—as overly ideological, arguing that political correctness has led to a dogmatic and intolerant climate, the destruction of all standards, and, more generally, to a crisis in the academy. Radicals have a long history of rejecting academic traditions and politics of the white, Western male elite as politically problematic—as sustaining and even fueling power structures of exclusion and hierarchy. They adopt the term as appellation for a critical and, therefore, desirable position. Political correctness is not only used in debates between left and right, however. Left-wing activists have frequently used the term to tar other activists who they consider to be overly fanatical, while others have used it to chastise the counterculture for neglecting more serious concerns. Thus, the phenomenon has been and continues to be a bone of contention among those on the same side as well as the opposite side of the ideological fence.

Feminism is a case in point. Within it, there have been different responses to the phenomenon of political correctness. Some have affirmed the vital importance of taking a hard line stance after an era of Reaganomics which has eroded feminist accomplishments and weakened women's general social position (the feminization of poverty, the withdrawal of men from the responsibility of fatherhood, the high incident of sexual violence and harassment of women, and so on). For example, Susan Bordo (1993) expresses this concern as she worries that the increasingly hostile political and cultural climate in the U.S. has transformed feminist thought into something which is scorned by its opponents as old-fashioned (the battle between the sexes is over, women are now free to do their own thing), psychologically motivated (hysterical, overly paranoid or humorless) or incorrect (lacking objectivity). She warns against the relativism of postmodernism with its "gender skepticism," "celebration of creative agency," and "plurality of options," and advocates keeping our eyes focussed on what is "relevant"—namely, the "institutionalized *system* of values and practices," and "*patterned*" relations of domination and subordination (Bordo 1993: 29–33, italics are hers).

Other feminists take a different stance. While they start from the same problem—namely, political conservatism and the polarization of feminists into opposing camps—they come to a different conclusion about the desirability of taking a correct line in feminist critique. For example, Marianne Hirsch and Evelyn Fox Keller (1990) reject a politically correct stance in favor of an "ethics of conflict" which looks for ways to deal constructively with often unreconcilable differences between the intellectual and political perspectives of feminism. While they acknowledge the sadness that accompanies giving up the dream of sisterhood and the unity of a shared political goal, they are wary of attempts to silence such differences under the banner of consensus. As Keller notes:

> Too often, the work of exploring differences among commonalities, and commonalities within difference, has been displaced by a defensive and anxious need to "choose sides." As a result, we are divided along lines that often seem to me more illusory than real, that may have little, finally, to do with any of the political or intellectual tasks that lie ahead (Hirsch and Keller 1990: 384).

Whereas one side looks to a tolerance for ambivalence, difference, and conflict, the other side finds solace in an increased attention to a shared political line. Both sides argue in the name of a strong feminist tradition and are directed at shoring up feminism against attacks from within and without. For dealing with ethically problematic issues like cosmetic surgery, both approaches have advantages and disadvantages.

The politically correct response to women's involvement in cosmetic surgery has been eloquently formulated by Kathryn Morgan and the advantages of her stance are clear. Her approach enables feminists to take a clear stand against cosmetic surgery as oppression, normalization, and ideological manipulation. It provides a way to denounce women's victimization without having to condone their own participation in it. Its adherents can tighten their ranks in a collective dismissal of cosmetic surgery and in an abstract solidarity with women as victims of medical technologies and cultural discourses. They also share distance from those less deserving of their sympathy: the wealthy, white, heterosexual, or embarrassingly addicted. Having established a position, they know what they are against and can exclude anything which detracts from or dilutes their critique. The feminist politically correct response to cosmetic surgery on the part of individual women is refusal and on the part of feminist scholars, a utopian revisioning of a world where cosmetic surgery and the problematic desires which keep it in place are a thing of the past.

Along with these advantages, Morgan's approach has some serious drawbacks, however. It makes it impossible to engage with the disturbing aspects of women's desire for cosmetic surgery. Rather than taking up women's experiences with surgery as an opportunity for further exploration, its adherents end up distancing themselves from experiences they don't like. They set up boundaries between themselves and other women—boundaries which prevent them from what Bat Ami Bar-On (1993b) has called "imaginatively entering the space" of other women's experience and from becoming "witnesses" to their suffering. Differences are squelched rather than explored. Instead of using women's claims as a resource for understanding the contradictions of feminine embodiment or the Janus-face of resistance and compliance, women's words are made to fit a theoretical framework or explained away for the sake of a straightforwardly critical analysis. While feminist visions of a surgery-free future are comforting, they can also close our eyes to the less dramatic instances of resistance, compliance, or discursive penetration which are part and parcel of any social practice. Our alternatives become nothing more than utopian—leaving us little to say of relevance concerning women's lived relationships to their bodies, their experiences with cosmetic surgery, or their doubts about the practices and ideologies which sustain it. Political correctness is a strategy of premature closure: it arrests our involvement with women who have cosmetic surgery, stops further theoretical elaboration of the phenomenon, and cuts off debate. In short, it makes us stop listening and, indeed, thinking.

It will come as no surprise that, while I have strong objections to the surgical alteration of women's bodies in the name of beauty, I am more inclined to an approach to the problem à la Hirsch and Keller. Taking cosmetic surgery as a dilemma rather than a form of self-inflicted subordination seems to me to be a more promising way to understand what makes it both desirable *and* problematic for so many women. In this inquiry, such an approach has enabled me to listen and take women's reasons seriously without having to agree with what they say. It has allowed me to explore their suffering, but also their resilience and creativity, as they try to alleviate pain and negotiate some space for themselves in the context of a gendered social order. By exploring their doubts about cosmetic surgery, I am able to understand how women can see through the conditions of their oppression even as they comply with them. I have been able to enjoy their small acts of defiance and resistance, even though they did not offer the promise of a future where women would not want to change their bodies or would refuse surgical solutions. Finally, approaching cosmetic surgery as a dilemma has provided me occasion to understand and explore the things that make it such a painful and intractable subject for analysis.

Obviously, there are also drawbacks to my approach. Any focus on the particularities of individual women's experiences with cosmetic surgery runs the risk of suspending attention from the systemic or structured patterns of women's involvement in the cultural beauty system—at least, temporarily. A concern for the complexity of women's desire to have cosmetic surgery makes it difficult to come up with either a blanket rejection or a gratifying resolution to the problems of cosmetic surgery.

The biggest disadvantage, however, is its insistence on engaging the discomfort and unease which cosmetic surgery will continue to evoke in all feminists. The politically correct response enables us a moment of respite, a sense that at least some of us have escaped the clutches of the beauty system, and a glimpse of a better future. When we view cosmetic surgery as a dilemma, however, we cannot escape the mixed feelings which assail us when we hear women proclaim their desire to have their bodies altered surgically. This view offers no respite from the uneasiness which goes along with their insistence that surgery is their best choice under the circumstances. And, finally, it does not try to make the situation more palatable by pretending that increasing numbers of women—including our own feminist friends—do not look to cosmetic surgery as a way to take their lives in hand.

Nevertheless, it is my contention that learning to endure ambivalence, discomfort, and doubt is the prerequisite for understanding women's involvement in cosmetic surgery. This approach not only prevents the premature theoretical closure which is antithetical to responsible scholarship, but enables us to keep the topic open for public discussion and debate. As concerned critics of the explosion in surgical technologies for reshaping the female body and of women's continued willingness to partake in them, we simply cannot afford the comfort of the correct line.

NOTES

INTRODUCTION: COSMETIC SURGERY AS FEMINIST DILEMMA

1. *Het Parool*, January 11, 1992.

2. An interesting case in point is a recent Oprah Winfrey program on cosmetic surgery. Having interviewed several scalpel slaves, Oprah asked women in the audience whether they would like to have cosmetic surgery themselves. Most replied without hesitation that they would, followed by a laughing rejoinder "if I could only afford it."

3. People showered me with stories about their problems with appearance, whether they had actually had cosmetic surgery or not. This shows how problematic looks are in contemporary life. This concern is by no means limited to women. Many men described the suffering and anxieties they experienced at becoming bald.

CHAPTER ONE: THE RISE OF THE SURGICAL FIX

1. This did not prevent surgeons from performing operations. See, for example, Dally's *Women Under The Knife* (1991) where she provides a chronicle of the gynecological and obstetric surgical experiments performed on women throughout the eighteenth and nineteenth century.

2. The number of reconstructive procedures performed in 1990 was 1,250,000—nearly twice the 640,000 cosmetic surgery procedures. *The New York Times*, February 23, 1992.

3. As evidenced by recent strides in sex-change operations—the most radical form of cosmetic surgery.

4. Pitanguy, a well-known plastic surgeon for the jet set has his private clinic on his own island and is reputed to treat celebrities and society women at the rate of two a day ("I feel I should spend as much time as a painter with a painting would, or a sculptor with a statue."). *The New York Times*, July 8, 1983.

5. *TV Guide*, October 26, 1991.

6. Taken from a Belgian women's magazine, *Flair*, May 3, 1991, which is comparable to *Cosmopolitan*.

7. *Newsweek*, Jan 11, 1988.

8. For a discussion of how Oprah's representations of women's experiences with their appearance and the practices of the beauty system can work to empower women, albeit in a somewhat ambivalent mixture of fluff and gravity, sensationalism and social analysis, the reader is referred to Squire (1994).

9. The prices vary depending upon the extent of the surgery, whether or not the patient is hospitalized, the reputation and expertise of the surgeon, and the geographical region. *Consumers' Digest,* July/August 1986.

10. Quoted from "Medical Economics" in *The New York Times,* February 23, 1992.

11. It is virtually impossible to obtain accurate statistics on the actual number of cosmetic surgery operations performed each year. In both the U.S. and Europe, statistics are recorded for operations performed in hospitals by registered plastic surgeons. Since the majority of the operations are performed in private settings and many operations are not performed by registered plastic surgeons, such estimates do not begin to cover the actual incidence of operations.

In The Netherlands, for example, the official estimate was 6,060 cosmetic surgery operations between 1980 and 1989, of which 5,925 were women (more than ninety-seven percent). However, since there are thirty-nine private institutes in The Netherlands performing cosmetic surgery, the actual number of operations is considerably higher. National health insurance experts have suggested that twenty thousand might be a "modest estimate;" i.e. nearly four times higher than the official figure!

12. *Der Spiegel* 32 (1992).

13. In addition to the difference in the number of cosmetic surgery operations performed on men and women, marketing strategies are very different for the sexes. For men, cosmetic surgery is presented as a means to enhance job performance and increase chances to compete, while women are targeted in terms of general attractiveness or changes in identity. I will be returning to this in the next chapter.

14. The types of cosmetic surgery are also ethnically specific. White women opt for liposuctions, breast augmentations, or wrinkle removal procedures, whereas Asian women tend to have double-eyelid surgery or nose corrections (Kaw 1993).

15. *The New York Times,* February 23, 1992.

16. In the U.S., at least ninety percent of the cosmetic surgery operations are performed in the physician's office or in a private clinic (American Society of Plastic and Reconstructive Surgeons 1988).

17. *The Los Angeles Times,* December 23, 1991.

18. A similar situation exists in The Netherlands, as illustrated by a recent inaugural address by a plastic surgeon who had been appointed professor in a university department of plastic and reconstructive surgery. He defended his discipline, explicitly setting it apart from the cosmetic surgery craze. He explained that plastic surgery, in contrast, was primarily reconstructive and aimed at "real problems" like replacing hands which had been severed during industrial accidents or alleviating birth defects.

19. *Consumers' Digest,* July/August 1986.

20. Cosmetic surgery on teenagers is up as much as three hundred percent, warns *The New York Times,* December 19, 1989. According to the American Society of Plastic and Reconstructive Surgeons, 73,250 nose jobs were done in 1988—the first year statistics were kept—and sixteen percent of those were performed on patients under eighteen.

21. *Self,* December 1991.

22. Breast augmentations are, of course, also done following mastectomies. In 1984,

breast reconstructions immediately following a mastectomy accounted for thirty/four percent of the ninety-eight thousand reconstructions. The rest were performed on healthy breasts for the improvement of appearance which makes breast augmentations one of the most common forms of cosmetic surgery. *Consumers' Digest*, July/August 1986. By 1990, the number of reconstructions for cosmetic reasons was up to eighty-five percent. *The Los Angeles Times*, December 10, 1990.

23. *The New York Times*, February 3, 1982.

24. ibid.

25. This was in response to the governor of California's proposal that in return for state-supported funds to reduce the cost of malpractice insurance, physicians would be required to treat indigent patients or patients for whom there was little medical care available. Grabbing his chance, this plastic surgeon proceeded to offer his services to female prisoners. By 1977, he had operated on more than seventy of them. *The New York Times*, July 25, 1979.

26. *Consumers' Digest*, July/August 1986.

27. Gabke and Vaubel (1983) refer to a barber surgeon who amputated the left breast of a maidservant, claiming that it had "assumed such great proportions that she could not support (it), neither standing up nor being seated" (p. 95).

28. *TV Guide*, October 26, 1991.

29. *The New York Times,* August 3, 1991 warns about a new "dilemma:" "How to wear the new short skirts without being called pudding knees, cottage cheese knees and such?"

30. *The New York Times*, June 29, 1988.

31. As one surgeon with a feeling for alliteration explained to me in an informal conversation, the "typical" candidate for a liposuction is "Fat, Forty, and Female."

32. Early on, eleven deaths were reported as a result of liposuctions. When this number was brought to the attention of a U.S. Senate ad hoc committee, it was pointed out that this is a very low mortality rate for a surgical intervention (.01 percent). However, since the patients getting liposuctions are otherwise healthy, this rate is clearly too high. *The New York Times Magazine*, February 28, 1988.

33. *Intermediar* (1991): 67.

34. *The Los Angeles Times* reports of a case of a thirty-five year old mother of four who was discovered unconscious in the recovery room of the doctor's office after a routine breast augmentation. She was taken by ambulance to a nearby hospital where she died four days later (December 24, 1991). There have been other fatalities, but statistics are not kept on deaths related to medical procedures.

35. *The New York Times*, February 3, 1982.

36. Genital excision is a case in point. Both The Netherlands and Great Britain are faced with the problem of Somalian and Ethiopian immigrants who want to continue the practice of infibulation on their daughters. In The Netherlands, a heated debate emerged when several Somalian mothers asked general practitioners to perform excisions on their daughters. Worried that the intervention would be carried out under unsanitary conditions, many physicians and social workers argued that a "ritual" cut on the clitoris might be a humanitarian way to prevent more drastic forms of genital mutilation. In Great Britain, the issue was tackled differently. Rather than advocating a medical solution to the problem of excision, grass-roots women's groups like the Black Women's Health Organization set up discussion groups for the mothers, attempting the slower and often painful process of reeducation.

37. The U.S. and South Africa are the only major industrial countries which operate under a market model of medicine.

38. With the notable exception of the critics of capitalist medicine. See, for example, Ehrenreich (1976), Waitzkin (1983), and Navarro (1986).

39. See Abel (1982) for a thoughtful discussion of risk in a market model. He shows how the political philosophy of liberal individualism individualizes risk. Individuals are given the opportunity to minimize their own risk taking, while little attempt is made to equalize the exposure of all citizens to risk.

40. The malpractice suit could only emerge in the U.S., where the medical profession is almost completely free of external regulation. In this context, public awareness of medical mistakes has to be expressed juridically. In the U.S., malpractice suits rose dramatically from a few hundred a year in the 1950s to ten thousand a year in the 1980s (Cockerham 1992, Chapter 13).

41. See Parker (1993: 63–64). For example, fibroid encapsulation—the single most common side effect—has been variously reported in fifteen percent (Meyer and Ringberg 1987) to seventy percent of implant recipients (Burkhardt 1988; Rheinstein and Bagley 1992). Pain or lack of sensation in the nipples ranges from ten percent (Meyer 1987) to thirty-eight percent (Ohlsen 1978). Cancer due to "gel bleed" has been disputed (Berkel et al., 1992; Fisher 1992) as has the actual incidence of implant rupture. The FDA advisory committee suggested that this occurs in more than 1.1 percent of "asymptomatic women," whereas Kessler (1992) estimates that it may happen in up to six percent of the recipients.

42. Recent surveys indicate that ninety-five percent of the augmentation candidates and eighty-nine percent of the reconstruction candidates report being "very satisfied" with the outcome of the surgery (American Society of Plastic and Reconstructive Surgeons 1990; Iverson 1991; Fisher 1992).

43. *The Guardian*, January 8, 1992.

44. *De Volkskrant*, February 24, 1992. Interestingly, the Public Health Department did send a directive to all plastic surgeons, family physicians, and hospital directors, requesting them to inform breast augmentation patients of the risks involved in silicone implants and follow up any complaints involving contracture of fibrous tissue and autoimmune diseases (January 1992). Whereas the letter was not exactly covert, it was also not made public.

45. This is an additional possibility for justifying cosmetic surgery. Dull and West (1991) have shown that in the U.S., plastic surgeons are limited to defending surgery in cases where the patient has "realistic expectations" and her body is "objectively in need of repair."

46. It is worth noting here that eligibility meant that cosmetic surgery was one hundred percent deductible if the patient met one of the three criteria. Otherwise, the patient had to pay half of the costs of surgery. In practice, this made cosmetic surgery highly available, even for patients who had to shoulder some of the burden themselves. The ruling also did not effect privately insured patients who obtained operations in private clinics without going through these channels.

47. Nearly two-thirds of all applicants received one hundred percent coverage, while one-third had to pay half of the costs of surgery themselves. Of the two-thirds, fifty percent fell under the heading "outside normal variation in appearance," thirty-four percent involved physical or functional disturbances, and only three percent severe psychological suffering. The rest involved second operations to repair scars—one of the most common cosmetic surgery interventions.

48. In 1991, a task force which had been set up by the Department of Health and Welfare (the Dunning Commission) published a report, *Kiezen en delen* (*Choosing and Sharing*) as an answer to the problem of an expanding medical technology and shrinking public resources. The report developed guidelines for setting limits to the development of medical technology and deciding how choices in the provision of health care could be made. The following criteria for decisions concerning which services should be included in the basic health-care package were suggested: Is the care necessary? Is the service effective? Does it do what it is intended to do? Could the care be provided through private means? It was assumed that by assessing the health care services presently covered by national health insurance along these lines, unnecessary services could be removed from the basic health care package, thereby reducing expenditure. There is no reason, of course, that cosmetic surgery could not have been subjected to this kind of assessment and it is quite possible that it would have been rejected anyway. However, the Council of the National Health Insurance System had already thrown cosmetic surgery out before the Dunning Commission had published its criteria for assessment.

Recent developments show just how shortsighted and premature this decision was. Since the 1991 ruling, the number of individuals seeking psychiatric treatment for reasons of appearance has doubled and more than half of all patients contesting decisions concerning coverage by national health insurance are applicants for some form of cosmetic surgery. Appeals tend to be denied in one of two ways: either the patient is labeled so disturbed that surgery won't help her, or her problems are described as not serious enough to warrant surgery. This damned-if-you-do and damned-if-you-don't argument provides a good look at the unwillingness of the medical profession to take the needs of cosmetic surgery candidates seriously. I am indebted to Marianne van Kan for this information. See also Davis (1992).

CHAPTER TWO: BEAUTY AND THE FEMALE BODY

1. This critique does not apply to feminist approaches to narcissism which place it in the context of the social constraints of femininity and power relations between the sexes. See, for example, Bartky (1982); Garry (1982); and La Belle (1988). Lasch (1979) also situates narcissism in a broader context by linking it to modernity and the problems of the the promiscuous and bored individual in search of intimacy and eternal life. See also Giddens (1991; 1993).

2. Frank also gives feminism some credit for bringing bodies back in. Feminist scholarship on the body has also struggled with the legacy of modernity in the face of the postmodern turn. Moreover, feminist perspectives on beauty generally situate beauty practices in Western consumer culture. Both sociological and feminist perspectives share a concern for how the social order is reproduced in the individual's embodied social experience. I will be considering feminist scholarship, including the split between modernist and postmodernist traditions, in the next section.

3. This point is made by sociologists who proclaim that we have entered the age of the postmodern as well as those who claim we are still hovering in the final stages of modernity. See Giddens (1990).

4. The point has been made—and it is an apt one—that, despite the centrality of the body in postmodern theory, material bodies seem to have disappeared altogether. The body is used to stand in for something else—the opposite of reason, the incarnate Feminine, or whatever. This same critique applies to much feminist postmodern theory of the body. See, for example, a recent issue of *Hypatia* on feminist theory and the

body as case in point. See also note ten in this chapter.

5. Like Featherstone, Giddens is more likely to emphasize that this imbalance is changing (1991: 105–106) or even that women have already succeeded in transforming themselves (Giddens, 1992).

6. Naomi Wolf (1991) does not belong to the group of second-wave feminists who were originally concerned with beauty. However, she does make similar arguments in her critique and, indeed, calls for a "feminist third wave" and some "generational mending" if we are to overcome the damage inflicted upon women by the beauty myth.

7. I have borrowed the terms "oppression model" and "discourse model" from Komter (1991) who has analyzed them in the context of recent developments in feminist theory in general. See also Davis (1991b).

8. Chapkis is one of the only theorists on beauty who link women's preoccupation with appearance to the struggles of transsexuals with their bodies. The theme of the ordinary body in a gendered social order links the experiences of women who have cosmetic surgery with those of transsexuals who have sex change operations.

9. I have translated Bordo's (1988: 90) term "axis" as "discourse." She uses axes to refer to "cultural streams or currents" which converge in a particular phenomenon. By exploring their interconnections we can understand why contemporary feminine disorders of the body emerge at this particular point in time, as well as make historical connections.

10. Bordo (1990b) is somewhat ambivalent about theorizing resistance. She is critical of postmodern cultural critiques which treat the body as a playground for experimenting with different subjectivities, while losing sight of the political valence of the options open to different groups. Moreover, she rejects the tendency within contemporary feminist theory to explore cultural representations of the female body without their relation to women's lived bodies. While she sees possibilities for resistance, she does not explore them herself.

11. This term was coined by Harold Garfinkel (1967) in criticism of functionalist or Parsonian conceptions of agency where the human actor has so completely internalized the norms and values of society that his or her activities become limited to acting out a predetermined script.

12. It is the contribution of the existential phenomenology of Merleau-Ponty and Sartre to discard the notion that the human mind is the locus of consciousness and the body the locus of experience. Instead, the subject is situated in the world and it is through this physical being-in-the-world, the "lived body," that we can act upon and give shape to our situations. According to existential phenomenology, it is the intentional or active capacity of reaching out into the world which enables us to transcend the body and to structure our situations, thereby becoming subjects. It is de Beauvoir's notable contribution to existential phenomenology to point out that subjectivities are structured by the situations in which we live. For women, the historical context of our subordination makes it difficult for us to transcend our bodies, to reach out, and, ultimately therefore, to become subjects. In addition to Young (1990b), see Allen and Young (1989), and Butler (1987) for a further discussion of feminist appropriations of phenomenology.

13. Young could be criticized for speaking of "typical" experiences of feminine embodiment—hers include throwing balls, pregnancy, or being breasted—given the enormous variability of bodily experience. She herself provides the necessary disclaimers, explaining that the tension between body as object and the subject acting on the world is a product of a specifically Western world view with its Platonic-Aristotelian doctrines of reason and substance and modernist conceptualization of a Cartesian egology (Young

1990b: 191). Nevertheless, her emphasis remains on the commonalities of embodied identities and on a politics of identity which focuses on collective difference rather than the particularities of individual body experience. See Young (1990a).

14. Obviously, men never fully transcend their bodies. The notion of the disembodied masculine subject—the mind without a body—is, like that of the objectified female body—the body without a mind—a fiction and has been amply criticized in feminist theory. See for example, Bordo 1987; Code 1991.

15. Although Smith claims a certain affinity with Foucauldian notions of discourse, she employs an ethnomethodological perspective which takes specific texts as a starting point for analyzing how people actually interpret texts and how these texts organize their interpretative practices.

16. In her discussion of racism, Young (1990a) makes a similar distinction between discursive consciousness and practical consciousness, whereby the former refers to aspects of experience which can be explicitly or easily verbalized and the latter to aspects of experience which are located at the fringe of a person's awareness. She uses this distinction to account for the involuntary aversion which members of dominant groups can experience toward other groups, even when this contradicts their conscious commitment to egalitarianism.

17. Bartky (1990: 10) uses this expression to refer to her own task as philosopher as well as to ordinary women's struggles with the contradictions of femininity. In her framework, any woman confronted with her demons and willing to reflect upon them should be able to engage in some feminist exorcism.

18. See, for example, a recent forum devoted to Bartky's work in *Hypatia*, (8 [1], 1993) where responses were mixed concerning her pessimistic approach toward transformation, ranging from regret that Bartky had neglected to provide "constructive suggestions of ways out from under" (Mickett 1993: 173) to praise that her analysis places estrangement and self-reflection at its center rather than a naive call for change based on a feminist identity politics (Bar On 1993a: 161).

CHAPTER THREE: PUBLIC FACE/PRIVATE SUFFERING

1. All names in the following chapters are fictitious. I have chosen names which can be either Dutch or American—in some cases, in collaboration with the women I interviewed. Excerpts are drawn from transcripts of interviews which were originally in Dutch.

2. Over ninety percent of the applicants were women. All breast corrections, abdominal surgery, liposuctions, and face lifting were requested by female patients. During the period in which I observed, surgery was requested for abdominoplasty or tummy tucks and liposuctions (twenty-two percent), blepharoplasty or eyelid reconstructions (fifteen percent), mammaplasty or breast augmentation, reduction or lifting (thirteen percent), rhinoplasty or nose corrections (nine percent), corrective surgery for scars (nine percent), and epilations (nine percent). The rest concerned otoplasty or ear corrections, liposuctions on thighs, buttocks, or upper arms, rhytidectomy or face lifting, and tattoo removal. The male applicants came for eyelid corrections or nose jobs.

3. Interestingly, if the Inspector had come up with "pertinent" cultural differences himself, the outcome of the negotiations might have been different—the tattoo example in Chapter One being a case in point. In the case of tummy tucks, the correct strategy for applicants seemed to be showing that they had dieted and lost weight and, therefore, deserved to have the surgery.

4. Feminist scholars have dealt extensively with the moral dimensions of slenderness. See, for example, Millman (1980), Chernin (1981) Orbach (1986) Bordo (1990; 1993).

5. The excerpts are drawn from both my initial "snowball" sample as well as the clinical study with women who had breast augmentations, see Introduction.

6. In 1968, the Women's Liberation Movement demonstrated at the Miss America Pageant, erecting a "freedom barrel" into which women could throw the various accouterments of their oppression: aprons and brooms, makeup and haircurlers, and, of course, the brassiere.

7. This was, of course, not surprising. My initial study began with friends and friends-of-friends (see Introduction). One of the surprises at the outset of this inquiry for me was that so many of my friends had had or were contemplating cosmetic surgery. They had, moreover, kept it to themselves, daring to talk about it only when they heard the subject broached by me in a sympathetic way. Chapkis (1983) also deals with the difficulties feminists have with appearance.

8. This is, for example, argued by Kathryn Morgan, who has described the rights orientation of many North American women who have cosmetic surgery under the motto "It's my body and I'll cut it if I wanna." I will be returning to this in more detail in Chapter Seven.

9. A current Dutch aphorism says it all: "Doe gewoon en je doet gek genoeg" or "Just be ordinary and you'll be crazy enough."

CHAPTER FOUR: FROM OBJECTIFIED BODY TO EMBODIED SUBJECT

1. See Kohli (1978); Bertaux (1981); Plummer (1983); Schütze (1983); Denzin (1989b) and Josselson and Lieblich (1993) for a discussion of narrative interview methodologies.

2. See Scheff (1988) for a description of how shame manifests itself in a clinical setting. Patients who are faced with the problem of having to disclose negative features of their biographies in institutional settings exhibit visible signs of being ashamed: they typically repeat their stories, engage in hiding behavior like speech disruption, lowered or averted gaze, blushing, or barely audible speech, or they rehash the pro's and con's of their behavior in lengthy monologues about situations where they have felt criticized or in error. Bartky (1990) transposes the demeanor of shame from institutional settings to the ways women generally feel in public contexts.

3. "Experience" is a problematic notion and has been the subject of considerable debate within feminist scholarship. Scott (1992), for example, provides a good critique of the problems involved in using women's experience as an authentic or particularly trustworthy source of knowledge. While this practice has provided the basis for much feminist research as well as for the philosophical critique of the exclusion of women's ways of knowing from authoritative forms of knowledge, postmodern feminists are, quite rightly, concerned about the twin specters of essentialism and foundationalism lurking just around the corner. While I agree with Scott that experience is a discursive event, inseparable from the language which is used to talk about it, I am more concerned than she seems to be in showing how experiences actually get constructed in women's narratives—or, as Young (1990b, 12–14) has argued—experience as "meaning in action." See also Code (1991).

4. In their analysis of how men and women tell stories about bodily experience, Gergen and Gergen (1993) conclude that women's stories are almost always about

embodiment (themselves in relation to their body) whereas men's stories tend to be about disembodiment (the subject who acts upon the world unencumbered by a body).

5. This format is also found in other texts about cosmetic surgery—from the plastic surgeon's slide show to the popular press with its surgical success stories. The format is also routinely—albeit more implicitly—implicated in women's beauty practices. As Smith (1990b) has pointed out, advertisements for makeup or fashion "work" because women are able to indexically imagine their present bodies (before) and how they would look following the application of eye-liner or the donning of a particular garment (after).

6. This term was originated by Anselm Strauss et al., (1985) to describe the process people with chronic or terminal illness go through as they lose control over their bodies and their lives. I have drawn here on the work of Riemann and Schütze (1991), who have applied the notion of trajectory more broadly to the analysis of bodily disorder and of suffering in individuals' construction of their biographies. I have found many of the same features in women's cosmetic surgery stories—not only how their problems with their appearance disorder their biographies, but how the experience of suffering can become a catalyst for the decision to have cosmetic surgery.

7. Obviously, there are other ways for getting out of trajectories and if cosmetic surgery were not an option, it is likely that other paths would be taken. For example, the suffering could be normalized as "just bad luck." Or, the person could go back over her whole life history, redefining herself as stigmatized because of the way she looks. Or, she might label the problem a matter of social injustice, become politicized, and band together with others with a similar plight. A good example of this kind of trajectory interruption is Irene (Chapter Six) who starts a self-help group for women who are the victims of silicone breast implants.

8. Argumentative sequences are part of any life story, along with narrative and descriptive features. They involve the narrator taking a meta- or theoretical stance toward the events in question (Schütze 1977; 1992).

In analyzing women's stories about cosmetic surgery, I have drawn upon the insights of Michael Billig (1987; 1991; Billig et al., 1988) as well. In his rhetorical approach to social psychology, he has devoted considerable attention to the argumentative features of discourse, claiming that, indeed, arguing is the sine qua non of thinking. Rather than relegating rhetoric to the realm of manipulation or disagreement, he posits it as part and parcel of how individuals deliberate about themselves, each other, and events in their everyday lives. In the course of thinking, individuals set up debates—either with themselves or with others—whereby particular positions are advocated in one moment, only to be taken apart in the next. In this way, an individual can think through puzzling, problematic, or controversial actions and events.

9. Benhabib (1992) is one of the few feminist theorists who does not reduce the significance of coherent individual identity to an Enlightenment fiction. She describes identity as a set of discursive practices which construct and sustain a coherent narrative of self. In order to do this, the individual draws upon a web of available cultural narratives which enable her to assemble a meaningful story—for herself and for others (p.198). It is in this discursive sense that I am using the term identity here as well.

10. It is not surprising that this experience occurs when Diana looks at her reflection in the mirror. La Belle (1988) provides a thought-provoking analysis of how women use the mirror as a way to get their bearings during periods of identity crisis. Looking in the mirror becomes a way to renegotiate a sense of self. Many of the women I spoke with described similar experiences of looking at their bodies in the mirror and attempting to integrate their appearance with their sense of self. ("Is this me?")

11. This term is borrowed from Giddens (1984) and refers to a person's capacity to put her awareness of the conditions under which she lives in discursive form. In my earlier work, I have explored women's discursive penetration of hierarchical relations as an important component of a feminist conception of power (Davis 1988; 1993a).

12. The business-as-usual phenomenon can be found in many instances of conversational discourse. Particularly in narratives about dramatic events, storytellers will often go to some lengths to normalize occurances that are especially painful, frightening, or, for that matter, exciting and exhilarating. See for example, Jefferson and Lee (1981) or Sacks (1984).

13. Categorization (that is, putting different people, events, or objects in the same category) is a common rhetorical strategy. It entails positing an essence (for example, oppression as the essence of anyone's experience of harassment) as a way of bringing otherwise disparate entities together. Given the argumentative character of most discourse, categorization opens up the possibility for controversy about the legitimacy of the category. Instances can be put forth which do not fit and so particularize the situation, or the nature of the category itself can be questioned. For example, the counterargument could be made that the experiences of harassment to which Diane refers are simply too different in essence to be compared. See Billig (1987, Chapter Six).

CHAPTER FIVE: DECISIONS AND DELIBERATIONS

1. Stomach stapling is a procedure which involves closing off a segment of the stomach with staples or a silicone ring. It is meant to aid weight loss by, literally, limiting the patient's capacity for food intake.

2. Just to give the reader an idea: in the U.S., there were sixty-nine programs on plastic surgery (as of November 9, 1992) and forty-seven on breast implants alone (as of January 6, 1993). This does not include Oprah Winfrey, Phil Donahue and Sally Jessy Raphael, who have also devoted considerable attention on their shows to cosmetic surgery (Journal Graphics, Inc., Denver, Colorado).

3. It goes beyond the scope of the present inquiry to deal with the issue of informed consent at length here. See, for example, Faulder (1985); Holmes and Purdy (1992); and Bordo (1993, 71–98) for thoughtful analyses of some of the issues involved.

4. See, for example, Gordon (1976); Dreifus (1977); Ehrenreich and English (1979); Petchesky (1986); Fisher (1986); Davis (1988).

5. The pathologization of a patient's concern with her appearance is not limited to female patients, although women—as the primary recipients of cosmetic surgery— tend to be dealt with most extensively in the literature. Male patients—particularly those who are dissatisfied with the results of cosmetic surgery—are also regarded as neurotic, however. For example, a male patient is said to experience the operation as "emasculating" and the surgeon as a persecutor—the primordial castrating father of his childhood (Gifford, 1980).

6. Parker's main focus is on how the construction of a distinction between the needs of reconstruction and of augmentation candidates perpetuates social biases about beauty. Whereas reconstruction candidates are seen as legitimate in their desire for surgery because they only want to return to their natural state, augmentation candidates are seen as perverting medical procedures to achieve what should have occurred naturally. Both views rest on social constructions of the female body and on conventional notions concerning female beauty and the range of (more or less effortless) actions

which women may permissibly undertake to achieve what is for them an acceptable appearance (Parker 1993, 70). The distinction not only masks the severe suffering which is experienced by many augmentation candidates (making surgery—for them—a matter of well being), but it obscures the fact that implant surgery is no less dangerous for reconstruction candidates than for patients seeking augmentation surgery.

7. See Giddens (1991, 109–143) for an account of risk assessment which does not lapse into an individualistic "rational choice" model, but places the process by which individuals make sense of risky undertakings in the context of modernity.

8. See Introduction. This clinical study was one of three studies which I conducted in the course of this inquiry; the other two studies involved doing biographical interviews and participant observations during consultations at the National Health Service.

9. Despite her defensiveness, this particular woman was the only respondent who did not wait for me to get in touch with her a year after the surgery for a follow-up interview, but instead called the outpatient clinic and got my home phone number in order to make sure she wouldn't miss the interview!

10. This lack of concern about the costs of the surgery has less to do with their own economic circumstances—which were, in the majority of the cases below the median income—but to the fact that cosmetic surgery was, at that time, funded by national health insurance. See also Chapter One.

11. This network phenomenon is obviously worth more attention than I can give it here. I did not discover it in my initial interviews with professional women who lived in urban settings. While they also described receiving support from a friend (see Diana's story in Chapter Four), they tended to emphasize how alone they were in making their decision. Interestingly, women who lived in provincial areas where family networks are more intact seemed more likely to know other women who had had cosmetic surgery. This, together with the coverage of cosmetic surgery through national health insurance, may explain the relatively large incidence of working-class women who have breast augmentations in The Netherlands. It may also account for some of the differences in how the operations were legitimated. Whereas all my respondents had reservations about the surgery and went to some trouble to defend it, the first group defended their decision to have the operation at all, whereas the second group seemed to have fewer difficulties with cosmetic surgery in general, but was concerned about whether it was justifiable in their particular case. ("Should *I* be having this done?")

12. Ironically, this sentiment was echoed in a recent Oprah Winfrey program about plastic surgeons who had operated on their wives. Both the surgeons and their spouses insisted that the decision had been the wife's and that he was perfectly happy with her as she was. While I am not suggesting that this insistence upon the decision being hers alone is the truth, it does provide an indication of how problematic it is for the husband of a cosmetic surgery candidate to admit in public that he is the driving force behind her desire for cosmetic surgery.

13. Carol Spitzak (1988) provides a chilling description of such a consultation. A feminist sociologist, she decided to go in for one of these consultations herself to see what it was like. She arrived with a fictive tale about a minor imperfection, prepared to see how the surgeon would react. She recounts sitting uncomfortably under florescent lights with mirrors placed strategically at multiple angles and finding herself confessing to more and more bodily defects, unable to stop herself under the doctor's critical gaze. Having reached a state of complete demoralization, she begins to feel that her entire body is deficient, and by the end of the consultation has forgotten her research interests and is almost prepared to pay the thousands of dollars "necessary" to fix her body.

14. See, for example, Spitzak (1988); Dull and West (1991); Balsamo (1993).

15. This is by no means limited to augmentation surgery. See, for example, Goldwyn (1980).

16. Only one of my respondents was privately insured and, therefore, had to pay the costs of the surgery herself. She did not go to a private clinic, interestingly, because she wanted a medical indication for the surgery. She was worried that it would "look like she just wanted to be a sex bomb." "In my case," she explained, "it was a psychological problem."

17. Take, for example, the now-classic study of Labov (1972) where he shows how Black youth living in the ghettos of New York chronicle their everyday lives, bragging about their daring escapades. Patients typically recount medical atrocity stories in such a way that their own active role in dealing with the medical profession is emphasized (Webb and Stimson 1976). The patient appears imminently rational and in control of the situation, thereby redressing a power imbalance between the doctor and the patient which has become too acute.

CHAPTER SIX: CHOICE AND INFORMED CONSENT

1. Evelyn Fox Keller (1983; 1985) makes this point in her discussion of gender and epistemology. She illustrates it by analyzing unconventional ways of doing science—as, for example, the work of Barbara McClintock.

2. This example makes sense in the context of the tensions of feminine embodiment described by Young (1990b). Whereas most women suffer the objectification which goes along with being treated as nothing but a body, women who have cosmetic surgery often see their bodies as the objects of their own actions and, consequently, seem to enjoy showing them off. While they have not escaped objectification, they seem to have escaped the experience of humiliation and of being "stuck" in one's body which often goes along with it.

3. This discrepancy between how a person looks to me and what she says about it herself is reminiscent of my field work experiences, described in Chapter Three. Intersubjective criteria for appearance cannot account for an individual's desire to have her body altered surgically any more than they can explain her perception of the outcome of the surgery. Susan's case seems to suggest that, like beauty, identity may also be in the eye of the beholder.

4. Of all the respondents, she is the only one whose operation at the time of the second interview could be regarded as a failure.

5. Plastic surgeons do not always suture incisions under the skin as this is more time consuming and more costly. Thus, many patients covered by national health insurance found themselves with unsightly scars following surgery—surgery, which was, ironically, being done for aesthetic reasons. Nearly twenty percent of all plastic surgery involves repairing previously done plastic surgery. During my field work, I was told of a well-known plastic surgeon who routinely botched breast corrections which a second, equally well-known, surgeon would subsequently repair—all under the auspices of the national health insurance system. Although the medical inspector was disapproving ("here we go again"), his medical code of ethics seemed to require a professional closing of ranks rather than taking action to prevent it from happening again.

6. This has been suggested to me by various readers and, indeed, the phenomenon has been given some attention in medical sociology under the term "decision

regret" which seems to occur in the context of medical procedures that are both elective and compelling: liver transplants, prenatal diagnosis, in vitro fertilization. See Bell (1982); Loomes et al., (1982); Tijmstra (1987).

7. According to Giddens (1991), fate and risk taking are central discourses of modernity. While traditional notions of fate ("God's will") have vanished, fatalism emerges in their place. Risk goes hand in hand with the belief that events must come as they may. In an uncertain or problematic environment, the individual learns to calculate her chances and the potential risks of a particular course of action. This "risk profiling" is part of the reflexive monitoring of daily life and, more generally, the overall reflexivity of a "colonizing of the future" which Giddens regards as a distinctive feature of late modernity.

8. In a survey on women's experiences with silicone breast implants following the FDA controversy, Scherpenzeel (1993) discovered that more than half of her one hundred respondents who had serious side effects from their implants claimed that had they known what they knew now, they would not have had the operation. The rest were undecided or suspected that they would have probably done the same thing anyway. This indicates that more adequate information does make a difference in how women decide, albeit less difference than might be expected given the risks. It does not prevent women from having breast augmentation surgery.

9. Plastic surgeons have traditionally regarded this as one of the more puzzling features of cosmetic surgery. In a uniquely self-reflexive document which chronicles the unfavorable result of cosmetic surgery from the surgeon's point of view, this puzzle remains unresolved (Goldwyn 1980). While the majority of recipients appear to be extremely satisfied with the results of the surgery (despite the drawbacks of most operations), those who are dissatisfied are, indeed, *very* dissatisfied. As Gifford, one of the contributors to Goldwyn's volume, puts it: "Why so many favorable results, even in patients with neurotic motivations and severe psychopathology, and why such emotionally malignant reactions in the rare failures?" (ibid., 11).

CHAPTER SEVEN: FACING THE DILEMMA

1. "Member's perspective" belongs to the tradition of interpretative sociology. As such, it does not refer to the way the world actually is, but rather how it is discursively constructed by individuals as they talk about themselves and their circumstances. Whereas the tradition of interpretative sociology has much to offer concerning the analysis of perspectives as social constructions, it is somewhat less reflexive about differences between members (shorthand for "members of society") who typically come with the specific accouterments of gender, class, ethnicity, and more. Feminist scholarship has, of course, been instrumental in deconstructing and elaborating the problematic aspects of taking the standpoint of another person. See, for example, Haraway (1988).

2. I say bracket because notions that women are victims rather than agents or are culturally scripted rather than free belong to the theoretical and political baggage of any feminist analysis—a kind of feminist common sense on how power works in a gendered social order. I have elaborated this elsewhere in Davis (1991a; 1993).

3. The embodied experience of being at home in one's body invites the comparison between cosmetic surgery recipients and those who are contemplating or have had sex change operations. Not only are their narratives similar, but both provide a particularly good place to explore the problems of embodiment in a gendered social order. See for example, Kessler and McKenna (1978).

4. See for example, Dull (1989); Balsamo (1993); Bordo (1993).

5. See Dorothy Smith (1990a, 1990b) for an excellent account of femininity as a textual practice and of feminist methods for recovering its construction from texts, which may range from personal accounts to literature, media representations, and scientific writing.

6. See, for example, Warnke (1993) for a good discussion of what a feminist hermeneutics would need to entail.

7. The concepts of identity, power, and morality, as well as the particular assumptions which Morgan makes about them, are not found only in her analysis. Many of the arguments I am making against her position could be raised in conjunction with other contemporary feminist perspectives on beauty, as I have shown in Chapter Two. I have chosen to explore Morgan's work, however, because she articulates particularly clearly both the strengths and the weaknesses of the feminist case against cosmetic surgery.

8. While identity is a central concept in feminist theory in general, it is also a highly contested one. Initially, feminist scholars tended to oscillate between a pessimistic conception of feminine identity as the distorted and damaged outcome of patriarchal relations (de Beauvoir, 1952; Millett, 1971) and the optimistic valorization of femininity as difference (Miller, 1976; Gilligan, 1982; Hartsock, 1983; Keller, 1985). Postmodern feminism, on the other hand, is more concerned with dispelling the myth of a unified feminine identity and raising the banner of fragmented, fluctuating, and multiple identities (Flax, 1990; de Lauretis, 1987; Butler, 1989). While Morgan tends to draw upon the more modernist arguments concerning femininity as uniformly repressive, she shares a postmodern indifference to women's actual bodily experience as well as to their attempts to create a sense of coherent, specific personhood (Benhabib 1992).

9. On this point, I am indebted to discussions with Natalie Beausoleil about her very interesting work on the makeup practices of Latina and Black women in the U.S.

10. The kind of conception I have in mind is eloquently formulated by Seyla Benhabib in her recent book, *Situating the Self* (1992).

11. Morgan is not alone in this. I have argued on another occasion that, despite the ubiquitous influence of Foucault upon recent feminist scholarship (Diamond and Quinby 1988; McNay 1992), feminists often draw upon a conception of power which is top down and repressive (Davis 1991a; 1993). This makes it difficult to explore the enabling dimensions of power as well as how women themselves participate in relations of power.

12. See for example, Bourdieu (1977); Giddens (1984); Lukes (1986); and Connell (1987) for approaches to power which explore the relationship between system patterns of domination and subordination and social practices of individuals. For a feminist reworking, see, for example, Felski (1989); Davis et al., (1991).

13. See Billig et al., (1988); Billig (1991).

14. Kathryn Pyne Addelson (1988, 108–132) makes a similar point in her discussion of the necessity of grounding feminist ethics in women's situated moral practices. See also Wolfe (1989, 212–236).

15. This goes against recent trends in feminist ethics which have been in the direction of a more contextual approach. See for example, Benhabib's (1992) communicative ethics or various renditions of an ethics of care and responsibility (for example, Kittay and Meyer 1987; Code 1991; Larrabee 1993; Tronto 1993).

16. See for example, Nancy Fraser (1989) for a good rendition of such an approach in her "politics of need interpretation." She advocates treating needs as essentially

contested, multivalent, and contextual. Need claims should be evaluated in terms of the questions they raise rather than looking for definitive solutions to them.

17. I have discussed the possibility of applying one of Young's feminist "thought experiments"—as she has done for ball throwing, pregnancy, or fashion—to cosmetic surgery in Davis (1993b).

18. See, for example, Bordo (1993, 20–33).

19. For example, one Dutch feminist journal gave a title to an article I wrote about cosmetic surgery as "The Right to Be Beautiful" (*Het recht om mooi te zijn*), which immediately evoked a critical rejoinder from another feminist scholar under the heading "The Right to Be Ugly."

20. Lisa Parker addressed the silicone controversy and made the same points which I have discussed in Chapter Five. She also expressed some concern that feminists, by treating cosmetic surgery recipients as more culturally scripted than other women, risk ignoring the rights of augmentation candidates to make decisions about their bodies.

21. I am somewhat reticent to use the term political correctness which has been so overused by the media and has become overladen with conflicting meanings. Despite this conceptual inflation, however, I still believe that the phenomenon to which it refers continues to deserve careful and critical attention by scholars and activists alike. See, for example, the recent discussion in a special issue on political correctness in *Partisan Review,* 4 (1993) as a case in point.

22. As long-time resident of Europe, I have adopted the view which tends to be taken here that political correctness is a typically North American phenomenon. Although similar controversies and rhetoric may be found in Europe, the term political correctness is not a part of the discourses drawn upon by traditional or radical groups to defend or criticize one another's positions.

BIBLIOGRAPHY

Abel, Richard L. 1982. "A Socialist Approach to Risk." *Maryland Law Review* 41:695–754.

Addelson, Kathryn Pyne. 1991. *Impure Thoughts: Essays on Philosophy, Feminism and Ethics*. Philadelphia: Temple University Press.

Allen, Jeffner and Young, Iris Marion (eds.). 1989. *The Thinking Muse: Feminism and Modern French Philosophy*. Bloomington and Indianapolis: Indiana University Press.

American Society of Plastic and Reconstructive Surgeons. 1988. "Estimated Number of Cosmetic Procedures Performed by ASPRS Members." Arlington Heights, Illinois.

American Society of Plastic and Reconstructive Surgeons. 1990. "First National Survey Asks Women How They Feel about Breast Implants." Chicago.

Ayalah, Daphna & Weinstock, Isaac. 1979. *Breasts: Women Speak About Their Breasts and Their Lives*. New York: Summit Books.

Baker, Nancy C. 1984. *The Beauty Trap: Exploring Woman's Greatest Obsession*. New York: Franklin Watts.

Balsamo, Anne. 1993. "On the Cutting Edge: Cosmetic Surgery and the Technological Production of the Gendered Body." *Camera Obscura* 28:207–237.

Banner, Lois W. 1983. *American Beauty*. New York: Alfred A. Knopf.

Bar On, Bat-Ami. 1993a. "Reading Bartky: Identity, Identification, and Critical Self-Reflection." *Hypatia* 8(1):159–163.

Bar On, Bat-Ami. 1993b. "Thinking about Women and Violence in Bosnia Herzegovina: On Trauma and Theorization." Paper Presented at Conference on Feminist Ethics and Social Policy. University of Pittsburg, November 1993.

Barthes, Roland. 1985. *The Grain of the Voice, Interviews 1962–1980*. New York: Hill and Wang.

Bartky, Sandra. 1990. *Femininity and Domination: Studies in the Phenomenology of Oppression*. New York: Routledge.

Baudrillard, Jean. 1988. *Selected Writings*. M. Poster (ed.). Stanford: Stanford University Press.

Belenky, Mary Field, Clinchy, Blythe McVicker, Goldberger, Nancy Rule, and Tarule, Jill Mattuck. 1986. *Women's Ways of Knowing: The Development of Self, Voice, and Mind*. New York: Basic Books.

Bell, D.E. 1982. "Regret in Decision Making Under Uncertainty." *Operations Research* 30:961–981.

Benhabib, Seyla. 1992. *Situating the Self: Gender, Community and Postmodernism in Contemporary Ethics*. New York: Routledge.

Berkel, Hans, Birdsell, Dale C., and Jenkins, Heather. 1992. "Breast Augmentation: A Risk Factor for Breast Cancer?" *New England Journal of Medicine* 326: 1649–1653.

Berscheid, E., Dion, K., Walster, W., & Walster, G. 1971. "Physical Attractiveness and Dating Choice: A Test of the Matching Hypothesis." *Journal of Experimental Social Psychology* 7:173–189.

Berscheid, E. and Walster, E. 1974. "Physical Attractiveness." In L. Berkowitz (ed.), *Advances in Experimental Social Psychology*. Vol. 7. New York: Academic Press. 158–216.

Bertaux, Daniel (ed.). 1981. *Biography and Society: The Life History Approach in the Social Sciences*. Beverly Hills: Sage Publications.

Billig, Michael. 1987. *Arguing and Thinking: A Rhetorical Approach to Social Psychology*. Cambridge: Cambridge University Press.

Billig, Michael. 1991. *Ideology and Opinions: Studies in Rhetorical Psychology*. London: Sage Publications.

Billig, M., Condor, S. Edwards, D., Gane, M., Middleton, D. and Radley, A. 1988. *Ideological Dilemmas: A Social Psychology of Everyday Thinking*. London: Sage Publications.

Bordo, Susan. 1986. "The Cartesian Masculination of Thought." *Signs* 11:439–456.

Bordo, Susan. 1988. "Anorexia Nervosa: Psychopathology as the Crystallization of Culture." In I. Diamond & L. Quinby (eds.), *Feminism & Foucault: Reflections of Resistance*. Boston: Northeastern University Press. 87–118.

Bordo, Susan. 1989. "The Body and the Reproduction of Femininity: A Feminist Appropriation of Foucault." In Alison Jaggar and Susan Bordo (eds.), *Gender/Body/Knowledge*. New Brunswick: Rutgers University Press. 13–33.

Bordo, Susan. 1990a. "Feminism, Postmodernism, and Gender-Scepticism." In L.J. Nicholson (ed.), *Feminism/Postmodernism*. New York: Routledge. 133–156.

Bordo, Susan. 1990b. "'Material Girl': The Effacements of Postmodern Culture." *Michigan Quarterly Review.* 653–677.

Bordo, Susan. 1990c. "Reading the Slender Body." In Mary Jacobus, Evelyn Fox Keller and Sally Shuttleworth (eds.), *Body/Politics*. New York: Routledge. 83–112.

Bordo, Susan. 1993. *Unbearable Weight: Feminism, Western Culture, and the Body*. Berkeley: University of California Press.

Bourdieu, Pierre. 1977. *Towards a Theory of Practice*. Oxford: Oxford University Press.

Bowlby, Rachel. 1987. "Modes of Modern Shopping: Mallarmé at the Bon Marché." In Nancy Armstrong and Leonard Tennenhouse (eds.), *The Ideology of Conduct*. New York: Methuen. 185–205.

Broverman, I.K., Broverman, D.M., Clarkson, F.E., Rosenkrantz, P.S. and Vogel, S.R. 1970. "Sex Role Stereotypes and Clinical Judgements of Mental Health." *Journal of Consulting and Clinical Psychology* 4 :1–7.

Brownmiller, Susan. 1985. *Femininity*. New York: Fawcett Columbine.

Burkhardt, Boyd R. 1998. "Breast Implants: A Brief History of Their Development, Characteristics, and Problems." In Thomas D. Gant and Luis O. Vasconez (eds.), *Postmastectomy Reconstruction*. Baltimore: Williams and Wilkins.

Butler, Judith. 1987. "Variations on Sex and Gender. de Beauvoir, Wittig and Foucault."

In Seyla Benhabib and Drucilla Cornell (eds.), *Feminism as Critique.* Cambridge: Polity Press.

Butler, Judith. 1989. *Gender Trouble: Feminism and the Subversion of Identity.* New York: Routledge.

Chapkis, Wendy. 1986. *Beauty Secrets.* London: The Women's Press.

Chernin, Kim. 1981. *The Obsession: Reflections on the Tyranny of Slenderness.* New York: Harper and Row.

Cockerham, William C. 1992. *Medical Sociology.* Fifth Edition. Engelwood Cliffs, N.J.: Prentice Hall.

Code, Lorraine. 1991. *What Can She Know? Feminist Theory and the Construction of Knowledge.* Ithaca: Cornell University Press.

Collins, Patricia Hill. 1990. *Black Feminist Thought: Knowledge, Consciousness, and the Politics of Empowerment.* New York: Routledge.

Connell, R.W. 1987. *Gender and Power.* Cambridge: Polity Press.

Coward, Rosalind. 1984. *Female Desire.* London: Paladin.

Crawford, Robert. 1984. "A Cultural Account of 'Health': Control, Release, and the Social Body." In J. McKinlay (ed.), *Issues in the Political Economy of Health Care.* New York: Tavistock. 60–103.

Dally, Ann. 1991. *Women Under the Knife.* London: Hutchinson Radius.

Davis, Kathy. 1988. *Power Under the Microscope.* Dordrecht: Foris Publishing.

Davis, Kathy. 1991a. "Critical Sociology and Gender Relations." In K. Davis, M. Leijenaar and J. Oldersma (eds.), *The Gender of Power.* London: Sage Publications. 65–86.

Davis, Kathy. 1991b. "Remaking the She-Devil: A Critical Look at Feminist Approaches to Beauty." *Hypatia* 6(2):21–43.

Davis, Kathy. 1992. "The Rhetoric of Cosmetic Surgery: Luxury or Welfare?" Paper presented at the Annual Meeting of the American Sociological Association, Pittsburg, August 1992.

Davis, Kathy. 1993a. "Nice Doctors and Invisible Patients: The Problem of Power in Feminist Common Sense." In S. Fisher and A.D. Todd (eds.), *The Social Organization of Doctor-Patient Communication.* 2nd edition. Norwood, N.J.: Ablex Publishing Co.

Davis, Kathy. 1993b. "Embodiment, Agency and Justice." In S. Sevenhuijsen (ed.), *Feminism and Justice Reconsidered.* Working papers. Anna Maria van Schuurman Center, Utrecht.

Davis, Kathy. 1994. "What's in a Voice? Methods and Metaphors." *Feminism & Psychology* 4(3):353–361.

Davis, Kathy, Leijenaar, Monique, and Oldersma, Jantine (eds.). 1991. *The Gender of Power.* London: Sage Publications.

de Beauvoir, Simone. 1952. *The Second Sex.* New York: Alfred A. Knopf, Inc.

de Lauretis, Teresa. 1987. *Technologies of Gender: Essays on Theory, Film, and Fiction.* Bloomington: Indiana University Press.

Denzin, Norman K. 1989a. *Interpretive Biography.* London: Sage Publications.

Denzin, Norman K. 1989b. *Interpretive Interactionism.* London: Sage Publications.

Deleuze, Gilles and Guattari, Félix. 1983. *Anti-Oedipus: Capitalism and Schizophrenia.* New York: Viking.

Deutsch, Helene. 1930. "Significance of Masochism in the Mental Life of Women." *International Journal of Psychoanalysis* 11:48–60.

Diamond, Irene and Lee Quinby (eds.). 1988. *Feminism & Foucault.* Boston: Northeastern University Press.

Douglas, Mary. 1966. *Purity and Danger: An Analysis of Concepts of Pollution and Taboo.* London: Routledge & Kegan Paul.

Douglas, Mary. 1973. *Natural Symbols.* New York: Vintage.

Dreifus, Claudia (ed.) 1978. *Seizing Our Bodies: The Politics of Women's Health.* New York: Vintage Books.

Dull, Diana. 1989. "Before and Afters: Television's Treatment of the Boom in Cosmetic Surgery." Paper presented at the Annual Meeting of the American Sociological Association. San Francisco, August 1989.

Dull, Diana and West, Candace. 1987. "'The Price of Perfection': A Study of the Relations Between Women and Plastic Surgery." Paper presented at the Annual Meeting of the American Sociological Association. Chicago, August 1987.

Dull, Diana and West, Candace. 1991. "Accounting for Cosmetic Surgery: The Accomplishment of Gender." *Social Problems* 38 (1):54–70.

Ehrenreich, John (ed.). 1978. *The Cultural Crisis of Modern Medicine.* New York: Monthly Review Press.

Ehrenreich, Barbara and English, Deirdre. 1979. *For Her Own Good.* London: Pluto Press.

Faludi, Susan. 1991. *Backlash: The Undeclared War on American Women.* New York: Crown Publishers, Inc.

Faulder, Carolyn. 1985. *Whose Body Is It? The Troubling Issue of Informed Consent.* London: Virago.

Featherstone, Mike. 1983. "The Body in Consumer Culture." *Theory, Culture & Society* 1: 18–33.

Featherstone, Mike. 1990. "Perspectives on Consumer Culture." *Sociology* 24 (1):5–22.

Featherstone, Mike.1992. "The Heroic Life and Everyday Life." *Theory Culture & Society* 9:159–182.

Felski, Rita. 1989. "Feminist Theory and Social Change." *Theory Culture & Society* 6:219–240.

Finkelstein, Joanne. 1991. *The Fashioned Self.* Cambridge: Polity Press.

Firestone, Shulamith. 1970. *The Dialectic of Sex.* New York: Bantam Books.

Fisher, Jack. 1992. "The Silicone Controversy: When Will Science Prevail?" *New England Journal of Medicine* 326:1696–1698.

Fisher, Sue. 1986. *In the Patient's Best Interest: Women and the Politics of Medical Decisions.* New Brunswick: Rutgers University Press.

Flax, Jane. 1990. *Thinking Fragments: Psychoanalysis, Feminism, and Postmodernism in the Contemporary West.* Berkeley: University of California Press.

Foucault, Michel. 1978. *The History of Sexuality, Volume 1.* New York: Pantheon.

Foucault, Michel. 1979. *Discipline and Punish.* New York: Vintage.

Foucault, Michel. 1980. *Power/Knowledge: Selected Interviews & Other Writings, 1972–1977.* New York: Pantheon.

Foucault, Michel. 1985. *The Use of Pleasure.* New York: Vintage.

Foucault, Michel. 1986. *The Care of the Self.* New York: Pantheon.

Foucault, Michel. 1988. *Politics, Philosophy, Culture: Interviews and Other Writings, 1977–1984.* New York: Routledge, Chapman, Hall.

Frank, Arthur W. 1990. "Bringing Bodies Back In: A Decade Review." *Theory Culture & Society* 7:131–162.

Frank, Arthur W. 1991. "For a Sociology of the Body: an Analytical Review." In M. Featherstone, M. Hepworth, and B. Turner (eds.), *The Body: Social Process and Cultural Theory*. London: Sage Publications. 36–102.

Frank, Arthur W. 1992. "The Pedagogy of Suffering: Moral Dimensions of Psychological Therapy and Research with the Ill." *Theory & Psychology* 2 :467–485.

Fraser, Nancy. 1989. "Unruly Practices: Power, Discourse and Gender in Contemporary Social Theory." Cambridge: Polity Press.

Freud, Sigmund. 1933. "On Femininity." *New Introductory Lectures in Psychoanalysis*. New York: W.W. Norton.

Freud, Sigmund. 1957. "On Narcissism: An Introduction." In *General Selection from the Works of Sigmund Freud*. New York: Doubleday/Anchor.

Freedman, Rita. 1986. *Beauty Bound: Why Women Strive For Physical Perfection*. London: Columbus Books.

Gabka, Joachim and Vaubel, Ekkehard. 1983. *Plastic Surgery Past and Present: Origin and History of Modern Lines of Incision*. Basel: Karger.

Garfinkel, Harold. 1967. *Studies in Ethnomethodology*. Englewood Cliffs, N.J.: Prentice Hall.

Garry, Ann. 1982. "Narcissism and Vanity." *Social Theory and Practice* 8(2):145–154.

Gergen, Mary M. and Gergen, Kenneth J. 1993. "Narratives of the Gendered Body in Popular Autobiography." In R. Josselson and A. Lieblich (eds.), *The Narrative Study of Lives*. London: Sage Publications.

Giddens, Anthony. 1984. *The Constitution of Society*. Cambridge: Polity Press.

Giddens, Anthony. 1990. *The Consequences of Modernity*. Cambridge: Polity Press.

Giddens, Anthony. 1991. *Modernity and Self-Identity: Self and Society in the Late Modern Age*. Cambridge: Polity Press.

Giddens, Anthony. 1992. *The Transformation of Intimacy: Sexuality, Love & Eroticism in Modern Societies*. Cambridge: Polity Press.

Gifford, Sanford. 1980. "Cosmetic Surgery and Personality Change: A Review and Some Clinical Observations." In R.M. Goldwyn (ed.), *Long-Term Results in Plastic and Reconstructive Surgery*, 2nd edition. Boston: Little, Brown & Co.

Gilligan, Carol. 1982. *In A Different Voice: Psychological Theory and Women's Development*. Cambridge: Harvard University Press.

Ginsburg, Norman. 1992. *Divisions of Welfare: A Critical Introduction to Comparative Social Policy*. London: Sage Publications.

Glaser, Barney and Strauss, Anselm. 1965. *Awareness of Dying*. Chicago: Aldine.

Goffman, Erving. 1959. *The Presentation of Self in Everyday Life*. New York: Doubleday Anchor.

Goffman, Erving. 1963. *Stigma: Notes on the Management of Spoiled Identity*. Englewood Cliffs, N.J.: Prentice Hall.

Goffman, Erving. 1967. *Interaction Ritual*. New York: Doubleday Anchor.

Goffman, Erving. 1976. *Gender Advertisements*. New York: Harper Colophon.

Goldblum, Randall M., Relley, Ronald P. and O'Donnell, Alice A. 1992. "Antibodies to Silicone Elastomers and Reactions to Ventriculoperitoneal Shunts." *Lancet* 340:510–513.

Goldwyn, Robert M. (ed.) 1980. *Long-Term Results in Plastic and Reconstructive Surgery*. 2nd edition. Boston: Little, Brown & Co.

Gordon, Linda. 1976. *Woman's Body, Woman's Right: A Social History of Birth Control in America*. Middlesex: Penguin Books.

Gurdin, Michael. 1972. "Augmentation Mammaplasty." In Robert M. Goldwyn (ed.), *Long-Term Results in Plastic and Reconstructive Surgery*. 1st edition. Boston: Little, Brown & Co.

Haraway, Donna. 1988. "Situated Knowledges: the Science Question in Feminism as a Site of Discourse on the Privilege of Partial Perspective. *Feminist Studies* 14:575–599.

Hartsock, Nancy. 1983. *Money, Sex and Power: Toward a Feminist Historical Materialism*. New York: Longman.

Hatfield, Elaine and Sprecher, Susan. 1986. *Mirror, Mirror: The Importance of Look in Everyday Life*. Albany: State University of New York Press.

Haug, Frigga et al., 1987. *Female Sexualization*. London: Verso.

Henley, Nancy M. 1977. *Body Politics*. Engelwood Cliffs, N.J.: Prentice Hall.

Hirsch, Marianne and Keller, Evelyn Fox (eds.). 1990. *Conflicts in Feminism*. New York: Routledge.

Holmes, Helen Bequaert and Purdy, Laura M. (eds.) 1992. *Feminist Perspectives in Medical Ethics*. Bloomington: Indiana University Press.

Huffstadt, A.J.C. (in collaboration with F. G. Bouman, N.H. Groenman, and H.M.A. Marcus-Timmers). 1981. *Kosmetische Chirurgie*. Alphen a.d. Rijn: Stafleu's.

Iverson, R. 1991. "National Survey Shows Overwhelming Satisfaction with Breast Implants." *Plastic and Reconstructive Surgery* 88:546–547.

Jacoby, Russell. 1980. "Narcissism and the Crisis of Capitalism." *Telos* 44:58–65.

Jacobus, Mary, Evelyn Fox Keller, and Sally Shuttleworth, (eds.). 1990. *Body/Politics*. New York: Routledge.

Jaggar, Alison M. and Susan R. Bordo, (eds.). 1989. *Gender/Body/Knowledge*. New Brunswick, N.J.: Rutgers University Press.

Jefferson, Gail and John R.E. Lee. 1981. "The Rejection of Advice: Managing the Problematic Convergence of a 'Troubles-Telling' and a 'Service Encounter'." *Journal of Pragmatics* 5:399–422.

Josselson, Ruthellen and Lieblich, Amia (eds.). 1993. *The Narrative Study of Lives*. London: Sage Publications.

Kaw, Eugenia. 1993. "Medicalization of Racial Features: Asian American Women and Cosmetic Surgery." *Medical Anthropology Quarterly* 7 (1):74–89.

Keller, Evelyn Fox. 1983. *A Feeling for the Organism: The Life and Work of Barbara McClintock*. New York: Freeman.

Keller, Evelyn Fox. 1985. *Reflections on Gender and Science*. New Haven: Yale University Press.

Kessler, David A. 1992. "The Basis of the FDA's Decision on Breast Implants." *New England Journal of Medicine* 326:1713–1715.

Kessler, Suzanne J. and McKenna, Wendy. 1978. *Gender: An Ethnomethodological Approach*. Chicago: The University of Chicago Press.

Kittay, Eva Feder and Meyers, Diana T. (eds.). 1987. *Women and Moral Theory*. Totowa, N. J.: Rowman & Littlefield.

Kohut, Heinz. 1977. *The Restoration of Self*. New York: International Universities Press.

Kohli, Manfred (ed.). 1978. *Soziologie des Lebenlaufs*. Darmstadt: Luchterhand.

Komter, Aafke.1991. "Gender, Power and Feminist Theory." In Kathy Davis, Monique Leijenaar and Jantine Oldersma (eds.), *The Gender of Power*. London: Sage Publications. 42–62.

Kunzle, David. 1982. *Fashion and Fetishism: A Social History of the Corset, Tight-lacing and Other Forms of Body-Sculpture in the West*. Totowa, N.J.: Rowman and Littlefield.

La Belle, Jenijoy. 1988. *Herself Beheld: The Literature of the Looking Glass*. Ithaca: Cornell University Press.

Labov, William. 1972. *Language in the Inner City: Studies in the Black English Vernacular*. Philadelphia: University of Pennsylvania Press.

Lacan, Jacques. 1977. *Écrits: A Selection*. New York: Norton.

Lacan, Jacques. 1982. *Feminine Sexuality*. J. Mitchell and J. Rose (eds.). New York: Norton.

Lakoff, Robin Tolmach and Scherr, Raquel L. 1984. *Face Value. The Politics of Beauty*. Boston: Routledge & Kegan Paul.

Larrabee, Mary Jeanne. 1992. *An Ethic of Care*. New York: Routledge.

Lasch, Christopher. 1979. *The Culture of Narcissism*. New York: W.W. Norton.

Laqueur, Thomas. 1990. *Making Sex: Body and Gender from the Greeks to Freud*. Cambridge: Harvard University Press.

Levin, Ira. 1972. *The Stepford Wives*. New York: Bantam Books.

Loomes, G. and Sugden, R. 1982. "Regret Theory: An Alternative Theory of Rational Choice Under Uncertainty." *Economic Journal* 92:805–824.

Lukes, Stephen. 1986. *Power*. Oxford: Blackwell.

MacCannell, Dean and MacCannell, Juliet Flower. 1987. "The Beauty System." In Nancy Armstrong and Leonard Tennenhouse (eds.), *The Ideology of Conduct*. New York: Methuen. 206–238.

Marwick, Arthur. 1988. *Beauty in History: Society, Politics and Personal Appearance c. 1500 to the Present*. Gloucester: Thames and Hudson, Hucclecote.

McNay, Lois. 1992. *Foucault and Feminism*. Cambridge: Polity Press.

Meredith, B. 1988. *A Change for the Better*. London: Grafton Books.

Meyer, L. and Ringberg, A. 1987. "Augmentation Mammaplasty: Psychiatric and Psychosocial Characteristics and Outcome in a Group of Swedish Women. *Scandinavian Journal Plastic Reconstructive Surgery* 21:199–208.

Mickett, Carol A. 1993. "Comments on Sandra Lee Bartky's *Femininity and Domination*." *Hypatia* 8 (1):173–177.

Millard, D.R., Jr. 1974. "Aesthetic Rhinoplasty." In M.Saad and P. Lichtveld (eds.), *Reviews in Plastic Surgery: General Plastic and Reconstructive Surgery*. New York: American Elsevier. 371–386.

Miller, Jean Baker. 1976. *Toward a New Psychology of Women*. Boston: Beacon Press.

Millett, Kate. 1971. *Sexual Politics*. New York: Avon Books.

Millman, Marcia. 1980. *Such a Pretty Face*. New York: Berkeley Books.

Mincer, Margaret and Scholz, Renate. 1988. *Schönheitsoperationen*. München: Mosaik Verlag.

Miller, T., Coffman, J., and Linke, R. 1980. "A Survey of Body Image, Weight, and Diet of College Students." *Journal of the American Dietetic Association* 17:561–566.

Morgan, Kathryn Pauly. 1991. "Women and the Knife: Cosmetic Surgery and the Colonization of Women's Bodies." *Hypatia* 6:25–53.

Navarro, Vincente. 1986. *Crisis, Health, and Medicine: A Social Critique*. New York: Tavistock.

Ohlsen, L., Ponten, B. and Hambert, G. 1978. "Augmentation Mammapolasty: A Surgical and Psychiatric Evaluation of the Results. *Annals of Plastic Surgery* 2:42–52.

Orbach, Susie. 1986. *Hunger Strike: The Anorectic's Struggle as a Metaphor for Our Age*. London: Faber and Faber.

O'Neill, John. 1985. *Five Bodies*. Ithaca, N.Y.: Cornell University Press.

Parker, Lisa (1993). "Social Justice, Federal Paternalism, and Feminism: Breast Implants in the Cultural Context of Female Beauty." *Kennedy Institute of Ethics Journal*, 3(1):57–76.

Peiss, Kathy. 1990. "Making Faces: The Cosmetics Industry and the Cultural Construction of Gender, 1890–1930." *Genders* 7: 143–170.

Perrot, Philippe. 1984. *Le travail des apparences: Ou les transformations du corps féminin XVIIIe–XIXe siècle*. Paris: Éditions du Seuil. (Dutch translation: 1987. *Werken aan de schijn. Veranderingen van het vrouwelijk lichaam*. Nijmegen: SUN.).

Perutz, Katherine. 1970. *Beyond the Looking Glass: Life in the Beauty Culture*. Middlesex: Penguin.

Petchesky, Rosalind Pollack. 1986. *Abortion and Woman's Choice*. London: Verso.

Pickering, P.P., J.E. Williams, T.R. Vecchione. 1980. "Augmentation Mammaplasty." In R.M. Goldwyn (ed.), *Long-Term Results in Plastic and Reconstructive Surgery*. Boston: Little, Brown & Company. 696–706.

Pitanguy, I. 1967. "Abdominal Lipectomy, an Approach to It, Through an Analysis of 300 Consecutive Cases. *Plastic Reconstructive Surgery* 40:384.

Plummer, Ken. 1983. *Documents of Life*. London: Allen and Unwin.

Probyn, Elspeth. 1987. "The Anorexic Body." In Arthur and Marilouise Kroker (eds.), *Body Invaders: Panicsex in America*. New York: St. Martin's Press. 201–211.

Reinstein, Peter H. and Bagley, Grant P. 1992. "Update on Breast Implants." *American Family Physician* 45:472–473.

Rees, R.D. and Wood-Smith, D. 1973. *Cosmetic Facial Surgery*. Philadelphia: Saunders.

Riemann, Gerhard and Schütze, Fritz. 1991. "'Trajectory' as a Basic Theoretical Concept for Analyzing Suffering and Disorderly Social Processes." In D.R. Maines (ed.), *Social Organization and Social Processes: Essays in Honor of Anselm Strauss*. New York: De Gruyter. 333–357.

Rubin, Gayle. 1975. "The Traffic in Women: Notes on the 'Political Economy' of Sex." In R.Reiter (ed.), *Toward an Anthropology of Women*. New York: Monthly Review Press. 157–210.

Sacks, Harvey. 1978. "Some Technical Considerations of a Dirty Joke." In J. Schenkhein (ed.), *Studies in the Organization of Conversational Interaction*. New York: Academic Press, Inc.

Sacks, Harvey. 1984. "On doing 'being ordinary.'" In J.M. Atkinson and J.C. Heritage (eds.), *Structures of Social Actions*. Cambridge: Cambridge University Press.

Sanford, L. and Donovan, M. 1984. *Women & Self-Esteem*. Garden City, N.Y.: Anchor Press/Doubleday.

Scheff, Thomas. 1988. "Shame and Conformity: The Deference-Emotion System." *American Sociological Review* 53:395–406.

Scherpenzeel, Roos. 1993. "Maak je borst maar nat. Een onderzoek naar ervaringen en verklaringen van vrouwen met siliconenimplantaten." MA thesis, University of Utrecht.

Schütze, Fritz. 1977. *Die Technik des narrativen Interviews in Interaktionsfeldstudien.* Arbeitsberichte und Forschungsmaterialien Nr. 1, University of Bielefeld, Germany.

Schütze, Fritz. 1983. "Biographieforschung und Narratives Interview." *Neue Praxis* 3:283–293.

Schütze, Fritz. 1992. "Pressure and Guilt: War Experiences of a Young German Soldier and Their Biographical Implications." *International Sociology* 7 (2): 187-208.

Schwartz, Howard and Jacobs, Jerry. 1979. *Qualitative Sociology: A Method to the Madness.* New York: The Free Press.

Scott, Joan. 1992. "Experience." In Judith Butler and Joan W. Scott (eds.), *Feminists Theorize the Political.* New York: Routledge.

Scott, Sue and Morgan, David (eds.). 1993. *Body Matters: Essays on the Sociology of the Body.* London: The Falmer Press.

Shilling, Chris. 1993. *The Body and Social Theory.* London: Sage Publications.

Smith, Dorothy. 1990a. *The Conceptual Practices of Power: A Feminist Sociology of Knowledge.* Boston: Northeastern University Press.

Smith, Dorothy. 1990b. *Texts, Facts and Femininity: Exploring the Relations of Ruling.* New York: Routledge.

Smith, Dorothy and David, Sara (eds.). 1975. *Women Look at Psychiatry.* Vancouver: Press Gang Publishing Co.

Spitzak, Carole. 1988. "The Confession Mirror: Plastic Images for Surgery." *Canadian Journal of Political and Social Theory* 12 (1–2):38–50.

Spitzak, Carole. 1990. *Confessing Excess: Women and the Politics of Body Reduction.* Albany: State University of New York Press.

Squire, Corinne. 1994. "Empowering Women? *The Oprah Winfrey Show.*" *Feminism & Psychology* 4 (1):63-79.

Starmans, P.M.W. 1988. "Wat gebeurt er met de esthetische chirurgie?" *Inzet. Opinieblad van de ziekenfondsen* 1:18–25.

Strauss, Anselm L. 1969. *Mirrors and Masks: The Search for Identity.* Mill Valley, California: The Sociology Press.

Strauss, Anselm, Fagerhaugh, Shizuko, Suczek, Barbara, and Carolyn Wiener. 1985. *Social Organization of Medical Work.* Chicago: University of Chicago Press.

Strauss, Anselm and Glaser, Barney. 1970. *Anguish: The Case Study of a Dying Trajectory.* Mill Valley, California: Sociology Press.

Suleiman, Susan R. (ed.). 1985. *The Female Body in Western Culture.* Cambridge: Harvard University Press.

Synnott, Anthony. 1990. "Truth and Goodness, Mirrors and Masks. Part II: A Sociology of Beauty and the Face." *British Journal of Sociology* 41 (1):55–76.

Turner, Bryan S. 1984. *The Body & Society.* Oxford: Basil Blackwell.

Tijmstra, T. 1987. "Het imperatieve karater van medische technologie en de betekenis van 'geanticipeerde beslissingsspijt.'" *Nederlands Tijdschrift voor Geneeskunde* 131 (26):1128–1131.

Tronto, Joan C. 1993. *Moral Boundaries: A Political Argument for an Ethic of Care.* New York: Routledge.

U. S. National Center for Health Statistics. 1987. *Detailed Diagnoses and Surgical Procedures*. Washington, D.C.: U.S. Government Printing Office.

Van de Lande, J.L. and Lichtveld, P. 1972. "Hypoplasia mammae, een psychosociaal lijden." *Nederlands Tijdschrift voor Geneeskunde* 116 (11):428–431.

Van Ham, I. 1990. "Borstvergroting en borstverkleining. Een literatuuronderzoek." *Huisarts en Wetenschap* 33:98–102.

Waitzkin, Howard. 1983. *The Second Sickness: Contradictions of Capitalist Health Care*. New York: The Free Press.

Walsh, Frank W., Solomon, David A., and Espinoza, Luis R. 1989. "Human Adjuvant Disease: A New Cause of Chylous Effusions." *Archives of Internal Medicine* 149:1194–1196.

Warnke, Georgia. 1993. "Feminism and Hermeneutics." *Hypatia* 8 (1):81–98.

Webb, Barbara and Stimson, Gerry. 1976. "People's Accounts of Medical encounters." In Michael Wasdsworth and David Robinson (eds.), *Studies in Everyday Medical Life*. Martin London: Robertson. 108–122.

Weiss, Rick. 1991. "Breast Implant Fears Put Focus on Biomaterials." *Science* 252:1059–1160.

Weldon, Fay. 1983. *The Life & Loves of a She-Devil*. Coronet Books.

Wilson, Elizabeth. 1985. *Adorned in Dreams*. London: Virago.

Wolf, Naomi. 1991. *The Beauty Myth: How Images of Beauty Are Used Against Women*. New York: William Morrow and Company, Inc.

Wolfe, Alan. 1989. *Whose Keeper? Social Science and Moral Obligation*. Berkeley: University of California Press.

Wolfe, Alan. 1993. "The New Class Comes Home." *Partisan Review* 60 (4):729–737.

Young, Iris. 1990a. *Justice and the Politics of Difference*. Princeton: Princeton University Press.

Young, Iris Marion. 1990b. *Throwing Like a Girl and Other Essays in Feminist Philosophy and Social Theory*. Bloomington: Indiana University Press.

INDEX

A

abdominoplasties, 26

adolescents: decision-making on breast augmentation, 124–25, 141

agency: femininity and, 60–62, 62–64; as theme of study, 11; women's decisions on cosmetic surgery, 117, 157

Andersen, Hans Christian, 65–66

anesthesia, 15, 27

antisepsis, 15

B

Bar-On, Bat Ami, 179–80

Barthes, Roland, 46

Bartky, Sandra, 51, 62–64, 172, 173–74

Baudrillard, Jean, 46

beauty: as cultural discourse, 54–56; femininity and politics of, 49–52; feminist critiques of cosmetic surgery, 172–75; history of in Western culture, 390–41; as oppression, 52–54; psychoanalysis and, 43–45; social psychology and, 42–43; sociology and , 45–49; women's decisions on cosmetic surgery, 88–92, 157

body contouring, 26–27. See also liposuction

body: cosmetic surgery and view of as commodity, 157; cosmetic surgery and women's experiences of embodiment, 96–114; sense of self in relation to, 59–60; social psychology and image of, 42; sociology and beauty, 47–49

Bordo, Susan, 54–56, 178

Branca (Sicilian physician), 14

breast augmentation surgery: history of, 24–26; narratives on decision-making process, 119–36, 137–58; side effects and dangers of, 27–28; women's decisions on cosmetic surgery, 3–4. See also silicone implants

breasts, femininity in Western culture and, 9, 60. See also breast augmentation surgery; silicone implants

C

Calvinism, 90

Chapkis, Wendy, 52–54

chemical peeling, 24

Cher, 4, 18

chivalry, medieval cult of, 39

choice: feminist critiques of cosmetic surgery, 164–72; women's narratives on cosmetic surgery, 137–58. See also decision-making

class: breast augmentation surgery and, 9; health insurance and cosmetic surgery, 6

clothing, sizing of and cosmetic surgery, 78–80

collagen treatments, 24

complaints, in women's narratives on breast augmentation surgery, 147–49

computer imaging, 17, 130

consumerism: media promotion of cosmetic surgery, 20; sociology and beauty, 47–49

cosmetic industry, 40

cosmetic surgery: as big business, 20–22; choice and informed consent in women's narratives on, 137–58; cultural critique of, 28–29; development of, 16; experience of difference in women's narratives of, 93–114; as feminist dilemma, 1–5, 56–59, 159–81; feminist satire of, 64–67; market model of medicine and, 17–18, 29–32; as mass phenomena, 18–20; methodology of study of, 7–11; Netherlands as focus for study of, 5–7, 34–38; new technologies in, 22–23; problem of "normal" appearance and, 68–92; side effects and dangers of, 27–28; welfare model of medicine and, 32–34

Crimean war, 16

criticisms, in women's narratives on breast augmentation, 147–49

culture: beauty as discourse, 54–56; critique of cosmetic surgery, 28–29; removal of tattoos, 36

D

decision-making, women's narratives on cosmetic surgery, 73–92, 115–36. *See also* choice

Deleuze, Gilles, 46

dentistry, cosmetic, 22–23

dermabrasion, 24

dermatologists, 21

diet industry, 26

disease, preindustrial models of, 15

Doda, Carol, 25

"double eyelid" surgery, 22

Douglas, Mary, 46

Dow Corning, 30–31

Dull, Diana, 19

E

ear surgery, 22

ethics, feminist, 175–77

F

face-lifts: history and techniques of, 23–24; side effects and dangers of, 27, 28

fashion–beauty complex, 51

fat removal, 26–27. *See also* liposuction

Featherstone, Mike, 20

femininity: agency and, 60–62, 62–64; beauty as cultural discourse, 55; breasts as symbol of in Western culture, 9, 60; concepts of identity, 168–69; morality and, 62–64; politics of beauty, 49–52; psychoanalysis and narcissism, 44–45

feminism: beauty as cultural discourse, 54–56; beauty as oppression, 52–54; cosmetic surgery as dilemma in, 1–5, 56–59, 159–81; and decision-making on cosmetic surgery, 86–87; scholarship on politics of beauty, 49–52

Finkelstein, Joanne, 23

Food and Drug Administration (FDA), controversy on silicone implants, 30–31, 117–19

Foucault, Michel, 47, 50

Frank, Arthur W., 46

French Revolution, 40

Freud, Sigmund, 43–44

G

gender: cultural constraints on women's choices, 158; difference and cultivation of appearance, 52–53, 54. *See also* sexual difference

Germany, statistics on cosmetic surgery, 21

Goffman, Erving, 46

Great Britain, statistics on silicone implant operations, 25

Guattari, Felix, 46

H

health care system: coverage of cosmetic surgery in Netherlands, 6–7, 34–38; cultural critique of cosmetic surgery and, 29; interviews with applicants for coverage of cosmetic surgery, 10–11, 68–73, 131–32. *See also* medical professions; medicine

heroic tales, women's narratives on cosmetic surgery as, 132–34

hierarchies: beauty system in Western culture, 51; women's choices and social order organized by gender and power, 158

Hirsch, Marianne, 178–79

hope, dialectics of in decision-making on breast augmentation, 134–36

I

identity: feminist critiques of cosmetic surgery, 163, 168–69; as theme of study, 11; women's narratives on cosmetic surgery, 98, 99, 104–14

ideology: and concepts of power, 169–70; national health insurance and cosmetic surgery in Netherlands, 37

immune system, side-effects of silicone implants, 30, 151

income, of plastic surgeons, 20

India, plastic surgery in, 14

informed consent: lack of information provided in consultations with surgeons, 131; silicone implants and, 30–31; women's narratives on cosmetic surgery, 137–58

insurance. See health care system

J

justice, in critiques of cosmetic surgery, 163

K

Keller, Evelyn Fox, 178–79

L

Lacan, Jacques, 46

Lakoff, Robin Tolmach, 41

Levin, Ira, 176

liposuction: development of, 26–27; side effects and dangers of, 27, 28

M

Madonna, 4

malpractice suits, 30–31

mammograms, 28

market model of medicine, 17–18, 29–32

mastectomy, 154

mastoplasty, 153

media: feminist critiques of cosmetic surgery, 166–67; popularization of cosmetic surgery, 18–20; sexualization of female body, 48

medical profession: barriers to breast augmentation surgery, 128–32; criteria for "normal" appearance, 69–73, 91; paternalism of and women's choices on cosmetic surgery, 118; public accountability of, 6–7

medicine: development of as a science, 15; market model of, 17–18, 29–32; welfare model of, 32–34. *See also* health care system; medical profession

men, cosmetic surgery procedures performed primarily on, 21

mind-body dualism, 54

modernity: cosmetic surgery as cultural product of, 17–18; sociological inquiry and the body, 47–49

Monroe, Marilyn, 42–43

morality: femininity and, 62–64; feminist critiques of cosmetic surgery, 163, 170–71; as theme of study, 11

Morgan, Kathryn, 164–72, 175–76, 179

N

narcissism, 43–45

nature, concepts of, 18

Netherlands: cultural discourse on cosmetic surgery, 90; as focus for study of cosmetic surgery, 5–7; national health care and cosmetic surgery, 34–38; silicone implant controversy, 33; statistics on cosmetic surgery, 21

O

opposition, in women's narratives on cosmetic surgery, 126–28

oppression: feminist critiques of cosmetic surgery, 165–66; feminist scholarship on beauty as, 50, 52–54

otherness, beauty standards in Western culture, 51–52

otoplasty, 22

otorhinolaryngologists (ENT-specialists), 21

P

Parker, Lisa, 117–19, 136, 175, 176

paternalism, women's decisions on cosmetic surgery and medical, 118

Peiss, Kathy, 40

Perrot, Philippe, 40, 41

plastic surgery: average income of practitioners, 20; history of, 14–16; increase in numbers of practitioners, 21

Plato, 39

political activism, 149–55

political correctness, 177–81

positivism, 46

postmodernism: feminist critiques of cosmetic surgery, 174; relativism of, 178; sociology and the body, 46–49, 50

power: beauty as cultural discourse, 54–56; beauty and oppression, 53; body in postmodern sociological theory, 47; cosmetic surgery and redefining of relationships, 106–107; cultural constraints on women's choices, 158; feminist critiques of cosmetic surgery, 165, 169–70; feminist scholarship on beauty, 50–52; sexual difference and social asymmetries of, 40

prisons, cosmetic surgery in, 24

psychoanalysis, beauty and appearance, 43–45

psychology, social, 42–43

R

race: beauty standards and otherness in Western culture, 51–52; cosmetic surgery in U.S., 21; justifications for cosmetic surgery, 2–3; standards for feminine beauty, 40

religion: Calvinism and cosmetic surgery in Netherlands, 90; preindustrial models of disease, 15

Renaissance, female body and beauty, 39

rhinoplasties: growth in cosmetic surgeries, 22; history of, 14

rhytodectomies, 23

risk: dialectics of decision-making on breast augmentation, 134–36; risk-benefit analysis in women's narratives on breast augmentation, 120–36

role socialization, 43

Romanticism, 39

S

scar tissue, 27

Scherr, Raquel L., 41

self: cosmetic surgery and construction of different sense of, 113–14; sense of in relation to body, 59–60. *See also* identity

self-consciousness, 80–82

self-esteem, 42

sexual difference: appearance and social asymmetries of power, 40, 52–53, 54; social psychology and beauty, 42–43

sexuality: reasons for cosmetic surgery, 84; women's narratives on breast augmentation, 140

shame: feminine experience and, 63; women's decisions on cosmetic surgery, 84–87

silicone implants: development of technique, 25; European reactions to controversy over, 33; feminist critique of FDA restrictions on, 117–19; hazards of and political activism, 149–55; informed consent and malpractice actions, 30–31; market model of medicine and controversy over, 31–32; side effects and dangers of, 28

Smith, Dorothy, 60–62, 172, 173–74

social psychology, appearance and beauty, 42–43

sociology: policy of credulousness in interpretative, 160–64; theories of appearance and beauty, 45–49

"Stepford Wives," 176

stomach stapling, 115–16

storytelling, narrative features of on cosmetic surgery, 96–98, 132–34

subject, cosmetic surgery as strategy for becoming embodied, 96–114

support networks, 125–26

syphilis, 15

T

tattoos, removal of, 36

textual practices, women's voices in media, 167

Turner, Bryan S., 45

U

United States: cosmetic surgery as big business, 20–22; cultural discourse on cosmetic surgery, 90; health insurance and cosmetic surgery, 6, 7

W

war, history of plastic surgery, 16

Weldon, Fay, 64–67, 106, 133

welfare model of medicine, 32–34

Winfrey, Oprah, 19–20

Wolf, Naomi, 20–21, 33

Y

Young, Iris Marion, 59–60, 172–74